Pg 38

W9-DBT-477

A NEW AMERICAN JUSTICE

DANIEL C. MAGUIRE

A NEW
AMERICAN JUSTICE

Ending the White Male Monopolies

Doubleday & Company, Inc., Garden City, New York 1980

Library of Congress Catalog Card Number 78-20084
ISBN: 0-385-14325-7
Copyright © 1980 by DANIEL C. MAGUIRE
All Rights Reserved
Printed in the United States of America

First Edition

To Tommy, my son, . . .

may he live to see the reconciliation
of justice and power . . .

ACKNOWLEDGMENTS

Gratitude is owed in abundance to
Preston Williams,
who in 1975 invited me to join a study group
at Harvard University on the subject of ethical theory and race.
My interest in the subject of this book was born in those sessions.

Marjorie, my wife and colleague in ethics,
for brilliant, painstaking, and sometimes painful criticism;

Ruth Whitney, Richard Schaefer, Nicholas Fargnoli,
John Yockey, Frances Leap, Joseph McGarvey,
and Theresa D'Orsogna,
who also befriended me with criticism;

Camille Slowinski and Colin Krodel,
who typed with skill, supportive interest, and good cheer;

Danny and Tommy, my sons,
who give me delightful daily lessons
on the preciousness of human life.

CONTENTS

A NEW AMERICAN JUSTICE

PART ONE

A Change of Epoch

Nations like persons must pay the price of a misspent youth. This American nation has just begun to pay. We have reached a turning point in the American story. The time of easy abundance is at an end. Social justice has assumed a new urgency. The current debate over preferential affirmative action is not merely a debate over a policy but the harbinger of an emerging consciousness and a new time. The crisis here is epochal, not episodic. It has no American precedent. It is akin to the discovery that the earth is not flat. That discovery was rejected by many in its day. Analogously, many today are entombed in flat-earth hypotheses. They have missed the dawning awareness that human life has turned a corner, that new modes of sharing are now needed if our species is not to perish. One new mode of sharing—preferential affirmative action—is the topic of this book.

Chapter One advises the reader in advance of the conclusions this book defends; Chapter Two takes a chastening and perspective-giving tour of American history; Chapter Three gets to the specific issue of preferential affirmative action and presents all the arguments—from the serious to the frivolous—that have been marshaled against it.

CHAPTER ONE

Conclusions

For two hundred years the United States has been operating under a rigid quota system. This quota system has insisted on and got a 90 to 100 per cent monopoly for white males in all the principal centers of power in government, business, and the professions, and in the competition for desirable jobs at every level. This white male predominance has been institutionalized and legalized. Now, belatedly, it is being challenged. White males are responding with a vociferous reliance on "meritocratic" ideals. Never in history has merit been so passionately befriended. The goal of the merit strategy is defensive. Its deeper implications, however, should not be missed since they are both racist and sexist. Insistence on merit subtly implies that merit has always prevailed—and thus that those at the top belong there while those at the bottom . . .

There is nothing evil about white males. They are only reacting as privileged groups always have when a threat to privilege appears. The challenge to white male monopoly has taken the initial specific form of preferential affirmative action. This means that, as a monopoly-breaking measure, members of disempowered and excluded groups will be given preference over white males in sufficient numbers to change the social patterns of distribution. This policy is not voluntary but enforced and it is based upon the philosophical assumption that individual rights and career opportunities may at times be sacrificed for necessary and significant social goals. The struggle involved in this exercise in social redistribution is young. The Supreme Court cases of *Bakke* and *Weber* are but the earliest skirmishes. The question faced in this book is whether such enforced preferential policy is just. So that what I am about might be clear, I shall state in this opening chapter the conclusions which I defend in what follows. The stakes in this debate are high and so are the feelings. I enter the kitchen fully aware of its heat. I enter it also as a white male who has enjoyed the preferential perquisites that accrue to my group. I write, however, not as a liberal on a self-indulgent guilt trip, but as an ethicist who hopes to do serious justice to justice in a time that requires nothing less. I lead with my conclusions in the hope that they will draw many into the most important debate of the next century. That debate is concerned with nothing less than the ending of the white male monopoly and thus the reshaping of both power and life on the American scene.

I acknowledge at the outset that "white male" is not a univocal term. Not all white males are equally endowed and some are drastically deprived. Jewish and Catholic white males, to give just two examples, often find doors and minds in the realm closed to them. Also, the impoverishment and disempowerment of poor Appalachian whites require special forms of redistributive relief. But no conclusion can be drawn from this diversity that the term "white male" has no substance or relevance to the reality of power. It is clear that from boardroom to pulpit, in the halls of government, business, academe, and church, "white male" is a warranted and meaningful generalization that points to an identifiable and controlling group.

The positions argued in this book follow:

American thinking on the concept of justice is muddled. The word runs like a greased pig through our political and legal discourse. Our long-standing philosophical poverty in this regard has not been alleviated by recent thinkers on the question such as John Rawls—and certainly not by Robert Nozick—hamstrung as these thinkers are by traditional American individualism. Neither does the Supreme Court operate out of a consistent theory of justice. This book will offer a wholistic notion of justice that includes the three essential forms of justice: *individual, social,* and *distributive.* Also the status of the phrase "to each according to his need" will be clarified as a principle of justice.

The affirmative action program has been bogged down by an absence of criteria regarding deserving groups. Preference cannot be given to "minorities" in general since we are "a nation of minorities." And yet, with the scent of preference in the air, minorities have lined up, and affirmative action listings promiscuously include everyone from Aleuts and Eskimos to Filipinos and unspecified "orientals." This, of course, gives grist in abundance to the critics of affirmative action. In this book, four criteria will be offered by which a group could qualify for preferential affirmative action. The criteria are stringent—so stringent that only four groups qualify: blacks, American Indians, women, and, among the Latinos, Puerto Ricans and Mexican Americans. No other groups, in my judgment, qualify for preferential relief.

Blacks should be the prime and paradigmatic recipients of preferential affirmative action. Dismantling the black/white caste system is America's most important redistributional business. Some would argue that it is a mistake to separate out one group as more deserving than others. My argument will be that only blacks are victimized by lowest caste status and that, unless their unique needs are seen as unique, they will continue to occupy the cellar as other groups move upstairs.

The current debate takes place in a context involving two new and critical complications: unparalleled economic crunch and a new and more subtle racism. On the economic side, we are entering a period of historically new economic constriction. The two-hundred-year joy ride is over. Terms of trade, cheap resources, competitive international advantages in business—all are taking an adverse turn.

The second complication is the emergence of Jim Crow, Jr. Gone is the candid racism of a Bull Connor. The new racism is distinguished and wears a mantle woven by the social sciences. It embodies a new school of studied social pessimism. The term "benign neglect" was not a chance comment fallen from a memo. It was rather the symbol of the new white response to the perceived inferiority of black persons. It signaled the latest strategy in the old "blame the victim" approach to the American caste system.

As a nation we are all too unsophisticated about how to move the Leviathan. We are fond of calling for *voluntary* solutions to intractable social problems. What this means in practice is that we will choose freedom even when it involves injustice whenever justice requires sacrifice, as it does in preferential affirmative action. This book will attempt to put freedom in its place vis-à-vis justice.

I shall argue that in affirmative action programs more, not less, enforcement is needed, given the successful resistance to affirmative action by so many corporations and schools. The present strategies of the federal agencies are inadequate. Litigation with delinquents on a one-by-one basis, with appeals to the rest for voluntary compliance, will not do. In the presence of evidence of non-compliance, a court-appointed corporate officer should be installed in the recalcitrant corporation (at the expense of the corporation) to preside over the affirmative action program and to discover how business is done both over and under the table. This would end the posturings of compliance which are broadly employed in lieu of the real thing.

In this book, also, the concept of the merit system is re-examined. Merit has its place. While there should be preference for admission to schools there should be no "quota" for graduation. And some positions that require special skill (brain surgeons, airplane pilots, professional basketball players, et cetera) should be filled purely upon a merit basis. However, merit has both a social and an individual meaning. Being black or a woman counts among one's merits or deserts in a society in which monopoly has suppressed black and female talent. Being black or female counts as a plus for the otherwise qualified persons, when the admission or hiring of these persons helps to end a stifling monopoly. Also, since we are not merely individuals but *social* individuals, rights too have a social meaning. Individual rights are conditioned by the common good. Regardless of individual merit and talent, no one has a *right* to be hired or to be admitted into a university without reference to the society of which that individual is a part. Most American discourse about "merit" and "rights" rests on the individualistic fallacy of seeing persons as asocial beings.

Finally, and summarily, this book will attempt to bring clarity to a number of areas where obfuscation reigns. Equality, for example, is often misused as a synonym for justice. Such it is not. Inequalities may be fair or unfair, just or unjust. There is and can be no pure egalitarianism. Also, preferential affirmative action is often confused with reparations for *past* offenses and it is no such thing. Affirmative action is concerned with present-tense disempowerment of certain groups in the society. The past has only evidentiary importance inasmuch as it illustrates the depths and nature of the problem. The notion of collective guilt also looms fuzzily about and must be clarified. Furthermore, the need for metropolitan solutions to community problems calls for attention. The suburbs are not morally free to be camp followers who use the city for their gain but do not bear the burden of city problems. Attention too will be paid to the role of the Supreme Court in social-moral discourse since that Court, quite uniquely, fulfills the philosophical function performed by the universities in medieval Europe. It is not merely a case court but an official philosophical forum—a forum, therefore, which should not be staffed with a 100 per cent quota of lawyers. Finally, it is necessary to distinguish between *remedial* affirmative action (special tutoring or job training, et cetera) and *preferential* affirmative action, which counts sex or race as a plus factor in hiring or admissions. Polls that report the public favoring affirmative action always refer to remedial affirmative action and never to preferential affirmative action. The failure to make this distinction is misleading.

The business of the book, then, is weighty and variegated. Its central thesis, however, is clear and direct. It is that a proper understanding of justice and a sensitivity to the new facts of our national existence show that affirmative action, of both the remedial and the preferential sort, is morally and legally required. Such action is, in fact, a modest approach to the major moral and political problem of the coming century—*redistribution*. American history does not prepare us well for handling that problem. Neither do the superficial understandings of justice that animate our debate stand us in good stead. There is no little urgency about meeting this basic problem head on.

CHAPTER TWO
Omnipotence in Demise

American society, like every society, sings lauds to justice but will settle for order and stability. American stability, however, because of fundamental defects in our conception of justice, was built upon a fault. For over half a century, with increasing intensity, that fault has been rumbling, and cracking, and splitting the social order. In this new time the effort to maintain stability by the bracing effects of traditional systemic injustices will no longer do. A qualitatively different situation requires a qualitatively different realization of justice. The truncated, individualistic "justice" to which we have been long committed will not maintain order or stability in this Republic any longer. A new and genuine justice must emerge, and it has haltingly begun to do so.

In a way that is stereotypically American, this new justice is emerging not as the fruit of coherent reflection but as a pragmatic response to realities that will no longer remain in compliant oblivion. Of such instinctive responses, however, a true revolution in justice will not be made. Only a fuller understanding of justice, wed to a more sensitive awareness of our societal plight (and opportunity), can direct the social processes toward improved social existence.

The purpose of this book is a defense of preferential affirmative action. The purpose of this chapter is to bring to that policy the meaning that only a historical portrait lends. More than we know, in our naïveté, we are our history. Only with a sense of our history can we penetrate the problems of the present or discover realistic solutions. The problem which preferential affirmative action addresses will be better understood when the parental influence of the past is clear. A historical character sketch which seeks out the themes of American consciousness is thus in order.

Summarily, our present situation is this: we are encountering *simultaneously* the end of free expansion *and* a demand for genuine social justice in a way that has no precedent in American history. Cheap abundance is no longer our happy lot. The big free grab is ended. We grew up, in the phrase of Frederick Turner, "at the hither edge of free land."[1] Using "frontier" in the broad sense, it can be said that all of our many frontiers are closed or closing. We are no longer on the hither edge of free land or free anything. We may expand, but it will not be free.

First, in the Civil War we lost the free labor of slaves. Then, in 1890, the Superintendent of the Census declared the end of the western frontier. Military conquests in which we briefly indulged in Cuba and the Philippines quickly became infeasible as a means of free growth. Economic imperialism remained as the last frontier. But that imperialism, which lived at the hither edge of cheap foreign resources, is also failing. Terms of trade, natural resources, competitive international advantage in business—all are taking an adverse turn.

With ironic inconvenience, it is at this very time that there arises from the newly articulate tongues of the dispossessed among us a passionate insistence on civil and human rights. Starting in 1954, the caste system that succeeded slavery and achieved a lot of slavery's economic purposes began to break up. A new generation of blacks, invigorated by the scent of justice, is bent upon the definitive dissolution of caste. Women, Chicanos, Puerto Ricans, and Indians are pressing their claims with a new sophistication and power.

The forces of this crisis are dragging us into a new epoch. We have not come this way before and there is no retreat. It is not, however, a hopeless situation. It would be hopeless only if we tried to face it with the tired old individualistic philosophy that stimulated us so during the two-hundred-year joy ride which is now at a belated end. The crisis is actually an opportunity for justice and for a prosperity based upon justice. Given all the ingredients of the situation, it would seem that we can best do well by doing good, and that's not bad. These worst of times are potentially the best.

These times, however, will not yield their promise if we heed the beat of the old drummers who are still with us, sounding out their deadly cadence. There has emerged in our day a neo-conservative literature of consolation, assuring us that there is no new and unprecedented crunch. The neo-conservative vision rests on a sanguine view of history. It claims that the "heresies" against the real American pattern emerge with seemingly overwhelming vigor, only to be repeled as a body repels a foreign substance. In this view, it was thus for slavery, for the Know-Nothings, for the American Protective Association of the 1890s, for the Ku Klux Klan of the 1920s, and for all the other "heresies." The consoling message is that, if we see massive and impressive evil now, have faith. It too shall be expelled like its vicious forebears and the central pattern of "all-inclusiveness" will re-emerge, glorious and immortal. Have faith in our folkways. Concentrate on individual rights and equal opportunity. Punish the malfactor; enforce non-discrimination on a case-by-case basis; but let the current patterns of distribution endure, for they are the sacraments of the salvific purposes that endow us with our identity as a blessed nation. The pattern of American social existence is an ever widening circle within which full access to political rights obtains.

One of the most zealous neo-conservative consolers, Harvard's Nathan Glazer, says in his book *Affirmative Discrimination* that this nation, animated by the faith of our founding creed, has been moving slowly but surely toward a day when none is denied access to the bounty of this promised land. We must not disrupt the continuum of success by new schemes for redistribution. Our history, according to Glazer, reveals a central pattern of "all-inclusiveness." No one shall be deprived or left out. Oh, of course, there have been historical deviations from this relentlessly benevolent central pattern. There was slavery and the subsequent caste system. And there was that nasty business about incarcerating the Japanese, the exploitation and lynching of Chinese workers, the race-conscious immigration laws, the systematic subjugation of Mexican Americans, the sexism, et cetera. In Glazer's view these are heresies and aberrations that do not reveal the all-embracing, all-inclusive heart of the American polity.

He warms us with the assurance that "The challenges to the central American pattern, brief and intense, were rapidly overtaken by the major tendency to a greater inclusiveness."[2] According to Glazer, the American polity has been defined "by a steady expansion of the definition of those who may be included in it to the point where it now includes all humanity . . . no one is now excluded from the broadest access to what the society makes possible. . . ."[3] Again Glazer: "The circle now embraces—as premature hyperbolic statements made as long as 200 years ago suggested it would—all humanity, without tests of race, color, national origin, religion, or language."[4] It is simply amazing to find Glazer saying that what was hyperbole two hundred years ago has now become a reality. But, like a religious zealot who can only admit the hyperboles of the past, Glazer professes that the latter days of glory are finally upon us. We are saved! Everyone is in the circle. And if we demur and breathe threats of redistribution in the name of social justice, we are accused of misreading history and of threatening the Providence that guides our ways with saving grace.

Let's face it. There is a delightful ring to that gospel—especially if you are not reading it in a decayed ghetto where there are more rats than people and where economic depression is and has always been statistically normal. For disempowered groups, this vision of America has all the realism of a report to the stockholders and all the compassion of Marie Antoinette's "Let them eat cake."

And unfortunately Glazer is not alone. He is but one of the denizens of the "neo-conservative chic." In Glazer we see the white male mind in its most inured form. The message from this untimely ideology is that more of the same will do. "Benign neglect" clearly was not a chance comment of a Daniel Moynihan but rather a phrase that captured the mood of retrenchment that has gripped quite a few of our contemporaries. Those who buy into the ideology that goes with this mood are optimistic about the problems of the disempowered and the poor and are pessimistic about government intervention in those problems. Old-time Lockean individualism plays a large part in this ideology. And, quite naturally, there is a repugnance for anything like preferential affirmative action, which would seek to change the patterns of distribution and challenge the white male monopoly that has long enjoyed hegemonic control of the principal centers of power and privilege.

Since this ideology, like any other, leans heavily upon a romantic reading of history, we can best address it by offering a history-based portrait of the American soul. The portrait will only be detailed enough to cast suspicions upon the unduly benign interpretation that undergirds neo-conservative visions. In this soul-searching venture I shall intentionally encourage a sense of guilt as an antidote to the abounding and abiding naïveté about social evil that fuels resistance to the redistributive work of justice. My attack on historical and social optimism does not lead me to pessimism but to tempered hope. I am not in the least disposed to deny or to relegate to cynicism the marvelous ideals that animated the foundation of this nation. These indeed are a treasure from which we can draw. Our national story has its glories. As a nation founded upon a creed, and not out of accidents of history, we have advantages in building a just society that are special. But lovely ideals do not easily become enfleshed in the resistant forces of societal living. Persons are more easily converted than peoples. The sum of egoism in a society is greater than the total of individual egoisms at work. The idea of a just society is eschatological, futurist. At this primitive point in moral evolution, justice is only approximated. Its roots are tender and slight. The greatest danger is to proclaim that we have attained to the final days, that the eschaton is now. Only history can give us some sense of our primitivity and of the actual forces that move us. Many of these forces are scarcely touched by the distant gravitational beckonings of our ideals. Prescriptions for the future must be conscious of the debits of the past that weigh upon our present possibilities. A second look at our psychic history is in order lest like the amnesiac, we forget who we really are.

EARLY ECSTASIES

There are some lofty prizes that can be wrested only by the naïve. The experienced and road-weary know more of price than of prize and in their timid fixation will miss the heroic opportunity. Young America enjoyed the requisite naïveté. Wizened old Europe with its eloquent intelligentsia could dream Enlightenment dreams, but young America had just the right combination of gall, detachment, wealth, and simplicity to give it a try. And so we followed our dreams with full confidence that the world could only applaud if it dared not follow. "There is no contending with omnipotence," is the recorded voice of early America; "our success is inevitable."[5] This was the vision of Benjamin Franklin that took so firm a hold on the social imagination of early America. Americans, Franklin promised, would "extend themselves almost without bounds" and "increase infinitely from all causes."[6] Don't miss the denial of limit that marked this vision: "omnipotence," "without bounds," "infinitely." The language takes leave of realism. Like the rich and spoiled young man, we set out on our adventure, confident that no matter what happened Daddy could and would pay. Daddy for us was the apparently inexhaustible free wealth of land and productivity that was always out there to help us in a pinch. All persons and peoples have an acquisitive bent. What distinguished our story and us was the abundance freely available for acquisition.

The acquisitive spirit in the American story is a peculiar thing, especially distinguished by a strong, isolationist individualism and by a faith in the sacramentality of wealth. First of all, let us admit to our acquisitive ways (since we have a long history of denying them and since they are now in for an unavoidable change) and then we can look to our peculiarities.

ACQUISITIVENESS

As much as any people, we have lived carnivorously. When our grabbing began, we went west for land (whether Indian-occupied or not) and east for Negroes. No effort to understand the American soul and story will be honest if it does not highlight our historical ability to buy and sell people as a major economic policy. In 1776 nearly one out of every six persons in the country was a slave. Americans, of course, did not invent slavery. The institution has a long and pathetic pedigree. But our brand of it did display some striking marks of the American way. The acquisitive and businesslike spirit in us contributed to what Stanley Elkins calls "the most implacable race-consciousness yet observed in virtually any society."[7] Other historical manifestations of slavery had their own cruelties, of course, but the status of slave normally had more redeeming ambiguities and fluidity. Elkins, however, sees the American system as unique. The property paradigm prevailed and produced a system that neatly and in the best mercantile tradition defined the status of the slave in relation to the master. As Elkins saw it, the American spirit of capitalism subdued humanistic impulses such as show up in most other slave systems, and stamped the status of slave with the chilling clarity of a depersonalized commodity.[8] The slaves were, in the crisp language of mercantile legality, "chattels personal . . . to all intents, constructions and purposes whatsoever."[9] The grab of black persons, in other words, was total and complete.

Neither did we as a nation entirely slacken our grip when the slaves were legally emancipated. What we did to the freed slaves was to institute a multidimensional process of social planning to "reenslave" them (to use the term of Mr. Justice Marshall in his opinion in *Bakke*). In the Jim Crow phase following "emancipation," the blacks were disenfranchised, stripped of their civil rights, and systematically and with the blessing of the Supreme Court put into the status of lowest caste. This set them up as the abiding exploitable base in our economic structure. In the second emancipation, beginning with the Brown decision in 1954 and the civil rights legislation of the 1960s, legal barriers against exploitation of the blacks were set up. Affirmative action programs have been an attempt to follow through on the implications of this second emancipation and prevent a second Jim Crow phenomenon. Because of the ingrained patterns and resistance, their success has been only partial. Jim Crow, Jr., is more subtly but effectively at work, and to his work I shall return when I spell out the actual present plight of American blacks.

The American Indians also know the tough acquisitive thrust of our history. As an indignant critic put it in 1842: "The people of this country would not be taxed without representation. They did not tax the Indians, without representation, but exterminated them and planted themselves in their territories."[10] Noteworthy in our attitude toward the Indian was the untroubled and premeditative right we felt to dispose of what was theirs. As early as 1776, "our Commissioners in France, finding it difficult to raise money abroad, distinctly proposed to Congress that 25,000,000 acres of the Indian lands should be sold 'to Europeans and Americans, to defray the expenses of the war.' "[11] History does not permit us to view that proposal as a "heresy," or incongruent with our behavioral record. We set out to "chastise those savages," as the idiom of the day had it, and in the process take what was theirs. Tragically, there was no necessity in this grim history of white acquisitiveness. As historians now point out, the number of Indians was small and the economic resources of the settlers was sufficient so that the Indians could have been fairly reimbursed for needed land. Instead, plunder was our preference.[12] William Penn's long success at peaceful accommodation with the Indians is witness to a gentler alternative, and yet our national option was for a bloody grab. Starting in Tidewater Virginia in 1607, all the way down to the massacre at Wounded Knee in 1890, we warred with the Indians.

This may be, as the neo-conservative consolers would have it, a heretical byway and not at all symptomatic of our actual benevolence and of the "central pattern" of all-inclusiveness that marks the true us, but almost three centuries of it give one pause. How this experience affected our national character is also worthy of some thought, since today is always, in significant ways, the resonation of yesterday. We must at least listen when Professor Richard Maxwell Brown suggests: "It is possible that no other factor has exercised a more brutalizing influence on the American character than the Indian wars."[13] No peoples are immaculately conceived. Neither are we, and it would be a self-serving "simplicity" that would assume that the darker side of our acquisitive history in no way infects our contemporary patterns and policies.

Our acquisitive spirit also reached for land. As to our expansion into the abundant West, the record and the results are clear. An observer in 1836 gives us something of the flavor of that great westward push.

It appears then that the universal disposition of Americans to emigrate to the western wilderness, in order to enlarge their dominion over inanimate nature, is the actual result of an expansive power which is inherent in them, and which by continually agitating all classes of society is constantly throwing a large portion of the whole population on the extreme confines of the State, in order to gain space for its development. Hardly is a new State or Territory formed before the same principle manifests itself again and gives rise to a further emigration; and so is it destined to go on until a physical barrier must finally obstruct its progress.[14]

The "physical barrier"—the Pacific Ocean—was reached some fifty years later but the "universal disposition" and the "expansive power" roared on. A new kind of expansionism followed. This expansionism was not seeking new soil to be tilled by American citizens. Rather, it sought trade centers, profitable plantations, and island naval bases in the cause of furthering trade and investment. As Charles A. Beard wrote of this expansionism: "It saw nothing out of the way in sweeping into the American orbit, distant lands with subject populations made up of aliens who for the most part did not yield readily to assimilation to American racial stock and nationality."[15] Cuba, Hawaii, the Philippines all attracted us. In each instance heavy ideological dressing was put on our public motives, but the practical import of it all was clear. By 1893 nearly two thirds of all taxable property in the island kingdom of Hawaii belonged to Americans. Within a few years nine tenths of all property was held by whites, nearly all Americans, with only a small proportion in the hands of native Hawaiians. Similarly in Cuba, American investments profited from forcible interventionism and expanded vigorously in the postwar period.[16] Also, in the Philippines, we did well while claiming to be doing good. A contemporary criticized President McKinley for his high-blown but widely shared pieties in explanation of the Spanish-American war, and noted that "when Spain was ready for peace, the Secretary of the Navy telegraphed to Admiral Dewey as follows: '. . . The President desires to receive from you any important information you may have of the Philippines; the desirability of the several islands; the character of their population, coal and other mineral deposits; their harbor and commercial advantages; and in a naval and commercial sense, which would be the most advantageous.' "[17] So it is not overwrought to say that the expansionist spirit of the frontier translated easily into fairly raw imperialism.

Military imperialism of the sort that we employed in the war with Spain came to be seen both as infeasible and unnecessary. There were other frontiers for the American imperialistic spirit more efficient than military conquest. An aggressive commercial establishment found it possible to exploit the cheap resources available in various parts of the world. The "terms of trade" worked to our advantage as we could buy primary resources cheaply and sell back manufactured products expensively. The new frontiers were, in fact, better than the old.

But this frontiering enterprise too has begun to run into barriers that are obstructing its progress. The balance of trade has turned against us. The Arab oil cartel signaled a new era. Cheap oil is no more. "Infinite" resources have revealed their finitude. All our frontiers have disappointed us. To make things worse, a senseless military budget bleeds us from within. And the multinational corporations, those newly born dinosaurs, whose ultimate loyalty is not fixed in either the home or the host countries, are in important ways out of control.

In summary, then, physical, social, and more broadly economic factors have risen to blunt our native, ingrained proclivities for no- or low-cost expansion. This is the new crunch—and the important word there is *new*. The 1890 closing of the western frontier was nothing in comparison to this. By that time, in fact, our industrial productive powers were beginning to blossom and so we could take the closing of the agrarian frontiers without breaking stride. This new crunch calls for a whole new stride and a whole new exercise in social imagination, especially since it is accompanied by an articulate and concerted refusal on the part of the exploited personal base of the economic structure to continue in that role. The passivity of the poor was an essential cog in the old economic machinery. Through their own impotence, the poor joined in the legitimation of the patterns of maldistribution. With blacks and women leading the way, that is increasingly no longer the case. Our acquisitive spirit, then, is called to repentance not only by justice but by the infeasibility of the old ways. The acquisitive American, however, will be one tough sinner to convert. We can see this by looking to two of his outstanding peculiarities: the glorification of individualism and the sacramentalizing of wealth.

AMERICAN SOLITAIRE

Horatio Alger is the true father of our country. Horatio was a self-made man. He was never on welfare. He sought justice not in accordance with his needs but in accordance with his earned deserts. This nation grew up around the myth of the "self-made man." (We were never so keen on the self-made woman.) There is, of course, a certain social alienation and detachment in the notion of the self-made man; the concept is isolationist and individualist in its essence. It idealizes "going it alone." Early America, drunk on its pristine abundance, was in an excellent position, nationally and internationally, to "go it alone." Indeed it self-consciously appropriated this as an ideal. George Washington referred happily to "our detached and distant situation," and asked rhetorically, "Why forgo the advantages of so peculiar a situation?"[18] We were, to say the least, comfortably overconfident in our solitary possibilities. The glorification of the achieving individual was quintessential *Americana*. We even made the illogical leap of identifying the interests of private enterprise with the good of the nation. What is good for Horatio Alger or General Motors is good for the country.

All this emerges paradigmatically in the remarks of Senator Chauncey M. Depew at Vanderbilt University:

> The American Commonwealth is built upon the individual. It recognizes neither classes nor masses. . . . We have thus become a nation of self-made men. . . . Commodore Vanderbilt is a conspicuous example of the product and possibilities of our free and elastic condition. . . . He neither asked nor gave quarter. The same . . . open avenues, the same opportunities which he had before him are equally before every other man.[19]

One need not imagine that the senator's Vanderbilt University audience winced or grimaced quizzically at these empirically unsupportable assertions. The good senator was merely and safely enunciating a national faith. There is, of course, a chilly core to his warm words. It leaves no apparent room for "to each according to his need." The message seems to be "self-make it or else." After all, the hero of the tale, Commodore Vanderbilt, "neither asked nor gave quarter." Of course, if there were a deep religious faith that the invisible hand of individualism would lead to an all-inclusive cornucopia, perhaps such a faith could console even the poor. Without such a faith, the spirit of the commodore is frightening.

One thing, of course, that "a nation of self-made men" would never want or tolerate would be an intruding government. After all, with the avenues of success open to every man, with Herbert Spencer's well-received assurance that "each adult gets benefits in proportion to merit, reward in proportion to desert,"[20] with omnipotence and infinity our national symbols, who needs a government to meddle in the naturally benevolent processes of distribution! These are the sentiments that insinuated their way into the depths of the American soul. James Bryce seems to have been on target when he wrote in 1888 that there were certain dogmas that one was almost sure to strike in plumbing an American mind. Prominent among these, he said, was a fear of centralized political power and the conviction that governmental functions must be kept at a minimum if the nation and the individual were to prosper.

This tradition took firm root. It is copiously manifested in our history. We see it blooming, for example, in the 1946 statement of the National Association of Manufacturers, a group that would appear to have fine credentials as to orthodox Americanism. Even the title of their statement is revealing: "The American Individual Enterprise System."

We became a nation of free men not serving political masters but ourselves, free to pursue our happiness without interference from the state, with the greatest liberty of individual action ever known to man. Individuals, conscious of unbounded opportunity, inflamed by the love of achievement, inspired by the hope of profit, ambitious of the comfort, power and influence that wealth brings . . . wanted little from the government beyond police protection while [they] confidently worked out [their] own destiny.[21]

Glaringly obvious in these words of the Association of Manufacturers is what Richard Hofstadter called "the ideology of self-help, free enterprise, competition, and beneficent cupidity upon which Americans have been nourished since the foundation of the Republic."[22] Once again, the esprit of this type of pronouncement would do little to warm the hearts of the poor on a cold winter's night.

We see this old-fashioned traditionalism again in the recent much-attended book by Harvard's Robert Nozick. Nozick's book, *Anarchy, State, and Utopia,* is strikingly unoriginal except in its packaging; it is significant because it cleaves so closely to the old tradition of the self-constituted man. He concludes "that a minimal state, limited to the narrow functions of protection against force, theft, fraud, enforcement of contracts, and so on, is justified; that any more extensive state will violate persons' rights not to be forced to do certain things, and is unjustified."[23] Nozick's work represents the mean stream of "don't tread on me" individualism that still courses through American veins. "There is no justified sacrifice of some of us for others."[24] With deadly seriousness he insists "that the state may not use its coercive apparatus for the purpose of getting some citizens to aid others. . . ."[25] He doesn't flinch at carrying this all the way to a position against taxes: "Taxation of earnings from labor is on a par with forced labor."[26]

It would be nice to see Nozick as a heretic, an apostate from the American way. But, as I said, he is unoriginal. If he cleaned up his jargon he could have been a speech writer for the old National Association of Manufacturers, for Commodore Vanderbilt, Senator Depew, Herbert Hoover, or any number of ancient or more recent representatives of the entrenched American ideology of self-made-man individualism.

The old individualism, however, has had its day. Faith in "beneficent cupidity" doesn't fit the new facts. We cannot realistically believe any longer that the more self-made individuals gobble up the better for the common good. We can no longer idealize the grabbers who neither gave nor asked quarter. Corporate power has shown that it can gobble up more than the common good can bear. This, indeed, has not come upon us of a sudden. Even at the end of the last century the tide was turning. As Hofstadter writes of that time, "the demand of the people for more positive controls of economic life gave rise to the Square Deal of Theodore Roosevelt and the New Freedom of Woodrow Wilson. . . . American capitalism had come of age, the great era of individualism, expansion, and opportunity was dead."[27] In 1931 the U. S. Chamber of Commerce Committee on Continuity of Business and Employment could declare: "A freedom of action which might have been justified in the relatively simple life of the last century cannot be tolerated today. . . . We have left the period of extreme individualism."[28] A nation that had wanted government only for few and guarded police duties came to hear cries for government takeovers of ailing businesses and for programs of relief. In the shambles of the depression there was little disposition to call government "a necessary evil," as an ebullient Thomas Paine could do in a simpler time. There were, of course, men like Herbert Hoover who could believe until much too late that the collapse of our economy was due to international ructions and not to our national faith in unimpeded "beneficent cupidity."

THE SACRAMENT OF SUCCESS

There was another critical element in the ideology of the acquisitive American spirit: the correspondence of success and merit. To have is to deserve. (The contrary of this is, of course, disheartening for those who do not have.) This is the sacramentality of wealth. (The sacraments were seen in theology as the efficacious signs of spiritual well-being.)

It is interesting that the literature on this aspect of American ideology turns naturally to the language of the religio-sacred: "The Gospel of Wealth"; "The Cult of Success." Professor Carnegie Calian has recently written a book entitled *The Gospel According to the Wall Street Journal*.[29] Such sacral language is appropriate. We are here in the realm of faith, of felt belief that, in the previously quoted phrase of Herbert Spencer, "each adult gets benefits in proportion to merit, reward in proportion to desert." This made for a kind of double indemnity in possessing wealth. It gave you the comforts and physical security available to the affluent and on top of that it marked you out as one of God's favorites. John D. Rockefeller could say: "The good Lord gave me my money." The money was thus a sacramental sign of God's esteem for Mr. Rockefeller. Having money was materially and spiritually salvific.

Small wonder then, with this in mind, that the powerful men of early America had such dread of the propertyless. Property was tied somehow to moral probity. Thus John Dickenson could speak of "men without property and principle." It was commonplace also to conjoin "property and character" in American speech. When John Hay looked disdainfully upon the labor riots of 1877, he felt that it was society's propertyless dregs that were rising up against the law of the land. According to his biographer, William Roscoe Thayer, Hay held: "That you have property is proof of industry and foresight on your part or your father's; that you have nothing is a judgment on your laziness and vices or on your improvidence. The world is a moral world; which it would not be if virtue and vice received the same rewards."[30]

The great American wager was that free, competitive processes would bring the greatest amount of good to the greatest number. As Ralph Waldo Emerson said in 1878, we open our doors "to every nation, to every race and skin." After inviting them into this land of opportunity, the rule of their survival, Emerson said, was this: "Let them compete, and success to the strongest, the wisest, and the best."[31] That is a happy thought for the successful because that would show that they are not only the strongest but also the wisest and the best. But, again, if you have not succeeded, the news is not good. You have had your equality of opportunity; poverty is failure. Implied here is an incredible faith that genuine fairness and equality of opportunity can exist in this or in any society. It is not even clear what equality of opportunity means. Human affairs are shot through with cronyism, clannishness, classism, and clubbishness—with all the favoritistic machinations thereof. To proclaim equality of opportunity is like proclaiming the imminent end of the world. The evidence is simply not there. I shall argue that equality of opportunity is the mask of social Darwinism—the survival of the fittest. It doesn't speak to the problem or to the worth of the unfit and the socially disempowered.

Calvinism has been blamed as the major culprit in the fostering of this mentality, and some forms of Calvinism were influential in this regard, but the proclivity has broader origins.[32]

In a further religious term, this conflating of economic and moral references amounted to a kind of cruel predestinationism. In its cruder form, predestination meant that some were chosen and some were not. It divided people into the elect and the damned, the saved and the reprobate. This allocation of good and ill was simply the will of God and there was nothing one could do about it. You were saved not by merit but by a divine choice over which you had no control. Thus the *theory* of predestination.

The practice, however, was not loyal to the theory. In practice, predestinationism prompted people to try to accumulate in their lives the signs of being among the chosen. In the American civil religion, which is rife with predestinational themes, wealth wrought of industriousness is a sign of salvation just as deprivation is the mark of the damned. The sacramentality of *having* and the ignobility of *not having* are thus deeply rooted in the American psyche. No realistic account of the current American crunch can ignore this forceful component of American mythology and ideology.

CONCLUSIONS ON THE AMERICAN STORY

It is unacceptably naïve to try to understand the United States or any nation by looking only at its professed ideals. Jefferson could write of liberty in a leisure bought by generations of slavery. Our founding fathers could proclaim all men equal while selling some as chattels. Virtue proclaimed is not virtue lived.

This nation is in a new kind of crisis. If you would plan for this crisis, you must take full account of all the complex forces that make this nation tick, above and beyond but also including its professed ideals.

Much of what we have is promising. We were, after all, weaned on a great vision of justice for all. There is much in our tradition to draw on in the struggle for social justice. But there are negative forces too that are intrinsic and endemic to us. And these are too lightly put aside by the critics of preferential public policy.

There is racism in the American character—profound and persistent racism. Three centuries of Indian wars show the mettle of this racism. Slavery and the abiding caste system are further witnesses. It also appears in all its ugliness in the history of race-biased anti-immigration policies which excluded southern and eastern Europeans and orientals, in the treatment of Hispanic Americans and Chinese, in the incarceration without trial of Japanese Americans during World War II. (We did not similarly incarcerate German Americans, who were also at war with us but who shared our whiteness and Western culture.) Sexism is also thoroughly American. So too are anti-Semitism and anti-Catholicism. Our zest for violence, which is highly indicative of our attitudes toward persons, has been much highlighted in recent scholarship. If a nation's prisons are mirrors of a nation's soul, as Dostoevski thought, ours tell a terrible story. And then, of course, there is our inveterate individualism with all of its implicit hostility to the other. Conjoined to this is the instinctive American call for a minimal state, which translates into an emasculation of the government. The government, however, with its unique access to carrot and stick, happens to be the most powerful and natural means for the achievement of social justice. Social justice is not the fruit of virtuous voluntarism, as well-heeled individualists would have us believe.

Slavery was not ended by appeals to virtue, neither does a nation mobilize for war or tax its citizens on a volunteer basis. At this point in moral evolution, commitment to the common good is not that strong or reliable. It is shallow utopianism to say that a caste system will be disassembled or that sexist power patterns will be changed by voluntary conversion and by litigating infractions on a one-to-one basis while leaving the regnant systemic injustices intact. Ensconced privilege has never yielded its place voluntarily in society. There is never an unenforced or painless transition from systemic vice to systemic virtue, nor will there be one now.

CHAPTER THREE

Justice for All Means Preference for Some

What does a nation do when suddenly it senses that it is caught in a double bind? On the one hand, free expansionism has ended, and at the same time the lassitude of the systemically deprived has changed into indignation. The combination of these two new realities opens up the unnerving possibility that the changes we need are not peripheral but structural. "The American way," with all that connotes, is on trial. Symbolically viewed, if we cannot tell the poor to go homestead on free land, we may have to share some unfree land with them. If we cannot siphon them off onto unclaimed territory, we may have to adjust our own claims to what territory there is. If we cannot provide for them freely, we may have to pay. In a word: the alternative to free expansion is *redistribution*.

Thomas Jefferson said that, whenever there are "unemployed poor, it is clear that the laws of property have been so far extended as to violate natural right."[1] It was Jefferson's view that it was the duty of government to promote the general well-being of the nation by doing those things that individuals could not do.[2] There are whole classes of people today who are disempowered and systemically impeded in their search for employment. One might well conclude that the laws of property have been overextended and that natural rights have been violated. Now how much should government do to promote the general well-being? What are the things it should do that individuals cannot do for themselves? This is the American debate that is now beginning afresh.

The growing awareness that such a debate is newly needed and that unavoidable change is now in prospect has stimulated two kinds of reactions. On the one hand, there is a fervid reassertion of the fundamental rights of the individual. These rights, it is said, may not be sacrificed to a greater social good. Stated in all of its purity in a *San Diego Law Review* article, this side of the argument holds that "the requirements of justice are based upon the principles of democratic-individualism, the fundamental ethic of Western man, which recognizes and affirms the ethical primacy of the concrete individual to the multitude of abstract groups of which he is a member."[3] Politico-moral discourse in America is cast in terms of "rights." Individualism insists that rights are vested only in individual persons. Thus if individuals have been persecuted and disempowered as members of a group—and not on a you vs. me basis—individualism has little to offer by way of solace to such individuals. Needless to say, problems suffered by individuals precisely because of group membership (being a woman, being a black) have no meaning in the individualist perspective. Groups are, as the quoted *San Diego Law Review* article put it, "abstract." As such they are not the business of government and are outside the sphere of rights. This curious doctrine, which, as I shall argue, no one could hold consistently, is alive and thriving in neo-conservative ideology and in some members of the Supreme Court.

There is, however, another reaction dawning in response to the epochal problems we now face. It stresses the claims of social justice and the necessity for a just society and its government to "promote the general welfare"—in the words of our Constitution—and not just to monitor one-to-one clashes of interest. This view is finding its principal expression in the debate on preferential affirmative action. Let me offer a brief word here on precisely what affirmative action is and whence it comes.

AFFIRMATIVE ACTION DEFINED

In general, affirmative action has come to mean any measure, beyond simple termination of discriminatory practices, which seeks to correct present discriminatory patterns so that discrimination will not recur. It seeks not just to spot misdeeds and correct them, but to alter the way of doing business so that some groups do not continue to benefit at the expense of other groups. Concretely, this means that white male monopolies are being challenged through systematic affirmative action.

On the eve of the Second World War, Franklin D. Roosevelt issued an executive order prohibiting racial discrimination in the employment practices of businesses that hold contracts with the government. Another executive order from Roosevelt sought to expand this, but these early efforts lacked both clout and follow-through. President Kennedy took a further step in 1961 by a new executive order directing contractors not only to refrain from discrimination but to undertake "affirmative action" to achieve equity in employment practices. This order showed the first awareness that a simple insistence on terminating overt discrimination might not end the systematic exclusion of certain groups from certain opportunities. President Johnson's executive order 11246 in 1965 put real muscle into preferential affirmative action. The perceived need was for some affirmative measures which would make job markets penetrable for the first time by certain groups of persons. Channels had to be opened for those for whom they had been, in complicated but effective ways, closed. As the U. S. Commission on Civil Rights put it: "In a society marred for years by pervasive discrimination in hiring and promotion, practices that are not racially motivated may nonetheless operate to disadvantage minority workers unfairly."[4] If those practices were not discovered and corrected, employers could piously rehearse a litany of compliance efforts that would effect no change in the actual employment of excluded minorities and women. Good intentions could abound without the slightest effect. Appreciation of this grew in the affirmative action program and in civil rights legislation and eventually found expression in the Supreme Court: "[G]ood intent . . . does not redeem employment procedures or testing mechanisms that operate as 'built-in headwinds' for minority groups and are unrelated to measuring job capability."[5] The Supreme Court has said that, in the absence of discrimination, it is to be expected that work forces will be "more or less representative of the population in the community from which employees are hired."[6]

There are basically two forms of affirmative action: remedial and preferential. Both forms involve positive steps to include previously excluded groups. Remedial affirmative action involves such things as collaboration with minority organizations and media, the use of minority recruiters, job recruitment at black colleges, revision of testing procedures, advertising targeted to minority groups, new training programs, and remedial education (including language education). Preferential affirmative action involves the use of numerical goals and timetables. Employers are asked to compare their utilization of women and minorities with the proportion of women and minorities available in the relevant labor pool. They are then asked to develop a plan involving reasonable and flexible goals and a timetable. The employer must never be required to hire unqualified persons or to compromise genuinely appropriate standards.

Most debate has centered on what I have called preferential affirmative action, since merely remedial affirmative action seems and is less threatening to white male privileges.[7] Debate heightened in the case of Marco De Funis and reached a crescendo in the cases of Allan Bakke and Brian Weber. For the Bakke case the greatest number of *amicus curiae* briefs in the history of the Supreme Court were filed. The Weber case excited similar concern since it moved from academe to the area of jobs, promotion, and seniority. Both cases provided workshops on justice for the nation. In both cases the nation struggled with some success for clarity on the meaning of justice.

Allan Bakke, who is white, was denied admission to the medical school at the University of California at Davis in 1973 and again in 1974. Bakke believed his rejections were due to the acceptance of less qualified minority applicants admitted under the university's special admissions program. Therefore he brought suit against the Board of Regents of the University of California. In the Supreme Court's decision in *Bakke,* the case for social justice and against narrow individualism found uneasy and uneven expression. Yet, in spite of all the stuttering and hedging the Court did in this case, I shall argue that American justice in *Bakke* took a gingerly but ultimately revolutionary step around a historic corner. *Bakke* is a landmark—albeit a shaky one. And so too is *Weber.*

Kaiser Aluminum and Chemical Corporation reached an agree-

ment with United Steelworkers to remedy the almost complete absence of black workers in skilled jobs in the aluminum industry. The
agreement amounted to a quota for the special training programs.
The program would be opened to whites and blacks on a fifty–fifty
basis until a representative number of blacks held skilled jobs. At the
plant where Mr. Brian Weber, a white man, was employed, the area
work force was 39 per cent black while only 2 per cent of the skilled
jobs were held by blacks. Two blacks with less seniority than Weber
were admitted into the training program and Weber brought a law-
suit in the district court charging violation of Title VII of the
Civil Rights Act of 1964. The district court held that the training
program was unlawful since the favored blacks had not been
specifically discriminated against by Kaiser. The court of appeals
affirmed this finding on the grounds that affirmative action programs
may only remedy discrimination against individual employees and
may not respond to societal discrimination. On June 27, 1979, the
Supreme Court reversed these decisions. Since this decision con-
fronted some of the principal presuppositions and arguments of
the opponents of preferential affirmative action, it furthered the
significant turn begun in *Bakke*.

Bakke and *Weber,* then, are early efforts to cope with the emerging conflict over redistribution. Recognition that much is at stake in
these decisions is shown not only by the record profusion of *amicus*
briefs and by the extensive and intensive attention given both cases
by the communications media, but also by the mounting of an extraordinary array of arguments against preferential affirmative action.
I shall turn first to those arguments since they are so revealing of the
current mind of America in this time of crunch. Then I shall analyze
briefly the Bakke and Weber decisions to show the progress made
there toward a new sense of justice.

IN DEFENSE OF THE INDIVIDUAL
QUA INDIVIDUAL[8]

Like bombs bursting in air, the arguments against redistribution
through preferential affirmative action are with us in force. Some of
these arguments are serious; some are narrowly legalistic; some are

silly but not for all of that unpopular. I have attempted to catalogue these arguments in five groupings: the philosophical, the pragmatic, the legal, the strategically naïve, and the *reductio ad absurdum* objections. Since all of these arguments are potentially or actually influential, and since all of them derive strength from their linkage with the old American folkways, all must be faced seriously. Here I shall simply state them; in the course of this book I shall ignore none of them. In the final chapter I shall speak to each of them.

THE PHILOSOPHICAL OBJECTIONS

1) The principal philosophical objection is encapsulated in the term "reverse discrimination." Preferential policies are an evil means to a good end. They discriminate to correct discrimination. They respond to injustice with injustice.

2) Preferential policies work on the assumption that groups have rights. They do not. Only individuals have rights. Thus an individual may litigate to seek redress but it is absurd to think of a group doing so. Also, there is no such thing as collective guilt. Members of groups may do wrongful things, but the group as such cannot be considered guilty.

3) Employment and admissions should be based on merit, not on irrelevant group membership. Indeed, as philosopher Alan H. Goldman says regarding employment, "the white male who has successfully met the requirements necessary to attaining maximal competence for a position attains *some right* to that position."[9]

4) Preferential treatment by its very definition is a violation of equality and equal opportunity. As Aristotle said, "All men think justice to be a sort of equality."[10] That must at least mean that some cannot be preferred to others simply because they are members of certain groups.

THE PRAGMATIC OR
CONSEQUENTIALIST OBJECTIONS

1) Even if one could justify theoretically a program of preferen-

tial redistribution, the backlash would be socially disruptive. Someone has to lose out when someone else is preferred. Since the preferment is in terms of group identities, this will exacerbate group tensions. The rash of "reverse discrimination" suits and the cooling of relations between blacks and Jews are seen as examples of this backlash.

2)   Preferential affirmative action leads to a situation of wrong victims and wrong beneficiaries. Well-off or middle-class blacks are likely to be preferred rather than poor blacks since poor blacks are less likely to qualify for skilled employment or admission to institutions of higher education. Likewise the whites who are rejected owing to a preferential program might be the most disadvantaged whites whose qualifications are marginal precisely because of their disadvantages. Also, in this plan, the unprejudiced might be punished and the prejudiced spared. There seems to be no workable way to avoid these apparent inequities.

3)   Because of all the supervision needed to see if affirmative action is working, government will intrude itself excessively into business and the professions. This would interfere with academic freedom and free enterprise.

4)   If race becomes a qualification for preference, we are faced with the fact that our definitions of race are not all that susceptible of simple application. This raises the specter of litigating the race of an individual. As John Kaplan writes in the *Northwestern University Law Review:* "One can well imagine a case in which testimony would be necessary from 'expert' witnesses as to the degree of kinkiness of hair, of skin color, of pinkness of palms, and many other factors which go into our definitions of a Negro."[11] The use of racial or ethnic review committees to screen claims of group identity, ethnic identification cards (with the possibility of a black market in some)— all rise as practical obstacles to preferential policies based on group identity.

5)   Preferential policies necessarily involve a quota or target number. But how can this be set? Should it be based on a national

average or simply local, on urban or metropolitan figures? How could we settle disputes about what percentage should be reached before cutting off the preferential program?

6)   How can we distinguish between benign and discriminatory monopolies? If, by way of tradition and ethnic preference, 80 per cent of the tugboat captains in New York are of Swedish descent and none are Jewish, black, or female, should we undertake to recruit and convince Jews, blacks, and women to "man" the tugboats? Affirmative action policies seem to point us toward purely statistical judgments of injustice, while, in truth, lopsided statistics are not always a sign of unfair advantages. We could end up requiring basketball teams to drop most of their blacks. In that instance affirmative action would be undermining the gains blacks have made on merit.

7)   From a Marxist perspective it is argued that race is not the issue; class is. Affirmative action, therefore, is a distraction from the necessary reforms of society which will be brought about not by fixation on the separate claims of racial and ethnic groups but by uniting all groups in a demand for more jobs and better education for all.

8)   If we admit more blacks into medical and law schools so that blacks in ghettoes will be better served, how can we know that the black doctors and lawyers will choose to serve the ghetto people? They are likely to be drawn as most professionals are to where the affluent remuneration is—and that clearly is not in the ghetto.

9)   Affirmative action programs lead to a parade of horrors and thus appear to be administratively infeasible. Unrealistic demands are made to hire from certain groups even though no qualified candidates from that group are available. Congresswoman Edith Green of Oregon, for example, reported in 1972 that a ship conversion plant in Portland had records to prove that they had hired 15 per cent minority people as a result of an active recruitment program. The Contract Compliance Office in San Francisco came to Portland and said they could get no federal contracts unless they had 15 per cent minority employees in every single job category. This placed an impossible burden on the company.[12] The number of stories like this in

circulation would indicate intrinsic problems in the affirmative action scheme.

THE LEGAL OBJECTIONS

1) The equal protection clause of the Fourteenth Amendment of the Constitution guarantees that no state shall "deny to any person within its jurisdiction the equal protection of the law." This clause gives constitutional status to the ideal of equality. It would seem to ensure that no person will be given preferential treatment and thus seems to clash at the conceptual level with preferential affirmative action.

2) Section 601 of Title VI of the Civil Rights Act of 1964 declares: "No person in the United States shall, on the ground of race, color, or national origin, be excluded from participation in, be denied the benefits of, or be subjected to discrimination under any program or activity receiving Federal financial assistance." These words seem to prohibit both discrimination against women or minorities and "reverse discrimination" against white males as part of a preferential program.

3) Title VII of the same act is even more explicit. It prescribes in paragraph 703 (j): "Nothing contained in this title shall be interpreted to require any employer . . . to grant preferential treatment to any individual or to any group because of the race, color, religion, sex, or national origin . . ." If this were not clear enough, the Supreme Court in *McDonald v. Santa Fe Trail* held that "Title VII prohibits racial discrimination against . . . white petitioners . . . upon the same standards as would be applicable were they Negroes. . . ."[13]

THE OBJECTIONS OF STRATEGIC NAÏVETÉ

1) Great progress was being made before all this affirmative action began. The best thing that could happen for blacks and all citizens is to abandon this exacerbating program and allow the normal democratic processes of a pluralist society to achieve the goals to-

ward which they had been moving. Those who see the situation this way are impressed with the possibilities of voluntarism, the enforcement of anti-discriminatory norms, and the providing of grievance machinery. Beyond this, nothing is needed.

2)   Affirmative action makes blacks *et al.* look bad. Those minorities and women who are qualified and make it in our society will be looked down on as having been favorites of the law who didn't really make it on their own.

3)   What the blacks are going through today is typical of the lot of the latest immigrants or migrants in our society. They will have to move ahead slowly as other temporarily disadvantaged groups did. Indeed, they have already begun to do so, indicating that this is no time to disrupt the process by lifting them out and placing them ahead of others.

4)   Since the government should be color-blind, it should find alternatives to affirmative action preferential policies. As Eliot Marshall, a senior editor of the *New Republic,* suggests, the government could, along with outlawing discrimination, "undertake a massive job guarantee program . . . it could stipulate that the poorest man's income would be no less than one-half as large as the richest man's. That would accomplish the same end as affirmative action, but it would do so without provoking the deadly passions of racial enmity."[14] (This is offered as a practical alternative to an ongoing program!)

5)   Blacks are culturally different. This shows up in their work habits and morals. They are often late, frequently absent, prone to stealing and insubordination. Edward C. Banfield, the Harvard urbanologist, says: "Men accustomed to a street-corner style of life, to living off women on welfare, and to 'hustling' are seldom willing to accept the dull routines of the 'good' job."[15] Banfield also tells us that efforts to overcome these problems have not been encouraging. In other words, there is not an awful lot we can do. Putting people in good jobs for which they are not ready will not work.

Added to this cultural problem is the recurrently touted possibility of the genetic inferiority of blacks. Arthur R. Jensen, for example, writing in the Winter, 1969, issue of the *Harvard Educational Review,* argued that the intellectual potential of the poor, and particularly of blacks, was due to inherent genetic limitations. He was explaining why domestic programs of the Great Society failed. His views find support in the positions of William Shockley, a Nobel Prize-winning physicist at Stanford University.

6) Affirmative action schemes are based on non-viable concepts like "societal discrimination" and "institutional racism." But as Mr. Justice Powell said in his decision on Bakke, "societal discrimination" is "an amorphous concept of injury."[16] And Nathan Glazer tells us that the whole idea of institutional racism is nebulous and unfounded and the use of such a term can only indicate that racism pure and simple is on its way out.[17] These sentiments of Glazer lead quite naturally to

THE *REDUCTIO AD ABSURDUM* OBJECTIONS:

1) Once you give preference to one offended group you will be besieged by all the others. Government directives mention as candidates for preferential affirmative action American Indians, Eskimos, Chinese, Japanese, Koreans, Filipinos, Mexicans, Puerto Ricans, Cubans, Central or South Americans, Samoans, and Aleuts. But why stop there? Short people, fat people, green-eyed people, gay people, South Side Milwaukee Polish-American housewives, and others can all make solid claims to have suffered from discrimination. The only way to avoid this chaos is to close the affirmative action pork barrel and treat individuals as individuals.

2) The very concept of affirmative action forces you to hire the unqualified. How can anyone know if the black airplane pilot or the black anesthetist got that position on merit and qualification or under government pressure? Only the traditional merit system is safe.

3) Professor Virginia Black of Pace University, Westchester, says that preferential affirmative action has its most obvious historic parallel in feudalism. She says: "I believe it is not too far-fetched to compare the case before us with those execrable bills of attainder marking legal distinctions between the protected and the unprotected

by hereditary birthright, and with feudal law of primogeniture in which inheritance passed to him who was favored by the contingencies of birth."[18] Professor Black also argues that the policies at issue here are also totalitarian and are examples of the primitive *lex talionis* in modern disguise.

4)   Professor Paul Seabury of the University of California at Berkeley compares preferential affirmative action to American foreign policy in Vietnam. Writing of HEW and university affirmative action goals, he says that only HEW wins. It wins because the "box-score is of its own devising. To the extent that its goals are met and the body-count proves this, it wins. But then, where have we heard *that* before?"[19] Miro M. Todorovich, co-ordinator of the Committee on Academic Non-Discrimination and Integrity, inclines to the same analogy. He sees affirmative action as betraying an overconfidence in the "manipulative abilities of social engineers that has characterized much of the worst (and most disastrous) in our recent foreign and domestic policy."[20]

5)   Preferential affirmative action seeks to compensate for *past* wrongs. However laudable in intent, this is impossible to achieve. Are we to hunt down the descendants of the Etruscans in the likelihood that some of our biological forebears maltreated them in times past? As Mr. Justice Powell said in the Bakke decision, this kind of compensation "may be ageless in its reach into the past."[21] We have enough to do to attend to the iniquities of the present without attempting to make reparation for all the evils that have been.

6)   Finally, in various ways it is argued that affirmative action programs are too complicated and difficult to administer. And even if we could be clear about how to give preference to whom, we would not know whether the system works since the good results may have come about through the natural democratic processes anyhow.

The above objections, I believe, are quite representative of the kinds of arguments that are brought against preferential affirmative action, though they take various forms with various authors. In fact, I do not know where in the literature a fuller listing can be found.

The problem of redistribution has achieved its most poignant focus in this debate, which offers us a distillation of just how the American soul is reacting to it at a time of unique and unparalleled economic crunch. This is the broader significance of these objections. However, they illustrate only one kind of response. The other possible reaction makes an important appearance in the pages of the Bakke and Weber decisions and opinions. I turn first to the Bakke decision. With all the indecision that the Court betrayed, American justice hobbled around an important corner in the case of Allan Bakke, and if we don't make careful note of this progress we may lose it.

BAKKE WINS, BAKKE LOSES . . .

The Bakke case produced a furor. Pending suits all over the country awaited its outcome. Public interest spread as the communications media visited the case with extraordinary attention. Projections of "landmark" status were proclaimed for the case months before the decisions were announced. Sixty-nine *amicus curiae* briefs were filed in this case—a record number for the Supreme Court. But then the decisions came, and no one was very clear about what had happened. Some supporters of affirmative action expressed gloom, others delight, and similar confusion could be found among opponents. Some cried "landmark"; others said the decision as rendered by Mr. Justice Powell didn't really touch affirmative action at all. The obvious question then is: What happened?

My own assessment is that progress happened. While Bakke the man won, Bakke the symbol of invidious individualism lost. While the Court showed itself quite unclear about the foundations of what it was doing, it still managed to say that properly motivated preference on the basis of race was neither unconstitutional nor unfair. Such color-conscious preference would not violate the equal protection clause of the Fourteenth Amendment or the civil rights of individuals who lose out because of the preferential policies employed. There is in the Bakke decision an admission of landmark proportions that public policy need not be color-blind and that preference might be given to members of certain groups *qua* members of those groups in certain circumstances. While throwing bouquets at individualistic meritocracy and equality, the Court came down on the side of an *inequality* that is commanded by social justice. The importance of this must not be underestimated. A report of the Carnegie Council on Policy Studies in Higher Education before the Bakke decision states quite accurately that the roots of this debated policy "extend downward into the bedrock of our moral and social philosophy, and outward into the economic and technological foundations of American Society."[22]

Although the Court made progress it did not escape a typically American ambivalence. A man caught on the horns of an apparently insoluble dilemma quite naturally shifts his weight to one side and then to the other. The Court decisions in *Bakke* reveal the inconsistencies and shiftings that such a predicament invites. Mr. Justice Powell wrote the judgment of the Court. And Powell, like our society, is torn between the ingrained ideology of individualism and equality and the pressing claims for a new realization of social justice with the inherent corrective inequalities that that entails. While on one horn of his dilemma, Powell decries the Davis program's "principal evil," which is to deny to an applicant the "right to individualized consideration without regard to his race."[23] Again he insists: "Preferring members of any one group for no reason other than race or ethnic origin is discrimination for its own sake."[24] An approved program must treat "each applicant as an individual in the admissions process."[25] His qualifications must be weighed "competitively" so that he will have no reason to complain of unequal treatment.[26] There must be no "disregard of individual rights as guaranteed by the Fourteenth Amendment."[27] Everyone must have the opportunity to compete for every seat in the class.[28] No individual should be insulated by any rubric "from comparison with all other candidates for the available seats."[29] The innocent should not be disadvantaged for whatever harm the beneficiaries of special programs are thought to have suffered.[30] Also, "societal discrimination" is "an amorphous concept that might be ageless in its reach into the past."[31] Says Powell of the Court, "We have never approved preferential classifications in the absence of proven constitutional or statutory violations."[32]

At this point, any Herbert Hoover individualist or Herbert

Spencer meritarian should be up and cheering. This seems to be "to each according to his merits" with no quarter given. No social planning or engineering seems permissible within this purview. Every man must stand or fall on his own merits. Color or sex does not matter. Only demonstrated worth counts within the purity of this competition. Where there are proven offenses, let reparation be meted out, but in the absence of such, let unimpeded competition reign. In such competition, neediness, it would seem, has no credentials.

But wait! There is another side to the Bakke decisions. While Powell looked earnestly backward, he still managed to move forward. Harvard College provided the crutch he needed. Powell decried the Davis program in language that would thrill any rugged individualist, but he then went on to praise the Harvard plan in a way that can give no pleasure to those who long for individualistic, meritarian competition.

Powell uses as his argument the educational value of diversity. A monolithic school, made up only of Boston Brahmins, would not prepare the students for the culturally diversified nation and world into which they graduate. Needed too are students from the East, the South, the Midwest, black students, white students, Jews, Arabs, and Irish. Achievements in art, social action, sports, and flute playing might figure in the calculation of appropriate "diversity" at the school. The Harvard plan, approved by Powell, has all of this in mind.

In the Harvard plan, "the race of an applicant may tip the balance in his favor."[33] It is fully admitted and countenanced that in this plan "race has been a factor in some admission decisions."[34] In the final determination of who shall be admitted and who rejected, race may function as a crucial "plus."[35] Other non-objective factors may also "tip the balance" in favor of one candidate over another. Among these: "demonstrated compassion, a history of overcoming disadvantage, ability to communicate with the poor, or other qualifications deemed important."[36] These last words, which are full of import for social justice, have been largely ignored in commentaries on the Powell judgment.

At this point, if I were a well-to-do white candidate, quite qualified for admission but down near the perilous cut-off point, I would be getting nervous. Certain things have entered the "competition" to which I have no access, and these things may be counted as "plus" factors and may "tip the balance" in favor of the person who does have one or more of them—even though his academic talents may be equal to or lower than mine! Through no fault of my own I may lack blackness, and that can "tip the balance" against me. Because I am affluent, I have not had the opportunity to acquire "a history of overcoming disadvantage" or "ability to communicate with the poor." The black candidate with whom I am in competition may have all three of these "plus" factors among what Powell calls "his combined qualifications" (merits?) and thus, even though he may be less impressive in his academic credentials, the balance tips toward him and I am rejected.

Where is my "right to individualized consideration without regard to . . . race" that Mr. Powell requires as the badge of constitutional propriety? And not only is race a "plus" factor that can count against me and keep me out of school, but possibly neither I nor the school have been proved guilty of constitutional violations meriting such retribution. And has Mr. Powell not just assured me that the Court has never approved preferential classifications in the absence of such violations? Yes, those are his very words.

However, there is more yet to fuel my white male malaise. The approved Harvard plan does not operate "without some attention to numbers."[37] Ten or twenty blacks would not be enough since "10 or 20 blacks could not begin to bring to their classmates and to each other the variety of points of view, backgrounds and experiences of blacks in the United States. Their small numbers might also create a sense of isolation among the black students themselves and thus make it more difficult for them to develop and achieve their potential."[38] So, not only are we allowed to take race into account as a balance-tipping plus, but we are also allowed to *count* the number of blacks to make sure it is more than a token force. This consciousness of numbers is legitimate, not because of "individualized consideration" or "competition with all other applicants," to cite two of Powell's meritocratic phrases, but because of *group* considerations. The justifying considerations here are related to the common good, not to individual rights—and certainly not to the individual rights of the rejected student. There are two groups to which individual claims are being subordinated. First, there are the white students at the school, who would not get enough experience of black life and culture with only ten or twenty blacks in a big white school. The second group is comprised of the blacks themselves, who if they are only ten or twenty will feel isolated and thus will be hampered in achieving their full potential. Group considerations are therefore interposed that will be for some students the decisive reason why they were rejected and, for others, the balance-tipping reason why they were admitted. In simple terms, the system approved by the Supreme Court will result in the inclusion of some and the exclusion of others on the basis of race and other group-regarding factors. Given the number of objective and subjective factors involved in admissions analysis, it may not be feasible to identify and name those who were not admitted because of the racial factor. But they are there. And these persons are individuals who are suffering because of group considerations beyond their competitive reach.

Mr. Powell, however, argues that the "applicant who loses out on the last available seat to another candidate receiving a 'plus' on the basis of ethnic background" will not have been treated poorly, since he or she had, in the approved Harvard plan, the chance to compete for every single place, while at Davis the student could not even be considered for a certain number of places.[39] But here, surely, Powell's logic slips. The ability to compete for every opening, when more than a token number of openings are going to be filled by qualified black candidates, and when "some attention is paid to distribution among many types and categories of students,"[40] is not an unalloyed and equal opportunity to compete for every opening. Down around the cut-off point, being black and qualified is better than being white and qualified, for some applicants at least.

But, argues Powell, there is no "facial intent to discriminate" in the Harvard plan. Of course, most discrimination can be achieved without "facial intent," so the statement is not impressive. What Powell seems to be saying here is that Harvard is doing what has to be done but is doing it with a touch of class, covering over the nonegalitarian preference operating here with a veneer of broad-minded educational concerns. What can be said is that *what* is going on at

Harvard and was going on at Davis amounted to the same thing. The *how* of it was different. In both schools race and other non-competitive factors counted as plusses; in both schools some qualified students who would have been admitted if racial and other factors were not counted won't get admitted; in both schools "individualized consideration without regard to . . . race" is programmatically excluded. Thus Powell had no grounds in logic or in law for approving one school's plan and declaring the other unconstitutional. Mr. Justice Powell should have joined Justices Brennan, White, Marshall, and Blackmun in approving the Davis plan. Then his logic, law, and ethical judgment would have been consistent. His endorsement of the Harvard plan, however, is a service to justice—provided that the import of what he did is not missed.

ACCENTING POWELL'S PROGRESS

It is easy to miss Powell's progress because of his legerdemain. In fact, Harvard professor of law Alan Dershowitz goes so far as to say: "At bottom, Powell's opinion really says nothing at all about affirmative action as such."[41] That is wrong. In principle, Powell said a lot about affirmative action. The confusion here, of course, is understandable. Powell's stress on the glories of diversity in a school context could easily imply that he was writing a piece in educational psychology. One can see reasons why Powell would be attracted to the educational diversity argument. Clearly this emphasis would be less disturbing to the public than an unvarnished facing up to the fact that the business at hand was not to clear the way for flutists at Harvard but to do something about the entrenched discrimination against blacks, women, and some other groups. Two important points must be noted about Powell's position:

1)   A year before the Bakke decision, Professor Thomas Nagel of Princeton University wrote: "The most important argument against preferential treatment is that it subordinates the individual's right to equal treatment to broader social aims."[42] Powell's diversity argument, for all its snobbishness, does subordinate "the individual's right to equal treatment to broader social aims." He departs from

meritarian individualism's "may the best man win" approach and says that *considerations of social good and of race may be factored into the criteria for admission.* Whether for reasons of jurisprudential subterfuge or from faintness of heart, Powell preferred to wax warm on the benefits of diversity at school. Yet the principal business at hand was the dismantling of a caste system in the United States. The history of the case and the multiple *amici* briefs filed show the real business that was up for decision in *Bakke.* The question asked of the Court was whether constitutional programs of admission must be color-blind, and the Court said no. The question also was whether you could prefer members of groups *qua* members of groups for reasons of the common good, and the Court said yes. It is not Bakke or the flute players who may get admitted at Harvard who are the big winners in this decision, but blacks, women, and certain other groups. Powell's fixation on the diversity argument should not obscure the point of principle that prevailed here. *Individualized treatment without regard to race is not required by the Constitution.* Considerations of the common good can override the right to such individualized treatment. Among the possible common-good considerations, diversity in an educational context is surely not the most important. Cities don't burn nor do unemployment figures soar nor do rats proliferate because of a lack of diversity in our colleges. But if the diversity need was the most that Powell could bear at this time, so be it. It is a matter of judgment whether educational diversity is a compelling social good. However, the critical principle that has survived this court test is that *something* can override the claims of individual merit. There can be a compelling social good to which the claims of the individual may have to be sacrificed. That is Powell's position and that is progress.

Because this principle was buried in the language of ideological individualism, Justices Brennan, White, Marshall, and Blackmun led off their lengthy opinion approving the Davis plan by expressing concern that "the central meaning of today's opinions" not be missed. What the Court had ruled, these justices pointed out, was that it is constitutional "to act affirmatively to achieve equal opportunity for all." Remember that, in the context of *Bakke,* acting "affirmatively" means preferential affirmative action. Furthermore, they said "Government may take race into account when it acts not to demean or insult any racial group, but to remedy disadvantages cast on minorities by past racial prejudice. . . ."[43] Both Harvard and Davis have preferential programs, and five justices approved of the Harvard plan and four approved of both. The issue of the day was preferential affirmative action and it passed muster.

IN THE CASE OF BRIAN WEBER

The Court's advances in the Weber decision are considerably more forthright than in *Bakke* and thus need less elaboration. The majority opinion, written by Mr. Justice William J. Brennan, Jr., does attempt to assert the "narrowness" of its inquiry. According to the opinion, the Constitution is not involved. The issue was simply whether private parties (in this case Kaiser and United Steelworkers) can reach the agreement they did without violating Title VII of the Civil Rights Act of 1964 and the Court's answer was that they may. Opponents of preferential affirmative action, however, are right in asserting that there is nothing narrow about that.

The two main elements of progress in *Weber* are these: it allows for a preferential quota that is even more unambiguous than that of the Davis plan rejected in *Bakke*. Approved here is a 50 per cent plan that will bring blacks from an excluded to an included status. It does not require that the individual blacks who are preferred be shown to have been discriminated against specifically by the corporation involved. That they are members of a group that has been traditionally segregated and discriminated against is enough. This throws out the one-to-one approach and the "reverse discrimination" and "color-blind" arguments so favored by opponents of affirmative action. Thus the basic notion of "discrimination" is effectively refined. The paralyzing idea that discrimination can be ended in society on a basis of individually litigated grievances is gainsaid.

Secondly, the Court gives a lesson in judicial interpretation that offers needed sophistication to the literalists who would sacrifice the meaning to the letter of the law. In *Weber,* the Court really does approve of a quota system as a mode of preferential relief. There are good reasons why "quota" became a bad word in American parlance. Quotas were used against Jews and certain kinds of immigrants in clearly unjust ways. The word "quota," however, has a native innocence. We may refer to "numerical goals" or "target numbers," but in any case we are talking about counting a certain number of people for a specific purpose. The agreed-upon plan at Kaiser came from a recognition that blacks as a group were egregiously excluded from desirable positions at Kaiser. The plan undertook a temporary shift in the patterns of selection to change the exclusionary patterns that heretofore reigned. This necessarily involved numbers. It also went beyond the handling of individual cases of proved discrimination to a tactic of social planning. Half of all candidates for the special training would be black till underrepresentation ceased to be a fact of life for blacks in this segment of the industry. It was to be understood that all persons who entered the training program must be qualifiable or they should be rejected and dropped from the program. But factors like seniority—which is seen as a meritarian element even though it merely means that you got there earlier—do not outweigh the need to end the exclusion of blacks. Setting a quota for blacks means that being black is a "plus" factor, in the language of *Bakke,* that can tip the balance. Being white can, for some such as Brian Weber, be a negative factor leading to exclusion at this time.

With this ruling, a number of classic arguments of meritarian individualism tumble. These arguments will, of course, rise to fight again since *Weber* will not end the debate and new forms of the same debate are already in the wings. But they have been dealt a mighty blow. The Court has brought new light to the meaning of discrimination. The discrimination against which the Civil Rights Act and this decision are directed is *unjust* discrimination. The word "discrimination" at root implies nothing bad. It simply means noting a relevant difference where there is one. "Discriminating judgment," in this root sense, is worthy of praise. The discrimination at issue in civil rights law, however, uses a characteristic such as race or sex to strip a person and even a group of persons of that which is their minimal due in justice. This distinction is completely missed by the literalists, such as Mr. Justice Rehnquist, who do not see that noting differences between black and white is just or unjust according to the circumstances. Rehnquist laments that employers are now permitted to consider race in making employment decisions. That is, of course, true. To change the patterns of employment based on color is no job for a color-blind person. Exclusionary color patterns of hiring and advancement based on color must be succeeded by inclusionary patterns based on color until color becomes an irrelevant characteristic in the process. Doing this hurts some of those in the previously advantaged group. However, their hurt is not the result of unjust discrimination but is part of the just reversal of existing discrimination. In the sense of civil rights law, there is no discrimination against Brian Weber although his color imposed a sacrifice upon him, any more than there is discrimination against a person drafted into military service because he or she happens to be a certain age. I shall argue all of this more fully later. For now, note that the Court has not blessed the white male cry of "reverse discrimination" or the belated call for color-blind justice.

In approving the 50 per cent plan at Kaiser, the Court has moved beyond the social myopia of individualism. It rejects Mr. Powell's dismissal of the notion of "societal discrimination" as amorphous. It recognizes the need to eliminate traditional "patterns" of racial segregation. It also recognizes the existence of hierarchies that kept the black person down. All of this shows a sociological sophistication not present in Powell's *Bakke* statement. The power that keeps blacks and others disabled is patterned, hierarchical, and systemic. It requires the kind of restructuring that the Kaiser plan provides. To achieve this necessary and significant restructuring some of the claims and opportunities of individuals such as Brian Weber will have to be sacrificed. Such is the nature of human society and social justice.

Because of all of this, the disclaimer of the majority opinion concerning the narrowness of their decision is unfounded. In their gently stated judgment, the majority cut through much of the barbed-wire defenses set up by the established powers in the society and worked out of a better conception of justice than did Powell in *Bakke*. While not speaking formally as social philosophers and while attempting to hew closely to the challenges presented by certain paragraphs of law, the Court acted out of the implied assumption that individual goals and opportunities may at times be sacrificed for significant social purposes. The quibbling over the exact meaning of certain legal language should not befog the achievement. Social justice was served in a signal fashion by the Court on this day.

In a way that is also laudable, the Court in *Weber* showed a mature understanding of its function and role in this society. In view of the letter of the law, the case for Weber and against preferential affirmative action was not without force—a point conceded by Mr. Brennan in his opinion. Some of the language in Title VII seems to state unambiguously that neither blacks nor whites should be preferred because of race. Also, the Supreme Court in *McDonald v. Santa Fe Trail Trans. Co.* held that Title VII protected whites as well as blacks from certain forms of racial discrimination. Yet here was Brian Weber being disadvantaged by reason of his whiteness. Being white with more seniority was not as good as being black with less. Could discrimination be made of sterner stuff?

Again, of course, the word on the loose in this argument is "discrimination." We might all agree that discrimination is illegal if we mean by it unjust discrimination. The precise point at issue, however, was whether preferential affirmative action is unjustly discriminatory. Many discussants of this case stand with Mr. Justice Rehnquist in assuming that it is. Their assumption would be true and Weber would triumph in reason and at law if justice involves treating everyone the same even though his or her situation is different. In *Weber,* the Supreme Court would have none of this.

In effect, what the Court did in *Weber* was to insist that distinctions be made where there are differences and that doing such is not unjustly discriminatory. There are differences between white and black power and status in this nation—differences that reach the qualitative level of caste. The Court does not use such language, of course, but in allowing the systematic disadvantaging of whites as a temporary process of reapportioning opportunities, it supports the position that preferential treatment may be just. This could be justified only if major differences exist between those differently treated. The Court was not just on solid philosophical grounds here; it was also showing legal realism. Contrary to the claims by Rehnquist and Burger that the language of Title VII is plain and unambiguous, the history of the Civil Rights Act shows no such thing. In a 1974 article Professor Alfred W. Blumrosen shows that the apparently anti-preference clauses of the act—despite their seeming clarity—contain their own "internal compromise," and must be understood only within the delicate balancing act involved in their creation. We do not have in Title VII the unnuanced view that blacks and whites must be treated the same and that it is forbidden discrimination to do otherwise. Such a position would have frustrated the whole Civil Rights Act of 1964. Also, as Blumrosen points out, the Congress in 1972 rejected proposed amendments to Title VII that would have prohibited so-called "discrimination in reverse," thus indicating that "Congress intended to permit effective affirmative action remedies where discrimination was found. . . ."[44] The Court in *Weber* was not, as accused, attempting to supplant the legislative process. It was simply recognizing as such a court should that the purpose and meaning of the law it was interpreting were to end the systemic, unjust discrimination against blacks. To side with Weber would have frustrated that law by using it to continue the evils it sought to end.

The purpose of the Supreme Court is not just to parse the law and diagram its sentences. It is not just an echo of the letter of the law. There would be no need to go to the living intellects of judges for that. *We ask the Supreme Court to find the meaning of the law in to-day's situation.* To interpret the Civil Rights Act as supporting the current caste system—i.e., by siding with Mr. Weber—would actually have been counterlegislation. It would have blunted the anti-discriminatory purpose of that law by forbidding means that are essential to that purpose. That, equivalently, would make a new law. If Weber and the minority on the Court had had their way, the Civil Rights Act would have been used to maintain the very white male monopoly that made a civil rights law necessary. Sticking to the letter is not conservative in this instance; it is rather subversive.

In both *Bakke* and *Weber* the Court, with all of its indirection, stammering, and disclaiming, stood up against the enormous weight of ideological individualism and took a major step toward a new American sense of justice and redistribution. Implicit in the action of the Court is a better moral philosophy of the just society that leaves behind egoistic individualism. In these cases the Court could not simply play amid the statutes and precedents or just tease the letter of the law. The answers could not be found in that wise. The Court had to philosophize and it did make philosophical gains. It did move toward a better appreciation of social justice. The gains here, however, are precarious and could be lost in another case, since the theoretical underpinnings were not firmly planted. It is to the establishment of those underpinnings in the higher court of ethical reasoning that I now turn. Moral reason is the ultimate appellate court to which even the Supreme Court must attend. The entire debate on affirmative action is predicated upon some notion of justice. Herein lies our major national handicap. There is no clarity as to what justice is. Shallow assumptions about what it might be rule the day. To a clarification of justice I now turn.

PART TWO

Doing Justice to Justice

If it is true that men of action are the pawns of men of thought, then thinking is serious business. Theory is not a luxury but is rather the stuff of life. If we attempt to do justice without a theory of what justice is, we will do it poorly. American thinking on justice is superficial. Confusing and often contradictory assumptions roam the American mindscape, whether one is reading a Robert Nozick, a Nathan Glazer, a Mr. Justice Powell, or even a compassionate writer like John Rawls. Individualism is the operating creed in this nation and the theories of justice that emerge from it are distorted and inadequate. The following three chapters do what cannot be safely avoided. They present a theory of justice and explore the multiple confusions that befog justice-talk in this land. Chapter Four gives the main lines of that theory; Chapter Five expands this by bringing some definition to the fundamental but loosely used concept of "the common good"; Chapter Six completes the theoretical discussion of justice by confronting the American temptation to confuse justice with equality, the problem of moving the massive Leviathan of the state to do justice, the unique role of the Supreme Court

as a philosophical forum, and the critical but often missed prob-
lem of how justice relates to mercy. These three chapters then,
with an honest effort to avoid the tediousness that often besets
theory, will offer a wholistic theory of justice that is related to
the American facts of life. With such a theory in hand the issue
of preferential affirmative action can be argued.

CHAPTER FOUR

The Nature of Justice

A MODERN PARABLE

Once upon a time, on the south side of Milwaukee, there lived a young man by the name of Wilbur O. Michowski. Wilbur looked like an ordinary sort of fellow, but he was not. In fact, by American standards, he seemed to have been conceived without original sin. He seemed free of all racism and sexism and betrayed no negative attitudes toward down-and-out groups. As a child, he had marched for civil rights with Father Groppi and bore the taunts of his peers for so doing. He was an active member of the National Organization for Women. Wilbur wanted to be a doctor, and when he said that his main motive was to help people, it was credible.

Wilbur was a solid student, though not outstanding. His application to the Wisconsin State School of Medicine did not put him at the top among those blessed candidates who would be swept into the medical school with little question. Wilbur was down in that central bulge where many are qualified and few are chosen. Wilbur was rejected. A friend of his in the admissions office consoled Wilbur with the news that he had been done in by affirmative action requirements. If only Wilbur had been black, or better yet a black woman, or better yet a black woman with one Hispanic parent! Wilbur was a realist. If he could not make it into his own state medical school (which had a preferential policy for state residents), it was unlikely that he would make it elsewhere. Wilbur would not be a doctor.

Well, Wilbur had to do something to make a living so he sought work at the local telephone company. The interview went fine but again Wilbur knew the pain of rejection. The personnel officer mumbled something about a "consent decree" and a court order to hire minorities. So Wilbur went on to business school and found contentment in accounting. All in all, he lived rather happily ever after.

The questions raised by the parable are these: Were the two rejections of Wilbur fair or unfair? Wasn't this good man discriminated against? Even if the medical school and the telephone company had good intentions in complying with the affirmative action program, wasn't this the classical case of an evil means to a good end?

My position is that both rejections of Wilbur were fair. I painted Wilbur in the parable as a sinless type to emphasize that, even in the purported absence of all personal guilt, sacrifices such as his are a matter of justice since there is more to justice than exacting restitution from the guilty. Life in a just society requires sacrifice even from the guiltless.

Before going on to argue my judgment that Wilbur was treated fairly, let me quickly add that I am assuming for the sake of argument that Wilbur was done in by preference for minorities or women. That is no slight assumption. Most white males lose out in competition with other white males, while "affirmative action" provides a convenient excuse for admissions and hiring officers. Also, I would insist that good government should attempt—if it is possible and as far as it is possible—to mitigate the disadvantages to all the Wilburs who suffer during this necessary and temporary restructuring process of preferential affirmative action. With that said, let me go on to justify the rejections of Wilbur O. Michowski.

JUSTICE DEFINED

Every word in the affirmative action debate hinges on the notion of justice. Justice, of course, is the permanent passion of public life. Every policy maker and litigant claims it. Everyone points to it to justify his or her claims. But rarely do we pause to ask the most fundamental question of our political existence: *What is justice?* You can do a lot of work with electricity without knowing what the essence of electricity is, but this is not the way with justice. In political discourse, one's conception of justice is crucial. If the idea we have of justice is superficial or sidetracked, our conclusions will be correct only by accident. There is a way in which the handling of justice and the handling of electricity are the same. In both cases mistakes can be lethal.

When you speak of justice, you are reaching for the foundations of human existence. Justice is not just one virtue among the lot. It is the cornerstone of human togetherness. To try to define it is to address the most profound questions ever to challenge the human mind. In the definition of justice is contained one's definition of *person* and of *society.* Also at issue is the *relationship of the individual to society.* May individual interests be sacrificed for social goals? Are state interests and social concerns always to be preferred to individual interests or do individuals have some sacred turf upon which even Caesar may not tread? Preferential affirmative action sacrifices the good of some individuals like Wilbur for the social goal of terminating crippling and unfair monopolies. The theory of justice behind it implies that such is quite fair in the absence of alternatives. Individualism argues against this, saying that Wilbur's right to meritocratic competition cannot be overshadowed by social goals. That represents a different theory of justice, and one which, I shall argue, is so shallow that it could not sustain a viable society.

The definition of justice begins with deluding simplicity. *Justice is the virtue which renders to each his/her own.* There are three ways in which this rendering should take place and thus there are three essential forms of justice: *individual justice,* which regulates relationships between individuals; *social justice,* whereby individuals pay their debts to the common good; and *distributive justice,* which concerns the distribution of goods by the representatives of the common good. To these three forms I shall return.

"To each his/her own" is the persistent core formula for justice that has spanned the literature from Homer through Aristotle, Cicero, Ambrose, Augustine, and Roman law, and is still seen as the axiomatic core of justice in our own time. (The Latin for "to each his/her own" is *suum cuique* which is neither sexist nor clumsy. With apologies, I shall avoid clumsiness by reverting to the all-inclusive "his" in this discussion.) The simplicity and consistency of this definition are welcome as a start, but it is only a start. It is like the skin which must then be peeled away to reveal the layers of reality beneath.

Justice is the first assault upon egoism. Egoism would say: "To me my own." Justice says, "Wait. There are other *selves*." Personal existence is a shared glory. Each of those other subjects is of great value and commands respect. The ego has a tendency to declare itself the sun and center of the universe. Justice breaks the news to the ego that there are no solar gods in the universe of persons. Justice is the attitude of mind that accepts the others—all others—as subjects in their own right. Justice asserts that one's own ego is not absolute and that one's interests are related. In the simple concession that each deserves his own, the moral self comes to grips with the reality and value of other selves. Justice is thus the elementary manifestation of the other-regarding character of moral and political existence. The alternative to justice is social disintegration because it would mean a refusal to take others seriously.

But let us peel away another layer. When you say, "To each his own," you face the question "Why?" Why take others seriously? Why not just "To me my own"? The move from pure egoism to justice is nothing more or less than the discovery of the value of persons, or, in the common term, the discovery of "the sanctity of life." Justice implies indebtedness. You *owe* his own to each. But indebtedness is grounded in worth. The each is worth his own. Justice is thus founded upon a perception of the worth of persons. We show what we think persons are worth by what we ultimately concede is due to them. Talk of justice would sound like gibberish if we had no perception of the value of persons.

All of which leads to a jarring conclusion. If we deny persons justice, we have declared them worthless! Justice, you see, is not the best we can do in reaction to the value of persons. Friendship is. Aristotle did well to point out that friends have no need of justice. In friendship a higher, more generous dynamism is operative. You don't

tell newlyweds they owe one another signs of affection in simple justice. Love will take care of that.[1] Justice, however, is the least we can
do for persons. It is the first response to the value of persons, the
least we can do in view of that value. In friendship and in love we respond lavishly. Justice is concerned with the minimal due. Less than
this we could not do without negating the value of the person. To be
perfectly consistent, if we deny justice to persons we ought to kill
them because we have declared them worthless. Their liquidation
would be perfectly in order.

These are grim tidings in the political order. Love does not make
the political world go around; justice is the most we can achieve.
Love can flourish at the interpersonal level, but it would be a mad
romantic who said that, at this point in moral evolution, love can be
the energy of the social order. In the political realm, only justice
stands between us and barbarity. In this realm, when justice fails,
persons perish.

Notice, I started out saying "To each his own," with a warning
that there is more to the phrase than meets the eye. This led to the
worth of persons as the only reason why we should acknowledge the
other *eaches* and render them at least their minimal due. Denying
that implies they are worthless, and is thus murderous in intent. All
of this, remember, is part of my defense of preferential affirmative
action as a work of justice. If I can show that such a program is necessary to meet the essential needs, the minimal due, of some persons
in our society, it would follow that those who reject this program and
offer no realistic alternatives are by implication attacking the human
worth of the persons in need. And this leads to the next key question:
How does *need* relate to justice?

Most would concede that justice means giving to each what each
deserves. Justice, in other words, is based upon deserts. Here quickly
the ways part between individualists and the defenders of genuine social justice. The individualist would say that your deserts and entitlements come from your own achievements or as gifts from other
achievers. The theory of social justice concedes this but goes on to
say that you also *deserve* in accordance with your *needs*. Needs too
give entitlement. The essential needs of each are also "his own." The
point at issue here is obviously essential to my position on affirmative

action. In affirmative action, need is a primary consideration because its beneficiaries are those who cannot achieve and therefore need. Their deserts are need-based. If this point cannot be made, the case for preferential affirmative action fails.

WHEN NEEDING IS DESERVING

"To each his own" translates into "To each according to his merits and earned entitlements" *and* "To each according to his needs." I contend further that not only is the latter formula a solid dictate of justice but that it can even at times override the entitlement formula. In other words, we might have to yield some of our fairly merited entitlements, in view of the needs of others. This yielding might even at times involve not only what we have but even life itself in the case of the supreme sacrifice. (The good news is that affirmative action does not require the supreme sacrifice.)

To each according to his need. This little formula, if you can forgive its use by Marx, has a fairly harmless ring to it. Why then the resistance of our cunning species to its use? The answer is that the formula contains a threat to self-interest. There is no immediate threat apparent in the idea that everyone should have what he earns (or is given), i.e., the entitlement principle, in the sense of earned entitlement. But if people have a right to what they need, that could hurt. Giving them what they have earned makes a kind of hard-nosed sense and it implies that I'll be able to keep what I earn. Giving them what they need is another matter. What I have earned may have to be balanced against what they need. Thus the formula at hand is no gentle piety. What it does is bring us face to face with a major question of justice. In the process of rendering to each his own, might individual interests have to be sacrificed for social goals and the common good? Need raises the prospect of such sacrifice. If the need of others is in some way my business, the plot of my life is thereby greatly thickened. If I can say "To each his own" and concede to the other only what he has earned, my life has all the simplicity that individualism seductively promises. But if I owe him what he needs, even if I did not cause his need, simplicity is no longer my portion and I am more bound up with others than individualism led me to believe. What then are the justice-credentials of human need?

To initiate this discussion, let me make the question of the rights of need very concrete by dipping into my own personal life for an example—even though in so doing I am breaking the sacred canons of authorship which insist that one should write as though one had no personal life. The example of rights generated by needs is provided by my six-year-old son Danny. Danny receives many extraordinary benefits from the American political community, particularly the city of Milwaukee. He is given door-to-door transportation to school by bus and, when necessary, by taxi. He thus rides in heated comfort through Wisconsin winters while other children walk. He is in an almost one-to-one teacher/student situation. Specialists are brought in to attend to his special needs. There is no public utility in this. Danny has an incurable, degenerative disease that is slowly ravaging his central nervous system and will make his life a short one. His mental age is now no more than fifteen to eighteen months and is diminishing. Danny can lay claim to no distinctive merits, works, rank, or earned entitlements. He is delighted with the efforts of his teachers and passionately reaches out for what they offer. He wants to be part of this world and his teachers are a medium for contact with the world and some of its meaning. His intellectual reach is slight and diminishing but his need for the stimulation of school is real and insistent. He looks for the school bus even on holidays and weekends. When he could still manage such a sentence, he would announce to people on the street: "I go school!" The human need here is essential, not frivolous. He wants to be with us, and school—at least for the present—is one essential link.

Yet with all of this it remains a fact that he is learning less and forgetting what he knew. His physical problems are alleviated by the physical therapy the school provides, but that too is a losing battle. The polity is investing enormously and will never get a productive citizen. The critical questions are *who* is paying for this and *why?* And is this cost borne out of justice or out of charity?

My taxes clearly do not and will not pay for what he is getting. Through law-based taxation, the people of the political community are required to pay. Some of those who pay are childless and are still required to pay for the education of other people's children. Those who have children in school are also paying for Danny to get benefits that their children do not get. And none of these people will get any calculable return from Danny. Most will never know of his coming or his passing, yet they are sacrificing for his benefit. Still, even amid a tax revolt, such aid to the handicapped is not in principle threatened. In cases like Danny's, the ruling perception seems to be that this little boy with blighted mind but exquisite affections deserves suitable though expensive care from the community. And the community makes it a matter of enforced law, not of optional charity. The care that Danny needs and I could not afford to give him is given him by the community as an expression of social justice. The "his own" part of "to each his own" includes need—personal need as well as group need, the needs of productive as well as of unproductive persons. The community has decided that Danny's "own" includes the development of whatever potential he has for as long as he has it. It is not his own because of a deal he struck with the community. It is not a reward, for he is without "merits." Neither is it reparation, for the community has not harmed him. It is also not an investment, for he will make no return. His own *worth* is the reason why he has a *right* to the essential care he *needs*. The enthusiasm and hunger he brings to his schooling show that it is an essential need for him to stretch his potential as far as it will go for as long as it will last. Helping him to do as much as he can seems the least that we can do. Meeting his felt need for development is his minimal due. He is worth that. The need here is essential. Essential needs are those without which self-respect and hope could not endure. Even the retarded have such needs.

Need gives entitlements because of the worth of the needing person. The judgment housed in the law and practice of the community is that to deny the needed care would be to deny justice. Hitler judged such life worthless, and then quite logically eliminated it. Our polity evaluates persons, and therefore justice, differently. We have decided as a people that the Dannys of the world are worth justice and so we render to them according to their needs. The working assumption is that we *owe* things to people in justice because of their need. People have *rights* because of their needs. Need, therefore, is a critical category of justice. Danny's case is particularly illuminating in this regard since his intrinsic worth is the only justification for meeting his essential needs. It may be socially useful to help a child with Downs syndrome since help may make the child somewhat independent rather than a future burden on the state. The Dannys of the world have rights based on need without reference to social utility— with reference only to their personal worth.

Need, of course, like all human categories, is slippery and calls out for distinctions. For one thing, need, like every term relating to persons, has both an individual and a social meaning. Both individuals and groups have rights—breeding needs. A starving individual has a right to "steal" a loaf of bread from a bakery if his death would otherwise follow. (He would not be *stealing* since he has a right to it.) A group which has been disadvantaged as a group needs reinstatement into the sharing patterns in which essential goods are distributed in a society. South African blacks, for example, have a right based on need—which in turn is based on personal worth—to a restructuring of the distributional patterns of their society. Identifiable groups have similar problems in the United States, as I shall argue anon.

Furthermore, the need in question may not always be guiltless in origin. Handicapped persons whose ailment was self-induced—by drug use, for example—have needs to which society is and ought to be sensitive. If they are rendered incompetent, we don't gas them and incinerate them, which we could do if they had no rights. We see them as having rights, based on need, based on enduring worth. It is generally seen as unjust to use criminals—even those condemned to death—as guinea pigs in medical experiments. This too is another reason why capital punishment is unjust since it implies that the person, who may indeed have lost his right to freedom, has lost all his rights and is therefore worthless. This, of course, is a gratuitous, unprovable assertion, and thus bears a burden of proof which it cannot meet.[2] Personal worth is not negated by the loss of some rights. No one can judge any human being completely worthless.

Some need is based upon mismanagement and even thievery, as when a major corporation sinks into financial distress. Sometimes it is judged that such a corporation should be allowed to die of its own mismanagement. At other times, *for considerations of the common good,* it is judged that unbearable harm would come to the economy, and a rescue operation is undertaken at public expense. If well advised and truly promotive of the common good, this is an act of justice. The common good has moral standing because that is one dimension of the good of persons. Every consideration of justice and morality is rooted in the good of persons. For that reason, the grounds for helping Chrysler and Lockheed and Danny are the same —if we presume that Chrysler and Lockheed had valid claims. All valid claims are traceable to the breeding ground of every right and entitlement—the perceived preciousness of persons.

Need sometimes relates to the dignity of an office. We provide our president with a mansion because we judge that, for practical as well as symbolic reasons, he could not serve the common good as well from an apartment on Q Street. We see this as a social need.

Also, we decide that farmers and small businessmen might need special aid and tax breaks for a vigorous overall economy. Crop failures and other natural disasters create needs to which society responds. The details of such things are subject to infinite wrangling, but the principle is that justice entails reacting to the needs of certain individuals and groups. As we become more sensitive to the value of persons, we perceive more needs. Only recently did we decide that defendants need and deserve a lawyer even if they cannot afford one. We are still debating whether persons need minimum health care just as much as they need minimum education. In the gory past we did not judge that persons needed a fair trial, freedom from slavery or torture, "social security," the opportunity to vote or run for office, et cetera. Social changes are based on a deepening perception of the value of persons. Because of their value, certain of their needs should not be unmet and certain things are inalienable rights. Persons should be literate; they should have safety and sufficient food; they should have some say over their political destiny; even when they are handicapped they should be able to activate their potential; if they have been ostracized by society, they should be reincorporated. They should not be tortured, et cetera. Social evolution is based on a growing appreciation of the worth of persons, which is the grounding of all moral and political life. Because of that worth, we must render to them their deserts. Deserts, however, are grounded both in their achieved entitlements and in their essential needs. To deny either would be to declare them worthless.

Of course persons do not have a right to everything they think they need. Some people think they need luxury. Hence the stress on *essential* need. Essential needs, again, are those without which life, self-respect, or hope could not endure. On this basis, we have guaranteed certain rights such as those contained in the Bill of Rights and provided for at least minimal health, education, and welfare. It is on this basis also that unjust monopolies should not be tolerated. This is true in the world of business. It is also true when white males have controlled all the power centers in the society from government to business to the professions in such a way that certain groups face head winds and barriers that prevent them from competing. This denies those groups both self-respect and hope and, as will be seen, even life itself. Changing this is an *essential need* and thus a matter of simple justice.

Needs, of course, like rights, can conflict with one another. Nazi Americans might feel a need and claim a right to march in Skokie. However the need and right of Jewish residents not to have insult added to their unspeakable injuries can outweigh the Nazi claims. In a time of acute scarcity, Danny's needs for special education may be superseded by more urgent need. Also, freedom of movement would be considered an essential need, but in the event of a rare and virulent disease, the need for quarantine might be justified. Needs and rights are not *acontextual*. They are marked by the relationality and sociality of human existence. This necessitates an eternal process of discernment and debate. The principle, however, is the thing. *Basic needs issue into rights when their neglect would effectively deny the human worth of the needy*. Or in other words, essential needs create rights.

The final point on need is this: meeting essential needs in society is not a work of optional charity or benevolence. It is often spoken of this way but this is loose and dangerous talk. Meeting essential needs does not make one a candidate for sainthood; it merely establishes one's credentials as human. It is a minimal manifestation of humanness, the alternative to which is barbarity. If we wish to make it possible for handicapped people, as far as is financially feasible, to move about in society, this is not heroic on our part. It is simply a matter of meeting essential needs of persons as best we can. As soon as we cast this obligation in terms of compassion or charity, we have declared it supererogatory and therefore dispensable. To neglect it would be ungenerous, but not morally wrong. When we are speaking about essential needs, such a view is nonsense. Such a view is also a radical departure from the Judeo-Christian idea of justice, which is supposedly normative for many Americans. In Hebrew and Christian thought, meeting essential needs is the soul of justice.

What I have said so far is fine for the Dannys of the world, but what about the Wilburs? To the Dannys we give; from the Wilburs we take. How is that just? Are Wilbur's essential needs being sacrificed as part of a do-gooder's scheme? Is Wilbur being denied "his own?" These are fair questions that must be answered. The answers lie in an understanding of

THE THREE SIDES OF JUSTICE

All of justice is divided into three parts. There are three ways in which we give "to each his own." To miss out on even one of these is to be unjust.

Having said that, I must immediately become defensive. Persons who may have stayed with my thesis thus far in the book might now throw up their arms and cry: "Here comes the inevitable pedantic quibble!" Permit me to enter a plea of innocence swiftly. What is involved here is no harmless numbers game. Errors would not be "merely academic," as that strange expression goes. If there are three ways we can be just or unjust, and if injustice may be lethal to human beings and disruptive of their environment, it is not unpractical to indulge in a little clarity on what justice is. Although it is rarely adverted to or understood, a rich variety of apparently disparate topics depends on an appreciation of the tripartite nature of justice. Though I am not considering all these issues in this book, I offer here a list of just some of the issues which require us to assume, implicitly or explicitly, a position on what justice is and how many forms of justice there are: universal health care, civil disobedience and the right to dissent, using organs from retarded donors, medical experimentation on children, limiting sales to blacks to prevent a neighborhood from "tipping" and going all black, international income tax for economically developed nations, progressive income tax, the right to take a child from parents who refuse medical care, drafting persons for an onslaught on poverty and illiteracy, and, of course, quotas for disempowered groups such as women and blacks. These seemingly unconnected issues are approached in varying ways in the different disciplines. All of them, however, are hinged to a conception of justice and its several forms, although, as I have said, this is broadly missed. Implicit in any conception of justice are assumptions about the nature of personhood and the rapport between the individual and society. All of the issues just mentioned involve just such assumptions. And unexplored assumptions are at the root of all intellectual evil.

For this reason, I beseech the reader to meet the theoretical issue of justice squarely. There could be nothing more practical than this theoretical exercise.

The heart of the matter is that we are not merely individuals; we are *social individuals,* and there are three fundamental modes of sociality to which the three kinds of justice correspond. These three are, as I have said, *individual justice, social justice,* and *distributive justice.* These are not three different categories but rather three ways in which the one category, justice, is realized. Justice does not admit of partitioning. Failure at any form of justice is injustice.

The beginning of most confusion occurs in a failure to recognize the tripartite nature of justice. Even Aristotle, whose influence has been so controlling on this subject, never managed to get it straight as to whether there were two, three, or four basic forms of justice. The experts on his work are still divided on that count.[3] Bad faith adds to the muddle. If one doesn't want to meet the demands of justice in some way, it is self-serving mischief to define that form of justice out of existence.

Quite simply, there are three forms of justice because persons relate to persons in three different ways.[4] We relate on a one-to-one basis (individual justice); the individual relates to the social whole (social justice); and the representatives of the social whole relate to individuals (distributive). When, for example, we talk about fulfilling contracts or repairing injuries done to discrete individuals, we are speaking of individual justice. When we speak of modes of indebtedness to the social whole exemplified by such things as taxes, jury duty, and eminent domain, we are speaking of forms of social justice. And when we speak of distributing the goods and bads of society fairly (largely through the instrumentality of government) we are speaking of distributive justice. Though social and distributive justice are distinct forms of justice, both relate to the common good and are thus co-ordinates. It is an act of distributive justice for the state to collect taxes; it is an act of social justice to cooperate. As I will argue, it is an act of distributive justice for the state to insist on preferential affirmative action. It is social justice for citizens to cooperate and even voluntarily anticipate this redistributive need. One may therefore speak of social-distributive justice without conflating these distinct but related forms of justice.

Therefore, it is in these three distinct ways that persons render to each his own. The dozens of species of justice that encumber the literature on the subject are all reducible to one of these three essential modalities of just rendering.[5]

Individual justice is basically simple in its concept. It is, after all, rather clear-cut that if I contracted to cut your lawn, I owe you a lawn cut, or if I stole your lawn mower, I owe you a lawn mower's worth of restitution. Justice at this level can often be captured in simple terms of mathematical equality. Also in individual, one-to-one justice it is only the ones who are interacting who are involved. If I made a deal to cut your lawn, that is a matter between you and me; the neighbor down the street is presumably in no way implicated. Social and distributive justice do not enjoy a similar basic simplicity. What is owed, by whom, and to whom are never as clearly delineated as in individual justice, and at the social level, justice is not reducible to simple equality since unequal demands may justly be made.

Social justice concerns individuals' debts to the common good. Fundamentally, this means that citizens owe a contribution toward making the social whole a context in which human life can flourish—a context in which respect and hope are present for all. That task is immense and never finished. No one can say he or she has cared enough, dared enough, been creative enough and thus has paid in full what is owed to the common good. The guilt of apathy and insufficient caring affects us all. Let's face it. Would whites have started the civil rights movement? Would males have started the women's liberation movement? In this sense, even the immaculately conceived Wilbur would have to say he still had debts outstanding to the common good. Voting, joining citizens' lobbies, cooperating with justifiable enlistment, et cetera, do not exhaust our debts to the needs of the social whole. Racism, classism, and sexism reign. Respect and hope for all persons do not obtain and we are all debtors on that account.

The prime subjects of *distributive justice* are the agents and agencies of government. But there are other economic and institutional powers that control some of the conduits through which the goods of society flow. All of these and the individuals who support them, at least by their apathy, are also subjects of distributive justice. It is not just the "powers that be" who control distribution. Individual citizens are implicated in some way in all the workings of distributive justice. To some degree government requires a base of contentment among the people. Otherwise the rule of the rulers will be rejected and the government will topple. Seven centuries ago Thomas Aquinas pointed out that distributive justice involves more than the princes. When the people are not rocking the ship of state, they are clearly satisfied . . . *contenti* in Thomas' term.[6] Their undergirding contentment shores up (legitimates) what the government is up to. Citizens may also participate in distributive justice by their influence on corporations. Such things as stockholders' resolutions, selective boycotts, and other forms of citizen and consumer pressure can have some influence on those corporate powers that are every day making decisions affecting the common good.

Again, as Thomas Jefferson wrote to James Madison, whenever there are unemployed poor, "it is clear that the laws of property have been so far extended as to violate natural right."[7] To change his language but keep his point, we could say that, whenever there are unemployed poor and massive dislocations of wealth and privilege, the distributional patterns of the society are unjust. Such a condition implicates the government, the agencies of corporate power, and the apparently decent citizens who legitimate the powers of distribution with their undergirding contentment. The subjects of distributive justice, therefore, are not only the persons who exercise governmental, corporate, and professional power but also the citizens who support the patterns of distribution by what they do, or, more significantly, by what they do not do.

These then, in brief, are the three forms of justice. Discussion of affirmative action or any other issue of justice will force you to assume some stance regarding the meaning and import of the tripolar category of justice. What stance you assume, however, will be influenced and possibly dominated by your cultural context. The American context is a breeding ground for special errors in understanding justice. This presents us with the dual task of cooling the pretensions of individual justice in American culture and of mounting a theoretical defense for social and distributive justice. With this undone, the case for affirmative action could not be made. Private entitlements and individual goals could not be sacrificed for broader social aims. In meeting the theoretical problems with justice that afflict American culture, I shall also be fleshing out the theory of justice in general.

THE PITFALLS OF INDIVIDUAL JUSTICE

If you don't know what individual justice means, you will soon have ample time to ponder its meaning in jail. This kind of justice is not likely to be neglected in any society; the individuals involved see to that. It will certainly not be neglected in an individualistic society which is fixated on this kind of relationship and only reluctantly concedes the existence of other forms of indebtedness.

Fixation at the level of individual justice, to which United States individualism is gravely prone, is beset by three radical problems: 1) mistaking a part of justice for the whole; 2) fomenting lawsuits and a spirit of litigiousness; 3) ignoring the social consequences of greed and the built-in necessity for redistribution.

First of all, therefore, by mistaking a part of justice for the whole, individualism falls into the same kind of error that collectivism does in ignoring other forms of sociality and justice. At the level of logic, the American individualist is a fellow traveler of a strict Maoist collectivist. Both are reductionists. Both simplistically bracket out the richness and complexity of human social existence.

Fixation on individual justice means that only one form of social relationship is acknowledged—the one-to-one kind. Such a fixationist could say, in fidelity to his own premises: "If I made a deal with you I will honor it; if I hurt you, I will make amends; but, if I did neither, bug off!" If there is only individual justice, those would be the words of a just man. The rigid collectivist is also fixated, but at the level of social and distributive justice. In the collectivist's view, individual dealings and relationships are faint shadows upon the grand substance of the common good, embodied in the state. A wife is more a political comrade than a spouse. All individual claims are subordinated to the collectivity. To change the image, as the waves of the sea are but mere fleeting apparitions of the sustaining, enduring ocean, so persons in the collectivist vision subsist in the state. They have no personal rights except by concession. Individuality is subsumed in the common good.

Fixation, whether collectivist or individualist, is by its nature unjustified selectivity. There is nothing benign about such exclusionary selectivity when the subject at hand is justice because the definition of justice is nothing less than the definition of social existence. Mistakes here introduce social distortions and strip persons of what is their due. Both collectivism and individualism lead to a social structure in which some persons, at least, will not get what they deserve. Pure individualism and pure collectivism never exist without inconsistency but they do exist as dominant biases affecting national institutions and laws. (The United States and China illustrate these two extremist deviations.)

The second related problem with fixation on individual justice is that it makes for a very litigious society. Individual claims and rights assume absolute value and the peace of the society will be fractured in their defense. Rights will be interpreted in the separatist, "don't tread on me" tradition and sweeter forms of reconciliation will be bypassed. Not surprisingly, the United States has close to 400,000 lawyers while Japan, with almost half our population, has fewer than 15,000. Culturally, Japan places more stress on harmony and sociality than the United States, and so a spirit of accommodation regularly limits the grasping quality of individualistically conceived rights. Indeed, the term "rights" in American vocabulary harbors a good deal of our native, countersocial litigiousness. "Rights" is heavy with defensive connotations in American parlance. "I have a right to it and you don't" is what it says. The chip is upon the shoulder and the frown upon the brow.

Beyond American usage, however, the assertion of rights implies an adversary situation. If one is receiving his due, there is no need to assert rights. Rights talk arises in the face of a denial of rights. In the United States, most of our justice claims are likely to be couched in rights language. Most Americans would be baffled by the fact that in Chinese there seems to be no word that exactly corresponds to our word "rights." There is, of course, a word for justice and a rich tradition surrounding it in the long history of China.[8] In fact, it is of no little interest to contemplate the paralysis that would beset our moral and political discourse if we were deprived of this our most hallowed linguistic tool for justice claims! I am not suggesting that those who either forgo or disparage rights language are well advised or better off for this. Indeed the collectivist or utilitarian temptation can best be met with a healthy dose of rights-talk. But at least we look to see what presuppositions dwell within this favored word of ours. When you marry a word, you may not want all the relatives, and the American relatives of "rights" are a mean bunch.

Professor Ronald Dworkin's description of rights shows the strengths and the weaknesses of the term. "Individual rights are political trumps held by individuals. Individuals have rights when, for some reason, a collective goal is not a sufficient justification for denying them what they wish, as individuals, to have or to do, or not a sufficient justification for imposing some loss or injury upon them."[9] Rights are "held by individuals" in a face-off with the group. Group rights are not excluded, but in an individualistic milieu they could be put on the defensive. Put such a description of rights into the hands of someone who tends to see all group claims on the individual as guilty until proven innocent, and the legitimate claims of social justice are imperiled. (My purpose here is not to negate individual rights but to keep them in necessary tension with the legitimate and neglected claims of the group.)

The liberation of the individual from submersion in the collectivity is a distinguished modern achievement and the language of rights served it well. However, when one is talking ethics out of a simplistic individualism, such a perspective must be redeemed by a vision of social obligation and of debts owed to the many by the one. The pendulum of human thinking swings too easily from one excess to another. A socially naïve individualism easily rises from reaction to overbearing collectivism. Individualism forgets that there is more to justice than rights. There is also need and need comes in individual and group form. This point is missed by individualists, especially when those individualists are talking about preferential affirmative action.

This leads to the third problem with a fixation on individual justice: its incomprehension of the might of greed and the need of redistribution. Let us imagine that the private dealings of individuals in a society are one and all scrupulously respectful of individual rights. At the one-to-one level, no one seems to be cheated. Let us further suppose, what is quite supposable, that as a result of these dealings power and wealth begin to concentrate in the hands of the few superdealers. The result is that the many can be gravely afflicted even with regard to their basic goods and needs without ever being defrauded on a one-to-one basis. They are done in by the monopolistic patterns that develop in the free trade atmosphere. Of course, no society runs on a completely free or individualistic basis. There is always some tempering of individual claims. The problem is one of bias and proclivity. A society which is addicted to unbalanced individualism will tolerate enormous amounts of human misery and the power patterns that sustain that misery before it will move to the necessary redistributive restrictions upon individual "rights." No society can be totally blind to redistributive needs—poverty intrudes itself upon our senses—but an individualistically biased society will console itself with "trickle-down" and "ooze-out" theories of redistribution. Here we are at the level of faith, and bad faith at that. We are confident that if acquisitive private dealings are uninhibited an invisible hand will guide the trickle-down excess to where it will do the most good. Meanwhile, the acquisitive society busily plugs the leaks through which trickling and oozing could occur!

All of this leads to injustice by ignoring the ensconced patterns of distribution that enrich some and disempower and deprive others. It represents a readiness to include the dignity and lives of persons in the check list of acceptable losses. The ethical primitivity here is also sociologically naïve. The point usually missed is that the common good is the setting and matrix of private, individual good. It is not a hostile and unrelated competitor. This is the hard lesson that sooner or later comes home to all elites—even when those elites constitute a national majority. Fixation at the point of individual justice, therefore, is unrealistic, self-defeating, and ultimately cruel however bedecked it is with claims to democratic respectability.

With all that I have said about the evils of reducing justice to the one form of individual justice, I do not thereby disparage individual justice. Without commitment at the individual level we are unjust. The most obvious manifestations of individual justice, as I have said, are at the level of fulfilling contracts and repairing injuries.[10]

More basically, however, individual justice represents an incipient form of mutuality. It recognizes the other as a legitimate source of moral claims. It is a beginning of the essential other-regarding pattern of genuinely human life. This points beyond external exchanges. What we owe persons is not just to follow through on our dealings. We owe them respect even when a deal has not been struck. In fact, we owe them more respect than we can render, given the value of persons. Goethe was being none too cynical when he said that being a man means learning to be unjust. This is why individual justice has also been called "compensatory justice." For this reason too some have said that the principal manifestation of individual justice is restitution. We do not react to the heroic value of persons with appropriately heroic response, even in our private dealings. We may at some level of our beings agree with the Jewish philosopher Martin Buber when he says that a person "is *Thou* and fills the heavens," but we don't always respond accordingly.[11] Thus a neat scoreboard of contracts kept and torts repaired does not mean that even individual justice has been met in all its demands. Therefore, far from disparaging individual justice, I am arguing that we don't even measure up to its awesome exigencies. And on that chastening note, I turn to the forms of justice that are more demanding yet.

JUSTIFYING SOCIAL JUSTICE

Social and distributive justice must be seen together since they represent the *to* and *fro* between persons and society. Both are based upon the pivotal assumption that persons are *social* by nature and not just *sociable*. Even the purest of individualists can concede elective sociability. Persons can interact and can even redistribute their goods on a consensual basis. To say beyond this, however, that society is the womb of personality, that persons are intrinsically and naturally social and political, is a qualitative leap beyond mere sociability. And a coherent theory of social and distributive justice is based upon that leap.

Recall that we are here comparing faith visions. The American-style individualist *believes* that rights belong only to individuals, that sharing with others is morally based upon consent, and that any forced sharing violates human rights. Individualism differs from a theory of social and distributive justice in two ways: first, regarding the nature of *personhood* and, secondly, regarding the nature of *society*. Individualism sees persons as basically separate atoms, individualized and detached entities, which relate to others only if they choose to do so and as they choose to do so. The state is not a natural reality but a voluntary contrivance of individuals. The wording of the Preamble of the Massachusetts Constitution of 1780 gives the individualist's view of society in a nutshell: "The body politic is formed by a voluntary association of individuals."[12] If the individuals did not voluntarily associate, there would be no body politic—only detached, individually compacted persons doing their own independent thing. There is no ultimate tension in this view between private good and public good, since the public or common good has no rights except those voluntarily conceded by individuals. Sacrifice of individual good for the common good makes sense only if individuals decide on it as a useful strategy. For the consistent individualist there are no debts to the common good; the common good has no rights. We can have debts only to other individuals; only individuals have rights. We are not a naturally sharing animal in this view—just an animal that might decide to share. If you carry all of this to its absurd extreme, as Robert Nozick does, even taxation is objectionable and on a par with forced labor.[13] Sharing is not natural; only being free to share or not share is natural. We are not social individuals; we are individuals who might socialize when it is in our self-interest. Dying for the common good would make no sense at all in this view and is a phenomenon that is theoretically unaccounted for in individualism. Also it would be unjust to subordinate Wilbur's desire to be a doctor to any social goals. The problems or needs of groups cannot get in Wilbur's way, since groups have no rights. Only Wilburs do.

Such a doctrine is nonsense and no state ever survived or ever could survive on such a theoretical basis. (Even Nozick with his dire view of taxes undoubtedly pays them since academics are not forced to practice the nonsense they may write.) Any surviving political community has somehow come to grips with the reality of persons as *social individuals*. Some forms of social and distributive justice are found in every society. What this signifies is that there are two elements in the meaning of personhood: individuality and sociality. To lop off sociality, as individualism does, or to lop off individuality, as collectivism does, makes for unbearable problems. A realistic theory of personhood (and justice) lives with the natural tension between individuality and sociality without apotheosizing or negating either. Such a realistic theory rests on the recognition that the human animal is

THE SHARING ANIMAL

Human life is shared life. It is this fact that grounds social and distributive justice. It is to this fact that I refer when I speak of our natural sociality. It is to this fact also that Aristotle referred when he said that "it is evident that the state is a creation of nature, and that man is by nature a political animal."[14] Human life begins and develops sharingly or it does not begin or develop at all. This does not mean that all sharing is good sharing or that we have to share everything we have. But it does mean, among other things, that our social individuality is naturally expressed in political form and that our privately and fairly made entitlements are not absolute or immune to demands from the common good. It means that we have reached the point where the individualist must choke or abandon his partiality and join us in a broader and realistic view of humankind.

It is because we are by nature the sharing animal that we cannot realistically imagine a "state of nature," as it has been called, in which self-sufficient individuals exist asocially. In this creation of deviant individualistic imagination, persons would be political by choice, not by nature. The state, in this view, would be created by a free compact made by individuals and would not be a "creation of nature." Such a "state of nature" is no more sustainable than a state of foodlessness or weightlessness. Persons flower into political existence or they wither. Obviously persons can survive without a political community longer than they can survive without food or oxygen because the need is different. It is, however, a natural need and what persons can become they will not become without the enabling matrix of a political community of some sort. Political community is not a jacket you put on if you think you need it; it is rather a body through which you live.

No coherent notion of social justice can emerge without an appreciation of our sharing social essence. From conception until death, human life unfolds under the physical law that to be is to share. Our social history is etched in our genes. Everything about us is social. The way we know, our language, our liturgies, friendship, sex, family —all are manifestations of unfolding sociality. And so too is the state. The formation of a political community or state is a natural and necessary law of survival and maturation for the human animal. Individualism's effort to see it as an adventitious device and not as essential and intrinsic to the human condition must implode under the pressure of its own inconsistency and unrealism. Even the rugged egoism that fuels individualism is ultimately frustrated by individualism's effort to sever individuality from its social moorings. Even private good is undone when its ties to common good are loosened or cut. "Man is by nature a political animal." His need for a state is not negotiable since the state meets certain human necessities that will otherwise not be met.

Two general necessities are fulfilled by the state: 1) meeting private and public human needs through state agency; 2) providing persons with a medium for self-definition. The meeting of these natural necessities permits persons to survive, grow, and thrive. None of this would happen if these necessities were unmet. This illustrates the naturalness of our sharing sociality and the politicality of our being.

First then to those services to human good that are specific for the state. There are indispensable needs that can be met only by the state. There are other needs that could be handled by the private sector but tend not to attract sufficient interest in a reliable and consistent way. A list of some of these will illustrate the indispensability of the state. Some of the state's functions are these: the regulatory control of the physical environment; encouraging the arts and research of all kinds since the arts and research can get lost within the narrow needs of the market place; ensuring adequate health care for all; drafting individuals when necessary into military or other public service roles; sustaining literacy and educative standards; providing for the handicapped; dismantling monopolies that impede a healthy economy; protecting against monopolies of information; dealing with multinational corporations; dismantling caste and elitist structures that may develop; chastening racist, sexist, or classist power structures; controlling energy use and development; issuing money; taxation; police protection; establishing and supporting courts; husbanding resources; directing disaster aid in a systematic way; traffic control; enforcing contracts; relating to foreign nations; managing trade patterns and international finance; issuing patents and copyrights; negotiating with other nations on space and sea rights; et cetera. I have said that some of these functions can be and are assumed by private agencies, and I also concur with attorney Jethro Lieberman's comment that "the boundary between private and public can never be marked with manicured shrubs."[15] But to say that the state is an optional extra or that we could choose a state of nature and do without the state is silly. Also, there is an incremental quality to the need for a state. We need it now more than ever and will need it more in the future. Our political sociality is growing. The expression of social-distributive justice is extending. In pre-industrial times, for example, the use of one's land rarely caused harm to others and so there was a minimal need to limit the use of one's property to avoid injury to others. Now the use of one's property might be lethal for present and future generations and a new and inexorable need for regulation exists in the modern state.

Increased state involvement has been the natural and inevitable result of industrialism. As Robert Heilbroner and other economists have pointed out, government has become more and more involved in the economic sphere in modern times simply to preserve that sphere. Government is involved in the unavoidable work of regulation in the area of ecology, environmental impact, and pricing. Corporations are in a sense creatures of the state, formed under state charters, governed by state laws and tax policy, and often working on government contracts. As Richard de Lone says: "The conceptual paradigm in which public and private spheres are separated has crumbled."[16] No force but the state could work toward full employment, bring about a national policy whereby firms would be required to invest a certain percentage of their investment capital in labor-intensive urban areas, provide for the jobless, or enforce affirmative action. Other possibilities of even greater government involvement in the economy are being experimented with in other countries such as Japan. It was felt in 1973 that energy-poor Japan would be devastated economically by the surge in OPEC prices. Such has not been the case. Instead a new kind of "corporate state" has been developing, involving a new and more intimate mode of collaboration by management, labor, and government. Koji Taira foresees a time when "negotiations among national-level interest groups, with the government's participation, may replace market forces and pluralistic (that is, free and decentralized) collective bargaining."[17] It clearly would be more difficult in individualistic America to achieve more fruitful realizations of cooperation among management, labor, and government.

All of the needs in my long but not exhaustive list of governmental chores could be classed as "pragmatic." This requires a word of explanation lest it give aid and support to the individualistic idea of the state as an incidental device. Clearly the state does have pragmatic value. However, we can distinguish between pragmatic luxuries and pragmatic necessities. In other words, contractarian theories of state assume that if we could find a way around it we could do without the state. That, of course, is about as realistic as saying that if we did not need to reproduce we could do without sex—missing the point that we do need and want to reproduce and that sex does a lot more in the world of persons than make babies. Similarly the state is not just a clever device to meet some needs that we happened to run into and might choose to ignore. Persons are self-transcending animals. They cannot pasture like contented cattle amid the actual; they are explorers of the possible. They are freighted with "divine discontent," which can sense the "not yet" beyond every achievement, the possible beyond the given. This self-transcending process of personal life would be frustrated and stunted if it were ripped from the enabling context of the *polis*. Thus the *polis* is a natural, not a contrived, need.

Politics, like technology, makes for a lot of messes. Abuse, however, does not invalidate use. Politics and technology can be abused. The "use" of politics, however, is natural to persons. Rejecting its naturalness and indigenous human status is a wild form of narcissistic imagination.

There are public and private needs that only government can meet. Without the empowering context of political community, atrophy would replace growth in the expansion of human potential. As A. D. Lindsay says in his *The Essentials of Democracy,* the state is the "hinderer of hindrances." The purpose of all its powers "is the setting free of the spontaneity which is inherent in the life of society."[18] The state, from this perspective, is as natural as is the setting free of our human possibilities, since these would not be set free without the state.

The second natural need met by the state is to provide persons with a medium for self-definition. By the nature of things, the state is not just a functional apparatus. It is also a system of symbols through which the members of the society interpret their meaning and destiny. Much is missed if a nation is seen only as a pragmatic agency. A nation also becomes a culture, a socially endorsed interpretation of reality equipped with an enshrined orthodoxy about what the good life entails. For this reason nationhood is always heavy with myth, symbol, and ritual. Patriotism is never a merely utilitarian emotion. If it were it could never inspire, as it does, supreme loyalty. A nation, in other words, is a creedal as well as a practical reality.

This mysterious but quite essential function of political community is illustrated by a thirteenth-century conversation between the Mongol leader Kuyuk Khan and Pope Innocent IV. Mongol expansion was threatening the Christian West. So the Pope sent a message to the Mongol court not only protesting the massacres in Eastern Europe but also requesting that the Mongols receive baptism and submit to papal authority. Kuyuk Khan was bewildered. "This your request, we do not understand it," he wrote back to the Pope. He could not, of course, understand it. Contradictory interpretations of reality were here contending. The military successes of the Mongols confirmed them in their assessment of things. It was "by the virtue of God" that "all realms" had been granted to them. The Pope should submit to them, and if he did not, he would be guilty of not observing "the Order of God."[19] Clearly there was more afoot here than military control. Each party was demanding that the other be baptized into another world view.

The heavily religious dressing of this exchange might make it seem an irrelevant period piece. However, as political philosopher Eric Voegelin observes, "The Communist movement is a representative of . . . truth in the same sense in which a Mongol Khan was the representative of the truth contained in the Order of God."[20] Similarly, the United States in its collision with Communism is concerned about more than markets and hard-nosed power politics. Each side wants to bury the other in the baptismal waters of conflicting creeds. Kuyuk Khan would have had no trouble understanding the rationale of the erstwhile House Un-American Activities Committee. The protection of orthodoxy was the issue and un-Mongol thoughts and activities would have been as sacrilegious to Kuyuk Khan as un-American leanings were to the priests of American orthodoxy. Contemporary clashes in Northern Ireland and the Near East could never be understood in purely legalistic or pragmatic terms. Visions of reality and even cosmologies are contending. Divergent views of meaning are vying. The separatist tensions in Canada also represent interpretational differences as much as tribal pride and the narrowness of vested interest.[21]

Obviously, all of this is dangerous. My point, however, is that, dangerous or not, it is the way we are and it is the way we *know*. Making sense of things is a political as well as private process. If we err by using the nation (or an international movement such as Communism) not as a heuristic vehicle of interpretation but as the definitive embodiment of truth, we slip into worship of the state (statolatry) and totalitarianism. If the process ceases to be self-transcending and does not point us toward a single global nation rich in diversity, then we will join the Khan and the Pope in falsely absolutizing partial visions of the real. But even if we achieve the ideal of a single planetary "nation," the knowing process will not lose its political dimension. We will still need to know ourselves through the political medium. Political community will still be a heuristic instrument of ongoing interpretation, given the sociality of our knowing processes.

In conclusion, then, social-distributive justice is based upon the fact that a person is a sharing animal. Sharing is as natural to this animal as are water and warmth to a tomato plant. This, however, isn't just an apolitical piety. It is rather the supreme political fact, the fact that makes us the "political animal." We must share politically and not just interpersonally. To some degree sharing must be public and structured as well as private and spontaneous. Societalizing (an admittedly clumsy word) or *polis*-making (clumsier yet) is nature's rule for the successful unfolding of human life. Human life becomes better and more human as the public and private sharing patterns do more and more justice to persons. Greedy monopolies obstruct sharing and are thus malignancies on the body social. Social-distributive justice attacks these malignancies. Thomas Aquinas came up with the conclusion that "justice consists in sharing."[22] Where monopoly causes a bypass in the proper sharing patterns a systemic problem exists that calls for a systemic solution.

But what is proper sharing? Does everyone have to get an equal share? Must we share everything—our spouses, our children, our homes? Equal shares are not necessarily fair shares since not everyone has the same merit or the same need. Neither should everything be shared. Just sharing rules out only the deprivation of others through exploitative monopoly. Exploitation is the key. Exploitation is the treatment of persons in a way that denies them their minimal due. If I deny you living quarters in my home, under most circumstances I do you no injustice. (In an emergency, it may be unjust to so deny you.)

Social and distributive justice require sufficient sharing to meet what is minimally due to persons . . . their essential needs. Again, generically speaking, the minimal need for persons is for an ambience marked by respect and hope, the essential ingredients of human life. We can do without anything, we can even lose life itself in the context of respect. When there is no respect, even the slightest inconvenience is unbearable. Insult—the absence of respect—is the cause of all rebellion. The absence of hope is also fatal for persons. Only hope moves us. Even Sisyphus had to be hoping for something or he would have left that stone where he found it. So if we would render to each his own, we owe our contribution to a social matrix in which respect and hope exist for all. If the plutocratic, acquisitive bent of persons has elbowed certain groups of persons out of competition by disempowering and excluding them from a fair share of the action, social and distributive justice require restoration. Disempowerment is worse than deprivation since it strikes at respect and hope. The deprived can put up with a lot if they haven't been stripped of the wherewithal to succeed. But power is the sacred source of both respect and hope. If society has exercised its perverse bent for building wealth upon exploitation, by blocking certain groups with built-in head winds and insurmountable barriers, those groups are radically deprived at the level of power, self-respect, and hope. The evil inflicted on them is worse than anything we can achieve at the one-to-one level because group action is more powerful and more pernicious. We are meaner together than we can be alone.

This kind of situation has another urgency built into it. Since the common good is the good in which all private good is set, we attack our own good when we do not pay our debts to the common good. If we exploit and disempower certain groups, depriving them of the essential ingredients of human life, we have blighted the common good in a way that is ultimately our own undoing. If we disempower and excommunicate some, we all lose what that group, empowered, might have contributed to the common good. Social injustice saws at the limb upon which we all sit.

The common good, then, is the cardinal category for social-distributive justice. Clarity regarding its meaning is requisite. If human good and justice are realized commonly as well as privately, if individuals are asked to sacrifice for the common good, then we ought to be as precise as we can about what the common good is. And so to the fair question that entitles the next chapter.

CHAPTER FIVE

What's So Good About the Common Good?

If private good and common good were realized in the same way, and if preferential affirmative action did not involve sacrifice to the common good, there would be no need for this corollary chapter on the common good. However, if, as is the case, the arena of the common and public good present distinct challenges to justice, the common good wins its case for special attention. Otherwise the discussion of social-distributive justice will be loosely hinged and lacking in sociological sophistication.

The common good is more easily spoken of than defined. It is also easier to say what it is not than to say what it is. Surely it is not "the greatest good of the greatest number" as the utilitarian would have it. For those not included in "the greatest number," that sort of common good might not be good at all. Actually, the utilitarian position is totalitarian in thrust, for all of its democratic pretensions. It provides for a tyranny of the majority and doesn't provide for the necessary and natural tension between the private and the common good, between minority good and majority good.

The common good is also not just the mathematical sum of individuals' goods. This ignores our sociality. It ignores too the practical political fact that every viable nation requires some surrender of individual good for the community. The common good is also not, as Josef Pieper tentatively suggests, "the social product, the total product of community life."[1] As Pieper himself concedes, this smacks too much of society in terms of productivity. There is more to us and to our personal and common good than production. And certainly the common good is not reducible to property, though some are strangely tempted in that direction. It is also not identifiable with the state or the "national interest," since the state might be so structured as to violate the common good. Also, the common good would appear to be broader and even international in its meaning, involving more than merely "national" interest.

The common good as I see it is a descriptive term that carries normative clout. It describes that which meets the needs of community existence and it implies that you ought to think of those needs when assessing your private goals. The term "common good" implies a dialectic between what might suit your narrowly personal needs and the requisites of a common life. The use of the term seems to import that individual good and community good cannot be conflated but must coexist in a perpetual bargaining posture. Just as the word "rights" implies a challenge to what those rights claim, so the term "common good" implies a reference to private, personal good as well as to the good of the social whole.

The common good is not something given, something already out there like a piece of property. Obviously there is some common good out there or we wouldn't be able to sit around chatting about it. But the term cannot describe something completed and done. The needs of thriving community existence are not all met. Clearly, we are not yet all that we might be. Reference to the common good is reference to what ought to be done to move us toward what we might be. A synonym for the common good would be flourishing sociality. That sociality which is of our nature implies that we will not reach fruition in solitude. Individual good is realized within the common good. Words like "womb," "matrix," "context" all describe what the common good is to individuals. We are naturally related to the common good because human good is not only private but common.

Still, it clearly is a lot easier to comprehend private good than common good. And it is a lot easier to understand how you could sacrifice something for another individual whom you know and love than it is to understand sacrifice for a common good involving persons you have never met. Two chores thus present themselves: to discern and spell out as far as possible the nature and workings of the common good by seeing what it is and what it is not and then to probe the meaning of sacrifice to the common good.

COMMON GOOD, COMMON BAD

Count Cavour once said that if he had done for himself what he did for Italy he would have been long since jailed as a scoundrel and a villain. Perhaps he should have been jailed also for what he did for Italy but that is not the point here. The point is that the count knew that there are real differences between the private and the public sphere and that representatives of the public order may do at least some things which would be irresponsible if done by a private citizen. Though both private good and common good are aspects of human good, the unfolding of good at the common (political, social) level is markedly different. If we are unaware of those differences we may go blundering forth to serve the common good with the tools and concepts of the private order. Our mission, then, no matter how well motivated, would be ill fated. I am pointing here to a common failing of critics of preferential affirmative action, whether on or off the Supreme Court. There is a mistaken idea abroad that you can move from discussion of private good to a discussion of common good without shifting gears.

Both good and ill are realized differently in the public sphere. Political life is not like life alone—or even like merely interpersonal life. Different realities develop that could not develop in private existence. Distinctive patterns of power form in a society and these patterns control the woe and weal of that society to a marked degree. Social coalescence not only creates liberating possibilities for the self-transcending human spirit, it also issues into distinctively sociopolitical problems that could not exist if we were but privately interacting atoms. The whole, again, is much greater than the sum of its parts. Coalescence magnifies the power of the participants, making social problems different in kind from private problems.

Let me list some of the differences in the way that power operates in the public sphere. This will show the peculiar problems of tending to the common good. First of all, public power is enormously more complex and influential. Compare the power of a nation or an international corporation with that of a private entrepreneur. The difference is qualitative as well as quantitative. In public power, agency and moral responsibility are diffuse. There is no easily determinable center of responsibility as in individual morality. Who causes inflation? Who started the Vietnam war? Who excluded women or blacks from the power centers of the society? Also there is a certain mindless quality to public power. Well did Reinhold Niebuhr speak of the feeble mind of a nation. Blind momentum and lack of focus and co-ordination are constant hazards. Egoism and meanness are more easily rationalized at the political level. Persons huddled and aggrandized into a group may make much of little or little of much in a way that would be deemed psychotic in private life. "Group think" sacrifices nuance to the joys of consensus. Guilt is more easily diluted in a group, and civil religion at the national level will dignify our basest purposes with sacral hues. Problems of representation beset public power. Efforts to interpret the public will and the public good are problems unlike anything met in private, interpersonal living. And through the processes of public power monopolies become entrenched, clogging the channels of distribution in ways that create excessive wealth for some and unbearable poverty for others. Private power is relatively helpless in the face of these societal realities.

The ancient Thales raised a large subject when he said: "If there is neither excessive wealth nor immoderate poverty in a nation, then justice may be said to prevail."[2] The problem to which the wise man alluded is that there is in social power an indigenous thrust toward excess in both directions. Power blocks form and gobble up "excessive wealth," creating "immoderate poverty." It is ever so. The most committed Communist states are consumed trying to fight this historical penchant of the human species. And the gobbling that thus goes on is nothing like a one-shot affair. Rather, a distributional pattern is created, directing the flow in one direction and blocking its movement elsewhere. It is as though certain organs in the body could effect a bypass so that they would receive a surfeit of blood while others organs would be left desiccated. The way this is done is as complex as society itself and changing it is a massive systemic challenge.

An example from one of the simpler forms of social power may illustrate the difference between problems that are social and those that are manageable and litigable on a one-to-one basis. Consider the difference between individual one-to-one crime and organized crime. Stopping individualized one-to-one crime and stopping organized crime are two different enterprises.[3] The difference lies in the sociological complexity of organized crime. You cannot end it by removing one or the other individual criminal. Indeed, you could take out the entire cast and not stop the show. Replacements would arrive almost like air pouring into a vacuum. What you are dealing with is not a mathematical accumulation of individual criminal actors but rather *socialized* crime. What would be needed to eliminate this social phenomenon would be a complex social restructuring. Organized crime fulfills a number of needs besides the financial enrichment of the principals. Involved here are ethnic pride and distrust of the dominant alien culture, a supplement to official administration of justice, a realization of historical hierarchical patterns, response to demand for illegal pastimes and services, an animating history of symbols and heroes, and momentum—the social name for habit and a basically blind and powerful force.

And organized crime is actually a simple problem compared to the concerns that underlie this book. Try the American caste system for a really impressive example of patterned social power. I shall return to this with further argument in Chapter Seven when I propose that blacks are the prime and paradigmatic candidates for preferential affirmative action. But as an example of socially achieved injustice, look at what white power has been able to do to blacks. I refer not at all to one-to-one hurts requiring one-to-one restitution. That is the simpler material of individual justice. I refer to the disempowerment of blacks as a group. This is the more complex material of social and distributive justice.

To see what socialized power can do, look to the power centers that control the good life in these United States. The patterning powers have been such that these centers are almost unanimously white male. So it is in Congress, the Supreme Court, the presidency, corporate management: look at leadership in the major religions, in the financial temples, the press, the professions generally and especially in those gatekeepers of power, the professional schools. White male power also has controlled the writing of history and the symbols of respect in literature and theater. Even in marriage, the touchstone of sociality and the most eloquent expression of acceptability, white exclusionism has very effectively barred blacks. The caste-making power here has even managed to reach into the source of all human power—self-respect—and take much of that away from black persons. As the report to the National Commission on the Causes and Prevention of Violence concluded, we have imposed "in the psychological legacy of slavery and caste a psychically crippling Negro dependency and even self-hatred which is largely immune to mere economic advance."[4] Compare all of this disempowerment and structured insult with a one-to-one robbery or even with organized crime, and know what problems justice faces in the social order. The sociological process by which a caste system has been created and maintained in this nation is as mighty as it is complex. It is a social achievement. It involves stubborn myths and ideology with all the ways of thinking, the symbols, the blind spots, the uncritical attitudes, the socially supported patterns of caring and not caring, and the overwhelming momentum of three centuries of belief in the inferiority of the Negro. To use the same principles to solve these problems that are used at the individual level of life would actually contribute to social violence. To say we must find the offenders against blacks one at a time and try them on an individual basis would be as realistic as saying that if you prosecute individual criminals when you happen to catch them organized crime will go away. Here is where Mr. Justice Powell showed extraordinary naïveté when, in *Bakke,* he dismissed the very idea of "societal discrimination" as "an amorphous concept." The state has an interest only in bringing remedies to "identified discrimination." Without "findings of constitutional or statutory violation, it cannot be said that the government has any greater interest in helping one individual than in refraining from harming another." Action can be taken only in "specific instances of racial discrimination."[5] Here is the voice of an unrealistic individualism. Both the sociology and the ethical theory operating here are unsound. The fixation is at the level of one-to-one individual justice. Such a constricted perspective is useless in the face of the actual problem. One cannot rechannel a river by scooping out buckets of water. We cannot dismantle a caste system any more than we can reform a sexist society simply by plodding from one specific violation to another, leaving the distorted and distorting structures substantially intact. Patterned injustice requires patterned redress. Social and distributive justice have to do more than take a tort-by-tort approach. We cannot "promote the general welfare," as the Preamble of the Constitution commits us to do, by chasing individual malefactors and leaving the unjust distributional patterns in control. The Kerner Report of the National Advisory Commission on Civil Disorders did not consider "societal discrimination" to be "an amorphous concept." Seeing the ghetto as the symbol of black disablement, the report concluded: "White institutions created it, white institutions maintain it, and white society condones it."[6] What is needed, said the report, is "to change the system" that is weakening our society.[7] Again, the problem is systemic and the change must be systemic.

Systemic changes are not wrought only by the government. Not even in the days of the most powerful king was all distribution within the control of the crown. In modern society much distribution and hence much distributive justice is in the hands of corporate powers, unions, and institutions which control many systemic developments. The hiring patterns and plant locations of corporations can reinforce sexual and racial caricatures, promote ghettoization, and prop up or divert the existing distributional patterns of a society. Management board rooms are models of caste consciousness and of sexism. Financial and lending institutions also have a major influence on housing patterns as recent discussion of "redlining" has brought to light. Realtors also have influence over important social trends. Graduate schools are an example of distributional power. Admissions policy in graduate schools presages the future shape of the society. As one study put it, graduate schools "encompass a predominant portion of the intellectual forces" of the nation and have therefore the power "to influence the social, cultural, and economic quality of national life, and to exert intelligent and effective leadership in world affairs."[8] These schools, in other words, establish an elite and decide the composition of that elite. Therefore they, as well as the government, have an obligation in simple justice to help dismantle monopolistic patterns of social distribution. Herein lies the absurdity of having the Supreme Court say that only where institutions have been found guilty of past discrimination may they be pressed to use preferential medicine. This comes down to saying to these institutions that they may not use their inherent powers for justice unless they are guilty of injustice. Only the guilty may do what distributive justice requires. When society has allowed massive and monopolistic dislocations of power to obtain, it is a work of social and distributive justice to correct these by helping to restructure the distributive processes in the cause of the common good. Distributive justice refers to the use of governmental and other corporate power in a society to attend to this work of redistribution.

In a word, then, common good and common bad cannot be understood in the simple terms of individual, one-to-one relations and dealings. Good and evil are different realities when socialized (collectivized, politicalized, institutionalized, or in-systemed). The common good, then, is sociologically complex and the promotion of the common good requires systemic changes as well as attention to individual complaints. These points are regularly missed by the opponents of preferential affirmative action.

THE BURDEN OF PROOF

Because human good is both individual and common, it is not enough for citizens, governments, and corporate powers to tunnel their vision toward the simpler world of one-to-one relationships. If our communal existence is marked by in-structured inequities and unfair monopolies, restructuring and redistribution are required by distributive justice. Indeed any government that lives comfortably with the maladministration of the common good has lost the grounds of its own legitimacy. It should be placed squarely on the defensive. Historically, however, this is not what happens.

In the typical perversion of power, it is the deprived who are asked to assume the initiative in correcting the social ill that afflicts them. For example, if blacks in the United States are unemployed at double the rates of whites, if they are segregated and cut off socially and professionally, the government has failed, and should be massively and immediately engaged in rearranging the distributional patterns of social life. If the government would even pretend to justice, it may not go forward with managerial grit, inviting individual victims to consume themselves in litigation, hoping all the while that, with the sweet passage of time, the dynamics that made the problem will somehow solve it! Unfortunately that description fits the history of this American Republic. Blacks, women, and other disadvantaged groups, as individuals or as pressure groups, are expected to attack the Leviathan and do what they can to budge it. The burden of initiative here is thoroughly misplaced. Patterned, institutionalized maldistribution is a governmental problem and the first duty of government is to correct it.[9] To tell individual victims of group discrimination to go out and litigate is unhelpful and unjust. The gains from this tactic are as obvious as they are base. Private litigation will not "promote the general welfare" if the phenomena of group control and group victimization go unaddressed. Addressing those phenomena, however, is admittedly a staggering task.

Understanding the common good, therefore, is an exercise in social theory. It requires sophisticated appreciation of the distinct ways of the collectivity as opposed to the ways of private persons. To a large extent, the concern for the common good puts us into confrontation with the common bad. No society has ever been free of exploitative monopolistic powers. Social justice and distributive justice are therefore often corrective. They involve efforts to correct the system.

The common good, then, refers to those things that permit our human nature to express itself in its private and social aspects. However much we understand of this, we remain unprofitable servants. The common good cannot be definitively understood. Like the meaning of personhood itself, the meaning of common good is always open to further penetration. No partial realization of it or no partial conceptualization of it may be absolutized as though it exhausted our possibilities. It must not uncritically be identified with any state, any cause, any movement, or any ideology. The human need for respect, hope, and fairness is never fully met. Therefore the very notion of the common good is always open to improvement and our debts to the common good are always outstanding.

THE ZERO SUM TEMPTATION

Because American thinking is a little soft regarding the common good, a warning is here in order. Because of our inveterate individualism, there is a strong tendency to think of our common life in sociologically naïve "zero sum" terms. In "zero sum," the cumulative gains are seen to equal the cumulative losses. More simply, your gain is my loss and vice versa. This idea looms in the current preferential affirmative action debate and represents a gross misunderstanding of the complexities of the common good.

The biases of such a notion are quantitative and individualistic. It understands human good in mathematical terms. It reduces the delicate relationship of the individual and the common good to mathematical subtraction and addition, ignoring the fact that sharing is the precondition of human flourishing. The fact that the affirmative action debate is so rife with zero sum simplisms signals the level at which that debate has largely transpired.

The enigmatic fact of life is that it is in receiving that we receive *and* it is also in giving that we receive. This is the way of our sharing relational nature and, however it frustrates our rationalistic need to make all things neat, it is a reality to be faced in any successful society. In very practical terms this means that, if individual acquisitiveness were unimpeded, even the acquisitive individual would suffer. Any society that is not based on patterns of sharing—sharing which is at times sacrificial and when necessary enforced—will not endure. Zero sum thinking leads naturally to a notion of society as a war of all against all. In this simplistic view, *mine* and *yours* are radically antithetical. In reality, because of our intrinsic sociality, my interests and yours are interdependent. Acquisition without sharing undermines the conditions for acquisition as well as for human development. If I fixate on my gains and take no account of your losses, my gains are eventually imperiled. This is a gospel that is hard to preach to the economically powerful and socially myopic, but history is replete with examples of its truth.

Zero sum thinking is a misconceived flight from pain. It represents fear of sharing. The social misconception involves seeing the human situation as comparable to the plight of persons locked in a cave with limited oxygen. In such a case it is true that every breath you take leaves less for me. Note the vicious core to this kind of thinking. In the competition it envisions, the death of the other would be in my interests. But the human scene is more comparable to cross-fertilization. If we exclude some from this process, there will ultimately be *less* overall rather than *more*. Zero sum thinking is right in one of its instincts. The sharing humanity posited by social justice theory does require sacrifice. Sharing can hurt. When a two-year-old first hears of sharing, he thinks it is the new word for getting. He will be happy to share what others have. Eventually and slowly he gets the message that sharing also has a sacrificial meaning. Even grownups resist that message. And yet, one way or the other, the law of sacrifice as a law of human nature will assert itself. To these painful tidings I now turn.

THE SACRIFICIAL BOND

Although individual good is set within the common good, the two are not identical. This raises the possibility that the two might conflict. Relative to preferential affirmative action, this leads to the critical question: *May individual rights be sacrificed for the common good?* To rephrase the question: Does it make any sense to say that individuals who have done no wrong or who have assumed no contractual obligations should, at times, be required in a just society to sacrifice their privileges, rights, possessions, or career goals for broader social aims? The answer to this question is yes. And, more disconcertingly yet, these sacrifices will not be required equally of all but only of some, and even then often somewhat happenstantially. Furthermore, any society that survives does so by living with this enigmatic fact of life—however many monuments that society may build to individual rights.

The truth of this may be seen in several ways. At a very practical and workaday level, that the common good can command sacrifice is assumed even by pragmatic, non-reflective persons. This assumption is housed in terms like "the national interest," "the public interest," "national security," or "the public domain." All of these terms denote something distinct from the private values of an individual—something to which some of those private values may have to be sacrificed. So strong are these convictions about these claims for the communally good that it has been necessary to draw up and doggedly insist upon Bills of Rights to protect the legitimate claims of individuals from being swallowed up in group concerns. Rights language is in fact largely concerned with this tension between what is owed to the common good and what the individual can insist on as his right even in the face of the public domain. Historically, the rights of the individual were only gradually even acknowledged. It is striking that even in individualistic America the code names for the common good are so powerfully endowed. The recent history of the terms "national security" and "national interest" shows this. Historically, then, we have never had any doubts but that the public domain can make demands upon us, and the prospect of the individual being inconvenienced or even subjected to the risk of death has not been allowed as a contrary argument. It is widely acknowledged now that this public power was absolutized, sacralized, and overextended. But even this new awareness of past excess and of the prerogatives of individuals in the face of state power does not negate the lived acknowledgment of the right of the state to make demands—even ultimate demands in cases of common defense.

The most salient manifestation of this aspect of human life is what is called the supreme sacrifice. It is an unrelievedly paradoxical yet practical fact of political life that you do not have a nation unless people are willing to sacrifice *and even to die for it*. For a state to be legitimated it must represent to a substantial degree the human ideals of the people. Without this the state is built upon sand and is a candidate for crisis and collapse. But if it does sufficiently manifest the ideals of people, it will command enormous, *self-sacrificing* loyalty. A lot of governmental iniquity and inefficiency will be tolerated, and ultimately, in a crisis, persons will die for that nation's cause or admire those who do so.[10]

This same self-sacrificing commitment also shows up in the reaction to government that does not win legitimation. People will die to topple it. In the preceding chapter I spoke of the need of persons to understand themselves and reality itself through the medium of political community. Thus, if a government is perceived as representative of a vision alien to that of the community, persons will be ready to die to remove this heretical pretender. What this again shows is that political stability rests on a broad base of sacrificial commitment. A government is legitimated only by sacrificial commitment. World government is not yet possible because no such commitment to transnational community yet exists.

Obviously, the commitment of which I speak can be misguided and manipulated, but that is not the point. The point is that sacrificial commitment makes political community viable. Most of the time that commitment is not unto death, but that supreme manifestation shows how far that commitment can extend. What this means is that all of us—even the individualists among us—are in debt to the common good and to the sacrificial commitment of other citizens to the common good. The common good is mysteriously constructed of many things, including as an essential element the unmerited and unmeritable sacrifices of many individuals. A viable society is served by meritocratic considerations, but it is not based on them. The common good subsists upon a base of sacrifices that could never be merited. Without a sufficient store of sacrificial commitment to the common good, even the individualist would not have the well-being and security to write his books about individualism.

So to the question *May individual rights be sacrificed for the common good?* the answer is *Yes,* or even *Fortunately yes,* since, without such, human life could not prosper. With that said, however, the pain of paradox remains. We are asserting here more than we can fully comprehend. Some things can be said to support the truth claim here. For example, it can be said that a coherent and fruitful human existence seems dependent on this sacrificial base, and coherence and fruitfulness are criteria of truth. It can also be said that, since to be a person is to be in debt to the common good, sacrifices required of us for the common good are a kind of repayment and are therefore just. This, however, does not settle all questions that arise, especially since sacrifices are not required on an equal basis. Not everyone is drafted into military service. Not everyone has to do jury duty. Not everyone experiences the pains that Wilbur experienced when a preferential policy led to his exclusion. Not everyone loses out to veterans when these are given preferential treatment. And certainly not everyone is asked to give the supreme sacrifice. Ultimately, the answer here will not dissipate all mystery since it touches the deepest regions of human experience. Ultimately, it is the worth of persons that is the root of all obligation including the moral obligation to sacrifice for the common good. That means that somehow persons are worth it. Having said that, we are as wise as we can be. But to deny it would be to deny the worth of at least certain persons, and doing that is barbaric and leads to intellectual inconsistency that is worse than the pains of natural paradox.

Here we see another attraction of individualism—its compelling simplicity. Its simplicity, of course, does not square with the complexity of personal and social life, but how alluringly tidy it is to say, "Give to each what he has merited and you will be just." Such a proposal, however, will not wash. Giving according to merit is a part of human life, but so too is sacrificing rights, opportunities, and even life for the common good.

Wilbur O. Michowski can be justly denied the two opportunities he sought. Even if Wilbur was the victim of affirmative action and not the victim of the myriad undetectable biases that always operate in hiring and admissions, the rejections can still be justified. Wilbur's social individuality makes him a natural heir not only to the glories of life but to its debts and requisite sacrifices. If systemic evil cannot be corrected without systemic restructuring that imposes sacrifices, then those sacrifices are part of the price of life. Somehow there is dying commingled in living, not just at the organic level but also in the social order. We can fight this law of our nature but we cannot conquer it. It is Wilbur's lot and ours too. This law too pertains to our common good.

CHAPTER SIX

The Realization of Justice

Though individualism is the generic malady of American thinking on justice, there are three specific soft spots in the American appreciation of justice that call for treatment. These three areas are not conceptually connected, and one requires considerably more treatment than the other two. All, however, loom prominently on the road to a better understanding and realization of justice in the United States. All, too, affect the specific issue of justice that is preferential affirmative action.

First, there is the confusion of justice with equality. Equality is an American god but it is not the same thing as justice. Justice may require inequality; equality may be unjust; and equal opportunity is not always fair opportunity. Secondly, freedom is another befuddling shibboleth which easily takes priority over justice in American thought. We are disposed to let freedom reign when only enforcement will bring justice. The problem here is a broad one since it leads us into the staggering question of how to motivate and move a massive society to justice. I shall speak here of the power of force, self-interest, ideals, fear, and guilt as social motivators. I shall also discuss the motivational role of organized religions and of the Supreme Court in American society. Finally, the American notion of justice is a chilly one that does not sense that there can be no justice without the seasoning of mercy. Here we face an anomaly that is both unavoidable and practical. Indeed, no treatment of justice can ignore the relationship of justice to mercy and be either practically or theoretically sound.

PUTTING EQUALITY IN ITS PLACE

I signaled earlier that social and distributive justice are more complicated and more demanding than individual justice. When such is the case, the human mind naturally seeks an escape hatch. It has done so in the case of social and distributive justice by turning hopefully to equality as the panacea for social ills. This goes to the point where equality and justice are taken as synonymous.[1] Aristotle led us down the path on this one. It was he who said: "All men think justice to be a sort of equality."[2] Those words have cascaded through the centuries, bedeviling many into equating justice and equality. This is wrong. There can be fair and just inequalities, and equal treatment can be unjust. Aristotle was here succumbing to Pythagorean influences which promiscuously commingled mathematics and ethics. Equality is primarily a mathematical term; it has limited adaptability to moral purposes. I am tempted to say that we could drop this word entirely from our moral and political vocabulary, return it to mathematics, and lose nothing in our understanding of justice.

Adapted for moral purposes, equality is valuable largely for what it is against. Our affection for the term is due to the fact that historically it has been used effectively against some bad things. When we speak of *equal* rights, we are actually opposing arbitrariness, prejudice, monopoly, and privileges of rank, sex, or class. Such opposition is a permanent necessity in human society. However what we really want is fair and just treatment, and this is not always equal. Equality imports sameness, and we cannot treat everyone the same if there are differences in persons' needs, duties, and merits. Equal treatment of the handicapped and the unhandicapped would be irrational and unjust. A tyrant could mistreat everyone, i.e., on a scrupulously equal basis, but no one would call this fair. Racist anti-miscegenation laws could be and have been defended on the absurd grounds that both races were being treated equally by such laws—both were being equally prohibited from marrying! The Equal Rights Amendment has long been impaled on this unfortunate and protean word, which to some imports sameness of bathroom privileges and everything else. What is desired is fair rights—fair being a synonym for just.

Equal treatment can actually preserve injustice. As professor of law Alfred W. Blumrosen points out, discrimination against blacks can be furthered, not eased, by equal treatment! He points out that if the employer promises equal regard for educational credentials, blacks will suffer, since as a class they have less education than whites. If the employer promises equal consideration of negative factors such as arrest records, blacks suffer again, since they are arrested more frequently, often on mere suspicion. If the employer requires on an equal basis that all live near the employment site, blacks confined to ghettos are again likely to be disadvantaged.[3] Thus black unemployment rates could remain double those of whites under a policy that is unwavering in its commitment to equality.

I am, of course, here caught in an anomaly. On the one hand equality stands high in our pantheon of social ideals. Its historical pedigree is impressive since it has been associated with moments of revolutionary progress. For many the word symbolizes all that is good and decent. In many simple matters it is equivalent to justice. Thus at the individual level equal pay for equal work is just. Reparation equal to the damage done is just. But when we move through the three fundamental modes of human interrelating we enter complexities where simple equality will not be simple justice. Also, no redblooded American really wants a society based on equality. As professor of law Monroe H. Freedman says, the American ideal is not equality at all. Rather it is to start out unequally low and end unequally high, Horatio Alger style. The classic American fantasy is that of the boy from the log cabin who becomes President.[4] The American ideal is upward mobility from one inequality to another. Thus our love affair with equality is fraught with infidelities. However, in the absence of a coherent understanding of justice, equality has been our stand-in.

What we have done is to strike a bargain with equality. Implicitly, realizing that a radically egalitarian society would be offensive to most Americans, and being quite put off with nations like Mao's China, which tried to live their egalitarian principle, we came up with a hybrid called "equality of opportunity." Here the word "equality" remains as an empty shell, with no equalness left in it. Equality of opportunity, for all of the democratic pretensions it exudes, is really a principle of aristocracy. It is, as I have said, the mask of social Darwinism, the cold doctrine of the survival of the fittest. It is based on the vicious imaginary figment that everyone has a chance to go as far as his abilities can take him. Rejoice! The deck is not stacked! The atmosphere is pure, and the competitive processes are greased with fairness! Thus let everyone come to the starting line—the old and the young, the white and the black, men and women, the handicapped and the well—and let the race begin! May the best *man* win!

Of what possible value is equal opportunity to those who are physically or socially or educationally handicapped? We do not come to the starting line equally endowed, because power and privilege, health and wealth, are not equally distributed throughout the society. The ideology of equal opportunity assumes that competition in the real world is pure. There is no bias. There are no carefully guarded monopolies of power. Sons of distinguished alumni and sons of peasants are all treated the same. Wealth and poverty are as one when the litmus test of merit is applied. That's the way it is.

The very slightest dose of experience would show that that is the way it isn't. What equal opportunity thinking does is confirm class structures and class consciousness—the very things against which the ideal of equality was unfurled in American history. The presupposition of "equal opportunity," that those who have deserve and those who don't have are inferior, is the basis of class and caste. The ideology of equal opportunity is an invidious pretension, calculated only to maintain inequities. It betrays no understanding of the meaning or the sources of justice.

Of course, what equal opportunity programs want is an end to monopolies and bias. Their ideals are perfectly in order. Their logic is not. What they want is a period of *unequal* opportunity so that the excluded may be let into the employment process on a fair basis. Preferential programs are housed under the equal opportunity rubric. Indeed, a chief agency for preferential affirmative action is the Equal Employment Opportunity Commission. Yet preferential treatment is not equal treatment. This simply fuels the "reverse discrimination" argument since it is all too obvious that those not being preferred and those being preferred are not being treated *equally*. This is not just a semantic problem. It is an American problem arising from our penchant for talking justice in terms of equality, even when justice requires inequality. I shall return to the category of equality. For now let it be seen as distinct from justice.

THE PERILS OF VOLUNTARISM

George Kennan once compared a democracy to a huge prehistoric monster with a brain the size of a pin.[5] The image is poignantly pertinent to anyone who contemplates a problem of public morality, such as redistribution. How do we teach the monster new tricks? How do we get him moving in new and better directions? Motivation is blessedly simple at the personal level of life! But how do you motivate a nation, or, we might ask, what does motivation even mean at the societal level? If you would move a nation "to establish justice," in the words of the Preamble of our Constitution, you had best begin by admitting the enormity of the enterprise. How much can we rely on freedom, how much on enforcement? The problem here is large and all of its facets must be seen.

As I have said, the original sin of political discourse is to attack the problems of the polity with the tools and categories of private, interpersonal life. This is particularly confusing when we try it with political motivation. At the interpersonal level, force is normally out of order. Persuasion, mutually advantageous exchange, and appeals to decency, ideals, and common sense go a long way. And where these things don't work, we disassociate as far as possible from those who don't know the rules or won't abide by them. Voluntarism, in other words, is the rule for private dealings. Pressures do operate in private life also; ridicule, stigmatization, lawsuits, and even violence do function as sanctions to render the contumacious more agreeable. But, overall, voluntarism is the norm.

So what happens when we move to the political order where most goals will be reached only by governmental and corporate power? The temptation here is to try the voluntarism that worked so admirably at home and in the neighborhood. It is a natural first reflex—

especially if one's own interests are not at stake. In areas where our own needs are involved, we are considerably less naïve about how life is lived and the good achieved in society. There are no calls for voluntarism when it comes to our needs for police protection or when we discover we are being hurt by price-fixing corporations. No one who needs Social Security has been heard to call for building that massive structure upon voluntary contributions. We don't leave it up to the good will of individuals to provide disaster relief. Taxation or military draft in time of war is never on a voluntary footing. A double standard does operate here; duplicity is a glaring fact of political conscience. But when our minds are not sharpened by need, the simplicities of voluntarism have great appeal as a way of handling social ills. However, in facing the problems of just redistribution in society, voluntarism won't work for two reasons: first, because of the intrinsic nature of the problem and, secondly, because of the primitivity of our political morality.

Social ills, as we have seen, are infinitely complex in their etiology and in their social support systems. Uncoordinated efforts will not solve them. Let us suppose that a corporation in southern California, suddenly enlivened in its social conscience, decides that it must recruit and train Hispanics and blacks who have, up to now, been almost totally excluded from their work force. Unless a similar moral conversion strikes all of its corporate competitors simultaneously— the probability of which is nil—the noble corporation will immediately be placed at a competitive disadvantage. Expenditures will increase; inexperienced hands will at least temporarily slow production; tensions with previously privileged candidates will have to be dealt with. The price of virtue will be high. And with all of its efforts, the noble corporation will also be tortured by the knowledge that its efforts are a drop in the bucket compared to the overall problem. This would add to motivational lag. Clearly, the nature of a social ill requires a coordinated response. Individual dabbings at the problem will not do.

Secondly, social ills have their grounding in our moral primitivity. It has been said that true justice obtains when those who are not injured react to the injury of others as they would react to injuries to themselves. The statement was made by the ancient Solon and it is clear that he was a visionary.[6] The end of egoism that he envisioned has yet to be. What he foresaw was the just society in which the reigning presupposition would be that persons are supremely valuable and in which the self and the other would be equally prized. In such a moral clime we would "weep with the weeping" and feel their wounds as our own. Only cynical smiles could greet the suggestion that we have arrived at such perfection.

The grim reality is that our capacity for empathy is feeble and primitive. Studies show that black problems are underestimated by whites and that the problems of women are downplayed by men.[7] The rule of life thus far has been that the sufferer must mount the campaign for his or her own redemption. All exceptions to this are only apparent.[8] History shows the truculence that is our enduring legacy. Through history our moral story has been one of tribal egoism. Outside the tribe, persons were at the level of exploitable means and even seen as a legitimate source of meat.[9] Significantly, the German word for peace, *Friede,* came from *fridu,* meaning a fenced-off territory, suggesting that peace can be expected only within the clan.[10] Justice, similarly, would apply only there. The problems of this intensified with the coming of mass society. As Eibl-Eibesfeldt observes: "Fear and mistrust formerly dominated man's relations only with members of alien societies. With the formation of anonymous societies we began to mistrust our neighbors as well."[11] Fear, he adds, tends to aggravate the struggle for power and minimize consideration of the plight and needs of others. How weird and unrealistic it is in such a setting to address major social dislocations with fervid appeals to mass benevolence. Such an approach is especially curious in a starkly litigious society such as ours where folks will sue folks at the drop of a hat, and then preach patience, trust, and forbearance to exploited groups. It has the ring of a drunken preacher calling for sobriety.

With all of this, voluntarism has been the medicine that white America persistently prescribes for blacks. One effect of World War II was to bring into some focus the gruesome reality of racism in this country. A flurry of efforts appeared to ease the scandalous situation. To prevent discrimination in employment, there were state fair employment practice laws, executive orders of various presidents, and judicial usage of the National Labor Relations Act. As professor of law Alfred W. Blumrosen says, these efforts "did not measurably improve the conditions of racial minorities."[12] Their defect? They were so generic as to be unenforceable. They outlined rights but ultimately relied upon a generous voluntary compliance that was not forthcoming. The accent was on persuading the discriminator without the use of legal sanctions. The result, in Blumrosen's choice words, was an "effort of immensely modest proportions."[13] The love of voluntarism also animated the federal anti-discrimination clause regarding government contractors. In response to President Kennedy's executive order of 1961, there appeared the "Plans for Progress," a voluntary coalition of major companies who agreed to promote minority employment without coercion. "Plans for Progress" was eventually exposed as a farce and so it was replaced by yet another voluntary program, the National Alliance of Businessmen. Twenty years of this toothless approach left American blacks just about where they were at the end of World War II in income, occupational distribution, and unemployment ratio.[14]

Professor Faustine Childress Jones of Howard University argues that not only has voluntarism been almost useless for minorities and the poor but even state and local government "enforcement" has had minimal effect. Only federally enforced gains have had any significance.[15] Thus, even with all of our Anglo-Saxon respect for law, the authority of state and local government is resisted. Only federal enforcement works, and even that meets sturdy resistance. After all, the Fifteenth Amendment in 1870 constitutionally provided blacks the right to vote. This right was in short order voided. In a true sense it was only with the passage of the Voting Rights Act of 1965 (ninety-five years later) that blacks in the South could safely and freely register and vote. And even now, with tougher enforcement in the affirmative action program, the resistance is formidable. In many corporations and universities the affirmative action program is a paper tiger. With all the posturings of compliance in these institutions, affirmative action plans and officers often serve as a shield for ensconced "old buddy" systems. As a rule, it is only when the government goes after a corporation in court, as it did with A. T. & T., that there is compliance. The message, therefore, is: the often painful work of redistribution will not take place through voluntary programs. Enforcement is the indispensable means of distributive justice. Obviously, the government should use both carrot and stick, and incentives could increase the amount of "voluntary" compliance. The stick, however, must be in evidence. Realism bids us admit that only enforced compliance will dismantle a caste system or reallocate goods and burdens in a sexist society.[16]

Force, then, is not a dirty word. It may be an instrument of justice in a complicated and morally primitive world. There are, however, three other ways to move the polity to new and just patterns of distribution. The first is an appeal to self-interest. Justice in the politcal order needs the bracing effect of perceived utility and gain. Secondly, an appeal to the ideals enshrined in the civil creed of a people can have an impact. And finally, an appeal to a realistic sense of guilt can have some motivating value.

These other motivating forces are not mere trimmings on the one and only true avenue to justice, which is enforcement. The enforcement is necessary because of the need for coordinated and patterned solutions and because of our recalcitrance. But justice cannot be imposed on a completely unwilling population. The enforcement by a legitimated government is itself educative and serves to engender willingness. It is imbued with the moral authority of the state and is thus not pure coercion.

Taxation is an example of legitimated enforcement. Clearly taxation is not a voluntary program. Yet it operates within a broad base of some bareboned willingness to contribute some of one's wealth to the common good. If there were no base of even halfhearted willingness, the enforcement process would become grossly inefficient.

Thus when we move to the painful business of preferential affirmative action, progress will slow intolerably without firm enforcement. But the enforcement itself will falter if the fairness of the redistributive process does not rise to some level of national consciousness. And so we must turn to *justice as profitable* (the utility motive), to ideals, and to the healthy recognition of guilt.

JUSTICE FOR PROFIT

If justice can be profitable and the polity catches onto this, justice is obviously enhanced. I have noted some rather uncomplimentary images of society and of the state. Reinhold Niebuhr spoke of "the feeble mind of a nation"; Thomas Hobbes compared it to the bulky Leviathan; George Kennan called it a huge monster with a pin-sized brain. More generously, I could say that a nation is a dolt, but a sufficiently cunning dolt that it can at times rise to the bait of its own advantage. It best understands doing good when the good is perceptibly tied to doing well. An important question, therefore, for distributive justice is: What's in it for all of us? If it is pure giveaway, a zero sum case of "you win, I lose," the forthcoming compliance will be so grudging as to be negligible. What, then, could be so *useful* about cutting the pie in a way that means some loss of pie to the previously privileged? In summary, the answer is that the sharing will actually enlarge the pie (!) and will also allow us to enjoy our share in peace.

More and more it is not land but mind that makes a nation rich and strong. The old adage "Waste not, want not!" applies more than ever to not wasting the surprising powers of the mind. We never know whence the genius and the triggering insight will come. Hard as it is for white male hubris to fully admit it, untapped technological and philosophical genius might be found in women and blacks and others who are outside the club. It was no flight of fanciful idealism but rather a pragmatic assessment of the national interest that Jefferson showed when he spoke of salvaging the talent that lies buried in every society.[17] In more cumbersome language, Herbert Marcuse was onto the same truth when he wrote: "A society is sick if its fundamental institutions and relationships (that is to say, its structure) are so designed that they do not permit the employment of the available material and intellectual means for the optimal development of human existence."[18] Here is where there is a bit of Hitler in every society. There are sources of discovery from which we expect nothing and so get nothing. Ideas, like people, must have the proper papers or they are rejected. Hitler banished and buried groups that could have helped him and added to his strength. Poverty, racism, and sexism likewise kill what is valuable to the polity. The syndrome of Auschwitz is to destroy what you actually need and we are all afflicted by this consumptive disease.

The nature of this disease, however, is such that a cure is begun by the very recognition of the malady. When we become aware that the current patterns of distribution, however generous they have been to us, are constricting our possibilities, we can view them in a new light. At this writing, the American business community is salivating at the opening of the China market. Cool heads, of course, are warning that the low level of affluence in China limits the market. Not until purchasing power grows will there be buyers. In the face of all of this, however, a warm and stubborn confidence obtains that the buyers will come and that American business will boom again.

The economic faith at work here seems to disappear when we turn to the home scene. What applies to the Chinese goose does not apply to the black American gander. Of course the fattening of the Chinese goose is not our problem and the advancement of the black gander is. So it is more congenial to dream dreams about China and ignore black America. Still the same economic principle holds and in this there is hope. If blacks did not even rise to white levels of affluence but merely rose to 80 per cent of white income, and if only a half of the black youths who are looking for jobs could find them, salubrious effects would soon roll through the entire American economy. Black unemployment is not even calculable since there is no way of accurately guessing how many have despaired of finding work. Aside from the cost in crime and welfare that attend unemployment and its accompanying despair, the loss of purchasing power is a noxious fact of American economics. Notice how zero sum thinking here would be misguided. Increased affluence expands the opportunities within the economy. The pie gets bigger. Black gain is not white loss overall since huge blocks of poverty slow the economy and drain it. It is not just the poor who suffer, though their suffering is obviously distinct and often fatal. The whole economy suffers. This is the thinking behind the call for a Marshall Plan for blacks in this country. As Judge Loren Miller wrote some years ago, "There is every evidence that raising the Negro's economic status would be good business indeed."[19] This was the kind of thinking that spurred programs of foreign aid. Destitute nations are not customers. If the business of America is business in the general mind, then let us go to the ghetto and begin the process of transformation. If unalloyed reverence for personal life does not move us, then let us put the hound of profit onto the scent of gain.

It is not only business that needs a profit motive. Our centers of reflection and learning, the universities and schools, could also do with some such reinforcement. These institutions are peering into a long tunnel of demographic constriction that will lower the student population well into the 1990s. By 1994 the number of non-white eighteen-year-olds will be close to 20 per cent in the United States.[20] Should not this convert admissions officers of our colleges into the natural allies of affirmative action agencies? In the light of these statistics, minorities may be seen not as threats to our privileges but as the *only growing market* for our educational product. These clients will not come to us like the fatted calves of suburbia. Because of the realities of caste and other prejudice, financial aid and remedial assistance will often be needed. But this should in turn make admissions people and other administrators turn to the federal agencies committed to preferential aid to minorities. The potential stimulus is here for a huge lobby committed to tilting federal funds to the educational needs of all minorities. Here is a war on poverty that has dollar gains on the bottom line for business and the educational establishment. If it becomes broadly clear that we need blacks as customers and students, and that the pains of redistribution are the price tag, progress in redistributive justice could more easily ensue.

There are other ways in which the utility of doing good can be perceived. Businesses and other institutions inevitably slip into administrative ruts. The accustomed way comes to be mistaken for the most efficient way. When presented with new challenges in the management of personnel, serendipitous gains in management skills are appearing. Many cries of pain have arisen in the enforcement process of civil rights. Yet gains are also being registered. As one commentator put it (with more than a hint of surprise): "Actually, the government is requiring us to do precisely the kind of detailed, critical analyses of our human resource needs and work force availabilities that we ought to be doing as a matter of self-interest. The minimal amount of extra work that is needed to meet their special procedural requirements is a small price indeed to pay for the education we are all receiving. Voluntarily or not, we are now learning how to manage human resource systems."[21]

In a word, then, if it could enter into economic orthodoxy that the advancement and economic activation of the growing non-white portion of our population is in the national interest, the case for justice could be better pleaded. If part of the solution to recurrent recession is in the ghetto, we must turn to the ghetto with the prodigious managerial genius of which Americans are so proud. Without putting it in so many words, this nation has lived with a utilitarian calculus regarding blacks. Our inconsistent and inadequate remedial efforts imply the belief that the plight of blacks must be tolerated for the greatest good of the greatest number—who happen to be white. This involves fictional economics. You cannot leave a substantial and growing minority in perpetual depression in a healthy economy. The economic strangulation of that portion of the citizenry creates expensive problems, leaves energies and genius untapped, and deprives the overall economy of significant purchasing power. Here bad business and bad ethics are as one.

THE POSITIVE SIDE OF FEAR

If gain is a fine supplementary motive for doing social and distributive justice, so too is fear. Fear is the beginning of wisdom, according to the Jewish scriptures. It is also a major motive for the doing of justice. Apathy, which is the principal form of social and distributive injustice, has a price tag. We ignore the rights of peoples at our own peril. It is in the interest of our ease to believe that Dr. Kenneth Clark was overstating the case when he said: "The dark ghettos now represent a nuclear stockpile which can annihilate the very foundations of America."[22] His words, however, have the ring of realism about them—indeed in two ways. First, as I have said regarding the utility of justice, the growth of ghettos is to the economy as the growth of cancer to the body. Ultimately even the greatest good of the greatest number is undone. Beyond that, however, great concentrations of alienated and disaffected people are a source of immediate threat to a community. Insult, after all, is the root of all rebellion. As Thomas Paine said, "Inequality of rights has been the cause of all the disturbances, insurrections, and civil wars, that ever happened!"[23] The dispossessed of our society are less and less a pliable, exploitable base. There is new literacy, a new sense of power, and a new capacity for indignation. Where insult, the denial of respect, is present, all deprivation assumes a compelling and intolerable quality. Following the case of *Brown v. Board of Education of Topeka* in 1954, and running through the 1960s, a new hope was born among black Americans. That hope is now turning to alienation and despair for many blacks in the face of mounting evidence of what Faustine Jones calls "eroding commitment."[24] Blacks are outraged by the new *myth* of black progress. There has been progress in education and in the number of blacks elected to office. However, there has actually been regression in unemployment, income, housing, family stability, health care, and in the deepening deterioration of the worst slums.[25] "Ethnic backlash," "benign neglect," cries of "reverse discrimination," and renewed interest in studies "proving" the genetic inferiority of blacks are turning hope into despair and anger.

A 1974 study on black attitudes at the Survey Research Center of the University of Michigan showed some ominous trends. From 1968 to 1971 the number of blacks willing to consider violence, if all other means failed, rose from 23 per cent to 44 per cent.[26] The study found young blacks considerably more alienated than older blacks, though it found all black respondents at least moderately alienated.[27] The primary resort of American blacks has not been to violence for social change. Appeals to conscience, to the courts, and to the national government have been most typical up to now. There are indications that an impatience with these means is building and a new rage is being born. If this alienation becomes mobilized, the dominant white society may wish, in the ensuing terror, that all we had to deal with was a moderate program of preferential affirmative action. The United States would ring with criticism of a foreign policy establishment that took no count of noxious and inflammatory conditions in some strategic nation when the explosions that were foreseeable occurred. Yet we live on in the bland and blind faith that our growing black population will be enduringly docile and compliant. There are indications that this will not be so.

IDEALS AS POWER

Next, in this complex problem of political motivation, there is the apparently feeble power of ideals. The impuissance of ideals is, of course, only apparent. In fact, only ideals can light the fires of revolution. People will not die for convenience or utility, but when a cause has been firmly identified with precious ideals, unlimited loyalty and enthusiasm follow. There is truth in what Harold Laski writes of Communism, saying that it "has made its way by its idealism and not by its realism, by its spiritual promise, not its materialistic prospects."[28] The same can be said of every revolutionary social movement. Every nation is assembled around a credo of ideals. Liberty, fraternity, equality, life, liberty, the pursuit of happiness; democracy, the revolution of the proletariat, et cetera. And nations are passionate, albeit unfaithful, lovers when it comes to their ideals. Ideals are potent because they touch at the sacred roots of human life. They are the epitome of the sanctity of life, expressing what most befits our being. They are our cherished dreams about the way life could and should be lived. Justice for all is a prime American ideal. It imports fairness and the right of everyone to a square deal. Admittedly, though we would die for that ideal, we would not and do not live by it. But, for all of that, it is a highly charged source of power in this society. Propagandists always know the power of ideals and seek to manipulate them to ideological purposes. The lesson is that the invocation of ideals is not useless. In so doing we touch tender centers of commitment. Much of the fury that greeted the mild cultural revolution of the 1960s in this country came from the favored tactic of casting the professed ideals of the nation before the wayward powers of the establishment. It is no indifferent thing to be called before the bar of one's ideals. The administration of justice in the polity can always do with a judicious smidgeon of preachiness.

HEALTHY GUILT

And finally to guilt. When we speak of motivating the political community to justice, we are in a conversation about power. In that regard, guilt might seem even more out of place than ideals. First of all, in the post-Freudian era, guilt itself has a bad name. It is redolent of neurosis and maladjustment. To speak of guilt, then, as a form of political power seems unpromising—especially since nations have uncanny powers of rationalization. History shows that groups can justify atrocities in ways that would seem psychopathic in an individual. Yet I insist, and must therefore argue, that the experience of guilt may be a powerful motivator not only at the personal level but also in the collective and political sphere.

To clear the air, I admit forthwith that guilt may be neurotic and sick. It might also, however, point to behavioral commitments that are incompatible with even the minimal standards of distinctively human existence. There is such a thing as evil, and we can get into it with gusto. Anyone who doesn't know that is naïve, a "deluded Pollyanna," in Abraham Maslow's phrase.[29] If we experience guilt feelings when there is no corresponding association with evil, that is sick guilt calling for therapy. If, however, we feel guilty when we are doing or endorsing that which is insidious and cruel, those guilt feelings should be as welcome as a good diagnosis. If we are treating persons as non-persons, it is good to know that. Guilt delivers that message. And the message is as important as it is painful. The experience of guilt is the indispensable prelude to moral and political evolution. As J. Glenn Gray writes: "If guilt is not experienced deeply enough to cut into us, our future may well be lost."[30] But if guilt is experienced deeply enough to cut into us, it becomes a source of power and motivation.

Moral values are terribly serious because they constitute what we are. They are not just adornments; they are constitutive of acceptable humanity. I may lack aesthetic values or athletic values without apology. The very lack, indeed, might be endearing. The lack of moral value is different. If I don't dance well, that is one thing; if I don't tell the truth well, that is another. The experience of guilt is the ex-

perience of the lack of moral values. This is a jarring, painful experience. The pain can be traced to a split between what I opt to be and
what I really am. If I seek gain through fraud or sexual expression
through rape, my native need for self-actualization through respectful
and friendly interaction with persons clashes with my behavioral op-
tions. Being and doing are in painful collision. Terms like inauthen-
ticity, bad faith, and guilt describe the resultant internal crisis. This is
a profoundly upsetting experience, and it is not surprising that guilt,
in its neurotic or in its healthy forms, features highly in the etiology
of much mental disturbance. The pain of guilt is such that we instinc-
tively withdraw from it either by moral conversion or by rationalization. If the rationalization is pierced, the pain returns. That
which can cause such pain is correspondingly powerful.

Personal guilt, of course, is more easily understood. But the question is, can there be such a thing as collective guilt? Whenever we
move from the personal to the collective we take a quantum leap into
complexity. The notion of collective guilt is not an easy one and it is
not helped by the fuzzy and even absurd notions of collective guilt
that have been proffered from time to time. Jews have been accused
of guilt for the death of Jesus. All whites without differentiation have
been seen as guilty of the death of Sitting Bull or of Martin Luther
King. Japanese Americans were cast under the cloud of collective
guilt and jailed during World War II in spite of their loyalties to the
American cause. This is nonsense. It blurs distinctions, confuses people alive with people long dead, and creates the problem of everyone
being guilty and therefore of no one being guilty. In this view, guilt
becomes a morass in which specific responsibilities are lost.

However, reflecting back to the sociality of our nature, note again
that human life unfolds collectively in distinctive ways. We can do
more and different things collectively. We can be better and worse
together. In terms of social and distributive justice, we can collectively fail to respond to the value of persons in ways that are much
more devastating to our victims than any number of uncoordinated
individual misdeeds or individual failures of response. Together we
can legitimate a society in which greedy monopolies and systemic insult obtain. Together we can lock doors that no individual can open.
As a group we can wreak deprivation upon a whole race or a whole

sex. And since rationalization works with psychotic force at the collective level, we can be blinder to our social guilt than we could ever be in private life. Collectively we are more distant from our victims and more enveloped in myth and image—we can be more abstract and therefore more cruel. As groups, we can act against whole groups—whether the grouping be in terms of class, sex, or race. Collective power is not only real but terrifying in its impact. Collective guilt—which could also be called political, social, or communal guilt —arises from failures in social and distributive justice.

The main form of collective guilt is apathy. The active practitioners of evil in any society will always be a minority. The guilt of the majority will be in terms of not responding, not resisting, not disapproving, not listening. Apathy is the catchall word for that. Apathy is not just an absence of caring and responsibility. It is at root an active form of complicity and a necessary supportive base for social evil. Non-resistance is gainful behavior. Discrimination is profitable, and the apathetic base of a discriminatory society knows it. Discrimination provides an exploitable economic substratum. It offers cheap labor. It affords someone to scorn, thus opening a negative route to improving one's self-image. Apathy is, therefore, a positive volitional force that is fueled by the perception of advantage. Its injustice lies in its politically supportive complacency before the denial of that which is due to persons. In a society where there is discernible sexism, racism, or class exploitation, collective guilt is a broad and real phenomenon.

From the viewpoint of political power and motivation, the challenge is to unmask that guilt so that its pain may be felt and thus become a potential form of motivational power. This kind of power is not without example in recent history. To some extent, the experience of guilt motored the civil rights progress of the 1950s and 1960s. The appeal to a sense of guilt is certainly a prominent part of the non-violent segment of the civil rights movement. In the case of Martin Luther King, the appeal to guilt was part of the educative strategy in his form of non-violent power. Some of the resistance to the war in Vietnam evinced socially experienced guilt of a powerful sort. The German experience after the last war and the international reaction to the holocaust of the Jews and the founding of the state of

Israel could not be understood without some reference to collectively experienced guilt. A growing sense of guilt about the treatment of the Palestinians is an important political development in the Middle East. There is power in each of these experiences.

Admittedly, the armor of hypocrisy that shields us from our guilt is not easily pierced. The first reason for this is the pain that attends guilt from which we can no longer hide. But, also, guilt introduces responsibility. It demands restitution. And restitution also causes pain. Restitution, however, is the only responsible reaction to the experience of guilt. Given the fact that none of us is without guilt in the social order, given the fact that none of us has done enough or been sensitive or creative enough regarding the social evils we have tolerated to our own advantage—given all of that, he who proclaims himself guiltless is a liar. But the prime duty of the guilty is restitution—another very painful component of the guilt experience. In the social order, where social and distributive justice operate, restitution is the elementary expression of justice. If there is social evil in a society and no active process of restitution in evidence, there is no justice because there is no effective recognition of guilt. The experience of guilt, however, is a necessary stimulant for social change.

Two final comments in this long discussion concern the role of organized religions and of the Supreme Court in the American realization of justice. Social motivation comes from many sources and we are wise to seek to know how these two sources of magisterial power operate in America. In the case of religious bodies and the Court, the appropriate questions are: How do they influence us, and How could they and ought they influence us?

RELIGIOUS DEFAULT

For many Americans, the strongest social allegiance is to their religion. These religions could be principal factors in social motivation. Unfortunately this influence is often not helpful or critical but simply endorses the prejudices of the status quo. In the debate on affirmative action the Christian denominations—excluding the black churches—have been all but mute. Scholars from the Christian churches have not been drawn to the discussion. Catholic scholarship and influence has been notably in default in this regard. This is especially lamentable in view of the theory of justice that has been elaborated in the Catholic tradition. As Protestant Emil Brunner wrote: "While the Catholic Church, drawing on centuries of tradition, possesses an impressive systematic theory of justice, Protestant Christianity has had none for some three hundred years past."[31]

Unfortunately Catholic thought in the United States has been too turned in upon itself and fixated on sectarian issues, and on moral issues to which they have committed their prestige, such as the abortion issue.[32] Christians in general, though, have been unaccountably ineffective in facing the crisis of redistribution. Given the central and definitive rights of the poor and the dispossessed in Christian teaching, this is a perplexing defection. Partly this can be explained by the fact that Christians have been distracted by love to the neglect of justice. Christians regularly miss the fact that in their moral credo, love is not the first order of business. Justice is. Preaching love bypasses the problems of the social order where love is not, and for the foreseeable future will not be, the energizing power of social existence. Interpersonally, love may reign; politically, there will be justice or degrading deprivation. American Christians, drunk on love-talk, have too often missed this. Put another way, justice is the form that love takes in the political order. Where there is full love, i.e. friendship, justice becomes irrelevant. In the political order thus far in moral evolution, justice is the most that can be hoped for. Thus the debate on redistributional affirmative action, which has been building in the legal literature for years and in the philosophical literature more recently, has not been well served by the Christian churches.

Jewish support for redistributional affirmative action—among both religious and secular Jews—has been disappointing also. To some degree this is as understandable as it is regrettable. Jews have suffered from *exclusive* quotas even recently, and thus are reacting adversely to the *inclusive* quota of affirmative action.[33] As recently as 1945, American medical schools were receiving applications annually from about 14,000 individuals. Nearly half of those individuals were Jews. The policy was to accept only a token number of Jews, regardless of their qualifications. Even at Howard University, then an all-black school, Jews were limited. Many Jews had to go to Europe, and even to Africa, to get their degrees in medicine.[34] It was not until the 1950s that Jews were received more freely into medical schools. Talk of numbers, therefore, makes many Jews nervous. Given the tendency for history to repeat itself, and given the deep anti-Semitism that still abides in the United States, care must be taken that Jews are not the first to have to yield in preferential programs. This concern should be built into anyone's concern for preferential affirmative action. The problem which the Jews face here, however, is not so unmanageable as to stand against the necessity to attack the caste system and the sexist structures that handicap the entire nation. There are strong reasons, in fact, why Jews should be vigorously supportive of preferential affirmative action. As recently as 1921 the argument was made that Jews (along with Italians and Poles) were feeble-minded, and that letting them into this nation in large numbers would dilute the mental acuity of the American populace.[35] The Jews, as well as anyone, should be able to empathize with the blacks, as new studies alleging the genetic inferiority of blacks emerge. Historically, Jews do have a distinguished record in the civil rights movement in this country. Two of the three civil rights workers who were slain in Mississippi, while working on black voter registration, were Jews. This was no anomaly but rather symbolized strong Jewish commitment to the cause of blacks. A slackening of that commitment now besmirches a great record, weakens the national coalition for civil rights, and thus damages the common good.

On top of this, Jews who join the attack on preferential affirmative action could also be accused of inconsistency if they are also supporters of the state of Israel. The creation and support of the state of Israel was, as Professor Faustine Jones points out, "an affirmative action by the international community to relieve the suffering of a group of people."[36] That action was not based upon the merit principle or upon an individualized comparison of rights. It was motivated by the prolonged suffering of the Jewish people and by the perceived need for structural change to ensure that such suffering would end. It was based upon the *needs* of a *group*. It did not create a state for the most deserving Jews or for those who had suffered the most, as individual meritarian approaches would require. It has been, quite simply, a case of preferential affirmative action based on group need.

More importantly, however, Jews who lambast preferential affirmative action for other groups, and gird themselves about with the wizened and mean-spirited categories of invidious American individualism, turn their backs on their own rich tradition of justice and the promotion of human good. They are thereby rejecting some of the noblest conceptions of the just and good society that have ever graced human history. There is a terrible sadness in this. Some Jews, in the words of the Hebrew scriptures, are selling their birthright for a mess of pottage.

THE SUPREME COURT
AND THE REALIZATION OF JUSTICE

The Supreme Court hovers over American notions of justice in a way that is unique among the nations. This is not sufficiently acknowledged either by the members of the Court or by the general populace. This Court is asked to do much more than pronounce upon the causes of litigants. It is asked, rather, to be a philosophical forum, to ponder the meaning and destiny of our common life. In this the Court reflects the mood at the birthing of this nation. The United States has indulged in juridical positivism—which confuses morality with mere legality—but it was not born of it. The Declaration of Independence and the various bills of rights, so jealously assembled by the states, were bright with convictions about that which was "just by nature," in Aristotle's phrase, over against that which was merely "legal."[37] The American Revolution was a product of this distinction. It was an appeal to justice, against what was then legal. The English King had legality on his side, but that was judged insufficient.

The creation of the Supreme Court was a high moment in political history. Nations have a perversely positivist bent. They are disposed to confuse their tribal laws with nature and to see morality and legality as one. However, much that is legal is wicked, and if you conflate justice and law, then law can crush you and you have no redress. Slavery, after all, was seen as legal and constitutional in our history.

The philosopher who criticizes erroneous or inadequate laws is a major patriot and civil servant.[38] His service is more basic than that of the judge since he puts the law and justice itself on trial in the court of moral reason.

The Constitution of the United States embodied our political philosophy, and the Supreme Court is asked to interpret that instrument. The task involved is thus primarily philosophical and not narrowly judicial. In an unparalleled way, our Supreme Court attempts to fulfill the striking vision of judgeship that Aristotle had when he called the judge "living justice."[39] Justice will never be fully captured in the crust of words. Particular laws are always approximations and unprofitable servants of justice. There is need in society for the "living intellect" to press beyond imperfect formulations to the sources of meaning.[40] Those who are deemed great justices have not been those clever dickerers who, with exegetical wizardry, made patchwork solutions from the decisions of the past. The great justices were the philosophical judges who moved within the spirit of the classical Roman jurists, believing that "law and right can and must always be sought for less in the detailed rules of the laws than in their foundation, that is, in the intrinsic nature of things, which is the perennial and inexhaustible source."[41] It is not enough to abide by the old axiom: *Stare decisis,* stand with that which has already been decided. Past decisions are illuminating but not definitive. The Supreme Court meets its real challenge when past cases do not offer adequate guidance, or must even be overturned. Past decisions emanated from some philosophical framework. That framework is also on trial in a new case. The philosophy of past decisions may have to be overturned if it does not do justice to justice. Aristotle put it very optimistically when he said: "To go to the judge is to go to justice."[42] What is more certain is that the justice must go to justice. Supreme Court members cannot assume that they are dispensed from the duty to investigate their own ruling assumptions regarding the nature of justice.

Not every case that comes before the Supreme Court has massive philosophical implications. But many do. Justices must be persons who can react with creativity and depth to these cases. As a nation, we have not thought deeply enough about the business we commend to this Court. If we did, we would see that it makes no sense for all of the judges to be lawyers. A number of other disciplines and perspectives should contribute to that philosophical forum that we call the Supreme Court. The 100 per cent quota of lawyers we have for this unique body tends to give a positivist cast to the Court and frustrate its prime purpose because of the mechanical jurisprudence that many of our lawyers have imbibed in their training.

Furthermore, since the realization of justice and the Supreme Court in this land are so tied, we should take instruction from the "Impeach Earl Warren" crowd. They at least knew that their foundational conceptions of the good life were being treated by the Court. Their argument was not with particular statutory issues but with the world view they saw emerging. They were Court-watchers in a way we all should be. For this remarkable institution to serve us better we must better know its function and potential. Reform of that Court so that it could better fulfill its function should be thinkable. Admittedly, it is not likely, since for many Americans that would be like trying to reform the work of God. At the least it can be said that a greater sophistication about the doings of the Supreme Court is necessary equipment for those who look to the realization of justice in this society. We should know the powers that move us and be critical of them.

In summary, then, motivation for distributive justice will be as complex as society itself. Moving the monster will not be simple. Enforcement is necessary because as a society we will not voluntarily be just and because even voluntariness would need coordination. Yet the enforcement process must be educational, showing the doltish collectivity where its interests lie and its ideals beckon. Thus is the process legitimated and made stable by at least a modicum of willingness.[43]

THE SEASONING OF JUSTICE

Justice, I have said, is the least we can do in response to the value of persons. Reveries of love are futile in the political order because love is not yet a functional kind of energy there. The powerless in society will have justice or they will die. With all of that affirmed and reaffirmed, we Americans with our tough, adversarial approach to justice must attend to the paradox that Portia signals when she says to Shylock: ". . . earthly power doth then show likest God's,/When mercy seasons justice."[44] Thomas Aquinas put it more directly yet: "Justice without mercy is cruelty."[45]

Justice untouched by mercy is minimalistic and stinting in its response to persons. Justice is incipient love and thus has some native ties to generosity and enthusiasm. A society whose "justice" is calculating, cold, and miserly will not rise to the needs of persons. (Old Ebenezer Scrooge may have paid his debts, but he would never be the symbol of justice.) An unfeeling justice will soon fizzle and the enforcement of it will soon flag. True justice must have at least a spark of great-souled appreciation of the preciousness of the persons to whom it attends. Where this is not present in a society, the extremes of poverty and wealth will coexist, exploitative power will wax strong, and the poor will wax weaker and poorer.

This link to mercy and enthusiasm is true for all forms of justice but is especially true for social-distributive justice which would direct powerful societal patterns of redistribution. American attitudes toward blacks illustrate the problem of unenthusiastic justice. White America has never mounted a massive, consistent, and strenuous effort to end the economic slavery of blacks and their incarceration in ghettos. The failure here is foundational. It is the failure of a land that lacks the mercy to be just.

Some civilizations have been so aware of this side of justice that they have attempted to institutionalize the quality of mercy in their reach for social justice. Ancient Israel is the most striking example of this. Every fiftieth year was proclaimed the Year of Jubilees. In this year all land that had been sold or foreclosed during the previous half century was to be returned to the original owner. Also, those whose poverty had forced them to sell themselves into servitude were to be freed during the Year of Jubilees. The effect of this was to restore the poor to their own productive capacities. The intention of such laws was to prevent the partitioning of society into the extravagantly rich and the drastically poor. The dealings that would bring about such a situation were all presumably "just" in a legal sense.

(There were other ways of handling fraudulent deprivation of land.) But, given the ways of power, the assumption was that these "legitimate" dealings would lead to a concentration of power and wealth in the hands of a few and the creation of deprived poor. The mandate of the law was: "There shall be no poor among you."[46] Poverty was seen as intolerable since "the poverty of the poor is their ruin."[47] Also in ancient Israel, every seventh year was a sabbatical year when all that grew spontaneously in the fields and in the orchards belonged not to the owners but to the poor. As Dr. Trude Weiss-Rosmarin says of this practice: "Obviously this was *expropriation*. But it was considered necessary so as to restore socioeconomic equity and equilibrium."[48] Another way of putting it was that the Hebrew people saw that justice must be corrected and fulfilled with mercy. This was clearly a form of preferential affirmative action. It had an inherent generosity and was not the conception of a wizened and parsimonious justice. It also was realistic. It did not pretend that the poor could litigate their individual grievances. Neither did it attempt to sort out the deserving poor and exclude the rogues and the lazy from the perquisites of a justice seasoned with mercy. *The burden of proof was not upon the claims of the poor but upon the accumulated wealth of the rich.* It did not assume that wealth came only through merit and virtue but saw that it was also the result of good luck, inheritance, and the native talents that are nature's unmerited gift to some. And interestingly, the redistributionary process of the Year of Jubilees was not looked on as a work of arbitrary benevolence but was rather seen as the consummation of justice.[49] In this Hebraic vision, justice showed its relationship to mercy. It is a practical fact of political life that all our plans and social schemes will fail and be survived by the problems they sought to address unless there is in them some of the fire that was in the spirit of the Jubilees.

PART THREE

The Challenge of Redistribution

Justice might require unequal and preferential treatment for some groups for a time. Yet not every group that lines up for preference deserves it. Chapter Seven offers four criteria that should be met to justify preferential relief. It is argued that only four groups qualify—blacks, American Indians, women, and, among the Hispanics, the Chicanos and Puerto Ricans. Chapter Eight, with reliance on the theory of justice developed in Part Two, tackles each of the objections lodged against affirmative action in Chapter Three above.

CHAPTER SEVEN

Criteria for Preferment

As Aristotle said, in an all too cryptic way, "it is by proportionate requital that the city holds together."[1] More simply put, it is by some preferential treatment and some fair inequalities that the city is held together. Undemocratic as that may sound, it is a fact of life in any viable polity. As mentioned in the preceding chapter, justice and equality are not the same thing. Inequality is our daily bread. The handicapped and the gifted, veterans, ailing corporations, and poor people all know the meaning of unequal and preferential aid. Progressive taxation is not equal taxation, neither are the benefits from the Social Security program realized on an equal basis. In all of this, "proportional requital" rules—not equality. The city holds together by recognizing differing needs, merits, and rights and by responding proportionately, and thus often unequally, to these unequal claims.

While the moral burden of preferential affirmative action rests upon the government and other distributional powers in the society that have fostered and sustained the disempowerment of certain groups, the obvious inequality of the cure is not always easily stomached. In its exciting history, "equality" was gallantly pitted against unfair preference based on bias and greed. In the popular mind explicit inequality is suspect. After all, we learned in childhood that a fairly cut pie had equal pieces. On top of that, we could hardly expect white males who have profited from keeping blacks and women "in their place" to cheer at the demise of their privileges. No privileged group in history has welcomed its dethronement. For all of these reasons, any group claiming preferential treatment in a society should be able to show that this preferential assistance is necessary for justice. Clear criteria for preferment are needed and have been sorely lacking in the affirmative action program. The line forms quickly when there is a whiff of preference in the air. We are a "nation of minorities" and there is no minority among us that could not point to some specific suffering. If each of these groups wins enforced preferential aid the result is chaos, since, when all are preferred, none are preferred. Most needs can be met by normal law enforcement and policies. But if there are groups which are not just slowed but disempowered, preferential social aid may be needed to empower them and end their excommunication from the common good. Preferential relief may even be needed on a permanent basis for those, such as the physically handicapped, who will never be able to compete. But in dealing with groups that have been disempowered by systemic prejudice and monopoly, the goal is re-enfranchisement in the normal competitive dynamics of society.

DISEMPOWERED GROUPS: THE BLACK PARADIGM

It is my judgment that there are four criteria for enforced preferential aid and that these four are fulfilled paradigmatically by blacks. No other disempowered group seeking integration within the American socioeconomic system meets the criteria as classically and fully as blacks do—although some other groups do fulfill the requirements in a way fully sufficient to merit enforced preference. These other groups are women, American Indians, and some segments of the Hispanic population. The plight of these groups is sufficiently close to the black paradigm to qualify them for remedial preference. The black problem, however, is worse and more intractable. It is my judgment—which I shall forthwith attempt to prove—that women, Hispanics, and even American Indians, whose plight most approximates that of blacks, do not serve their cause or justice by assuming that all beleaguered groups are equally disadvantaged. A major part of the black problem is that it has been trivialized by treating it as just one of many problems. Its uniqueness has never been systematically faced, and thus blacks have remained the permanent underclass and lowest caste. Again, I am not treating here the plight of the physically and mentally handicapped who require enduring preferential relief. The handicapped do not yet receive all the help they need, and many of their problems are crassly ignored by the hale and well. Still, their cause enjoys considerably more public favor than that of the socially handicapped. As Judge Loren Miller writes: "Large-scale hire-the-handicapped programs are undertaken without objection; yet loss of a leg is often less of a handicap than being born with a dark skin."[2] So what then are the four criteria that blacks fulfill in a unique and paradigmatic way and American Indians, women, and some Hispanics also fulfill to the extent of meriting enforced preferential assistance?

THE FOUR CRITERIA FOR PREFERENTIAL AID TO DISEMPOWERED GROUPS

To qualify for enforced, temporary preferential affirmative action, it must be established that 1) *no alternatives to enforced preference are available;* and 2) *the prejudice against the group must reach the level of depersonalization.* Social and distributive justice must respond to the needs of all the poor with welfare, educational and medical programs, job training, et cetera. The problems of the poor are a prime concern in a just society. However, we are dealing here with the special needs of discrete groups that call for further relief beyond the usual ministrations of just government, social agencies, and just persons. Strange as it may sound, there are some things that are worse than poverty—worse for individuals and for society. As professor of law Owen M. Fiss says regarding blacks, "Blacks face disabilities not encountered by the poor."[3] The proof of this is seen in the incentives white poor have to disassociate themselves from black poor. Lumping the blacks together with all "the poor" again misses the special qualities of the black situation.

I stress depersonalization here also since mere prejudice, such as that which greets the latest immigrants, will normally have shallower roots. The inconvenience and resentment engendered by the new arrivals is more amenable to the integrative dynamics of the society. When prejudice, however, attacks a group at the level of their personal dignity, the possibilities of assimilation or acceptance are blocked. All prejudice is a problem; depersonalizing prejudice is a radical disease requiring special remedies.

3) *The bias against the group is not private or narrowly localized but is rather entrenched in the culture and distributive systems of the society.* The prejudice must not be such as to remain in the heart but must have insinuated itself into the laws, institutions, and myths of a people. It is this in-systemed, in-cultured prejudice that makes a group *disempowered*. When members of such a group seek to compete, they run into strong head winds and obstacles that others—even other poor—do not encounter.

4) *The members of the victim groups must be visible as such and thus lack an avenue of escape from their disempowered status.*

BLACKS AND THE FOUR CRITERIA

Tragically, American blacks have no trouble qualifying under these four criteria. As to the first condition, that there be no lesser remedies of an effective sort, reliance by blacks on simple enforcement of non-discrimination is not a serious alternative. As University of Wisconsin president Robert M. O'Neil observes: "The short answer to this suggestion is that 'nondiscrimination' has been tried and found wanting."[4] The path of voluntarism has been tried and found wanting. And even when the federal government has insisted on the rights of blacks through executive orders, rulings of the Supreme Court, and formal legislative action, resistance has been formidable. Dilatory tactics and outright obstruction have greeted every federal action in behalf of blacks. Appeals for voluntary solutions to the black problem, therefore, amount to acquiescence in American apartheid, that continuing and deepening division of this nation into two separate societies. Blacks would truly be naïve and inferior if they trusted the good will of the nation that stole them from their homes, stripped them of their language and alienated them from much of their culture, enslaved them and re-enslaved them economically after abolition, ghettoized them, branded them and treated them as inferior, and resisted their every claim for justice. Still, white appeals for voluntarism dare, in the face of that record, to say: "Trust us!" Enforced redistribution is the only alternative for blacks.

The second condition relates to negative bias extending to the point of depersonalization. Depersonalizing prejudice is the ultimate insult. It tells the victim that his very humanity is deficient. The prejudice against blacks that besets American culture is an epic of depersonalization. The historic roots of the prejudice are deep and generously nourished by both religion and myth. Christian Europe believed that after Noah the lines of human descent passed through Japheth, Shem, and Ham. Japheth became the ancestor of nobles; Shem was the father of clerks; Ham, who was cursed, became the parent of serfs. Eventually this took on racial categorizations. Japheth was the ancestor of whites, Shem of the yellow race, and Ham of blacks.[5] The serf-black connection was thus widely accepted. There was even strong feeling that blacks might not descend from a common parent. Voltaire, for example, adopted and voiced this persuasion, saying that "bearded men, fuzzy Negroes, the long-maned yellow races and beardless men are not descended from the same man." Blacks again came at the bottom of the ladder. There was more readiness to accept the American Indian as racially akin to Europeans.[6] The American Indian was even idealized as the embodiment of original innocence in European literature. Not so the black African. As Voltaire saw it, whites are "superior to these Negroes, as the Negroes are to the apes and the apes to oysters."[7] Edward Long's *History of Jamaica,* which was considered authoritative for more than a century, divided the genus homo into three species: Europeans and related races, Negroes, and orangoutangs. He saw Negroes as closer to orangoutangs than to Europeans. He wrote: "In general, they are void of genius, and seem almost incapable of making any progress in civility or science. They have no plan or system of morality about them. . . . They are represented by all authors as the vilest of the human kind, to which they have little more pretension of resemblance than what arises from their exterior form. . . ."[8]

Slavery, of course, is the living proof that these ideas did not remain at the level of salon talk or academic rumination. The United States was destined to be one place where these sentiments would be translated into social reality. The subpersonal status of blacks became explicit in the institution of slavery. In the Dred Scott decision of 1857, Mr. Chief Justice Taney does us the service of summing up the common thinking of Americans vis-à-vis the black slaves at the time of the foundation of this nation.

> [Negroes] were at that time considered as a subordinate and inferior class of beings, who had been subjugated by the dominant race, and, whether emancipated or not, yet remained subject to their authority, and had no rights or privileges but such as those who held the power and the Government might choose to grant them. . . . They had for more than a century before been regarded as beings of an inferior order, and altogether unfit to associate with the white race . . . and so far inferior, that they had no rights which the white man was bound to respect; and that the negro might justly and lawfully be reduced to slavery for his benefit. He was bought and sold, and treated as an ordinary article of merchandise and traffic, whenever a profit could be made by it. This opinion was at that time fixed and universal in the civilized portion of the white race . . . intermarriages between white persons and negroes or mulattoes were regarded as unnatural and immoral, and punished as crimes.

The conclusion of the decision was that blacks were not seen by the framers of the Constitution as citizens or potential citizens.[9]

The depersonalization of slaves was woven into American law. "Slaves have no legal rights in things, real or personal; but whatever they may acquire, belongs, in point of law, to their masters."[10] The glorious proclamation that "all men are created equal" and are self-evidently endowed "with certain inalienable rights" applied only to white men and has not been effectively extended to blacks even to this day.

From 1619 to 1865 blacks were held in degrading bondage, possessing no rights that whites were bound to respect, denied the blessings of family life and education. From 1865 to 1877 there was a period of some respite and promise. The Thirteenth, Fourteenth, and Fifteenth amendments were added to the Constitution of the

United States. The Freedmen's Bureau was established and it had some salubrious impact on the lives of black persons. In 1875 a civil rights bill was passed. However, in 1883 the Supreme Court declared that bill unconstitutional. The *Plessy v. Ferguson* decision of 1896 sanctioned the separate and unequal conditions in which blacks would live until 1954 when the Warren Court overturned *Plessy* in the Brown decision. In the wake of *Plessy,* as Mr. Justice Harlan predicted in his dissenting opinion, the states in the North and the South went on "to place in a condition of legal inferiority a large body of American citizens."[11] Jim Crow laws spewed forth, segregating not only trains and schools but also waiting rooms, bathrooms, phone booths, textbooks, court Bibles, jury boxes, and places of prostitution. The vote was denied to many blacks. The federal government under President Wilson began to require segregation in government buildings, curtaining off desks of blacks, providing separate bathrooms and cafeteria tables, and even segregating the galleries of Congress.

Perhaps one incident in 1918 will sum up the virulence of the racist venom that fills our history. Lerone Bennett, Jr., recounts the story of Mary Turner.

The Mary Turner lynching of 1918 was undoubtedly one of the most barbaric acts ever committed in a civilized country. Though pregnant, the Negro woman was lynched in Valdosta, Georgia. She was hanged to a tree, doused with gasoline and burned. As she dangled from the rope, a man stepped forward with a pocketknife and ripped open her abdomen in a crude caesarean operation. "Out tumbled the prematurely born child," wrote Walter White. "Two feeble cries it gave—and received for answer the heel of a stalwart man, as life was ground out of the tiny form."[12]

The tragedy is that the incident fits. It is not discontinuous or heretical in our story. It flows naturally from our long and deadly serious denial of human status to black adults and children.

Has racism in our day, however, taken a 180-degree turn? Has it been washed away in the baptismal waters of civil rights legislation? Has it melted in the glow of liberal chic? No. Moral conversion has a broad arc. Such powerful poisons are not easily evacuated from our systems. History commends the probability that such ingrained attitudes when challenged only change their appearance and their tactics. Our racism abides but in new dress. Part of the new dress, in fact, is to admit the horror of the past. That done, we can go forth like exuberant new converts, bent on sinning no more, confident that the damned spots of our guilt have been purged by some miraculous moral detergent. From there on, "the past" becomes a bad word. Yes, it was just awful! But what possibly can be gained by bewailing what was? We must leave aside the sins of our ancestors and get on with doing good in this new order which somehow or other has been inaugurated.

The core problem is that being against the old overt racism becomes stylish. As Professor Derrick Bell says, there was a glory for many whites in those days "a decade ago when they could jet-ride South and walk arm-in-arm 'with Martin and the others' through the streets of some dusty southern town and sing the songs that equated freedom and brotherhood, suggesting that the time for both was at hand."[13]

There is, of course, a wispy quality to any "chic." The chic of today is the banality of tomorrow. Social problems, however, are made of sterner stuff and they are scarcely jostled by unsubstantive and temporary indignation. Temporary indignation can stimulate important legislation and stir the hearts of judges but cannot "change the system." It cannot convert the goals of law or judicial ruling into reality since it lacks tough and enduring determination. It is just such determination that has always been lacking in American history.

The new racism is subtle. It doesn't smash against our sensibilities like Bull Connor's dogs and vile-mouthed mobs. The new racism is likely to come wrapped in the prestigious robes of social science and to be heavily anointed with liturgical commitment to the ideals of integration and justice for all. This is what makes it so much more likely to succeed. The results of this new racism, however, are not new. It brings deprivation with insult and depersonalization to black citizens. The persistent and widespread imputation of inferiority, which is the soul of racism, is still with us. Only the way it is expressed has changed.

Sometimes the social-scientific dress of that racism is not at all subtle. Arthur R. Jensen, an educational psychologist at the University of California at Berkeley, reopened the question of the genetic inferiority of blacks in a 1969 article in the *Harvard Educational Review*. Jensen saw the causes of low income and lower social status to be mainly nature, not nurture. The conclusions from this, of course, are devastating. If blacks are down because they are inferior, then down, alas, is where they have to be. Jensen was interested in explaining why the programs of the Great Society failed. His answer was most consoling to those who found such programs inconvenient. Clearly there is no moral obligation to treat an incurable disease— and genetic inferiority would be incurable. Jensen did not groan alone on this topic. William Shockley, a Nobel Prize winner in physics from Stanford University, concurred. Popular journals and newspapers gave these ideas broad circulation. The ideas were welcomed and took root. In 1971, Dorothy Burnham, in an article entitled "Jensenism: The New Pseudoscience of Racism," argued that within only two years of the publication of the Jensen article "Head Start and other compensatory programs had been scuttled, funds for education at every level had been cut, welfare and medical programs had gone by the board, contributions of the federal government to the health and welfare programs of the beleaguered cities had been drastically cut." As Burnham saw it, a "totally false theory had been used as a part of the program to deprive the disadvantaged of their right to education."[14]

A subtler form of the new racism finds twisted ways to blame the victim for his plight. Nathan Glazer deftly invokes a number of myths in discussing black unemployment. He alludes to or quotes others alluding to "the existence of *attractive* alternatives to working," to "the alternative *attractions* of welfare," and to "illicit activities" as "an *attractive* alternative to work" (emphasis added). Glazer concludes that the "tangle of pathology in the ghetto" has never been convincingly explained but that "it is hard to believe it is anything as simple as lack of jobs or discrimination in available jobs."[15]

How far are we from Jensen here? The repeated use of the words "attractive" and "attraction" is telling. Attraction, as opposed to addiction, implies freedom. It involves being drawn to one among several actual alternatives. If you were to say that blacks, despairing of finding work after repeatedly running into the "built-in head winds" and the "artificial, arbitrary, and unnecessary barriers to employment" acknowledged by the Supreme Court, have turned to crime or welfare reliance as the only alternatives to destitution, that would be a very different statement from Glazer's. In that case, crime or welfare reliance might not be attractive at all. Crime and welfare might be chosen mainly because the *attractive* alternatives were unavailable. Glazer here is judging motives in the name of social science and in so doing adds injury to insult. It is insulting and simplistic to infer that blacks—large numbers of them—find crime and the absence of gainful employment congenial and attractive. It would make them a different kind of being. And it is injurious to truth and scientific method to ignore evidence that this is not the case. A study done by Leonard Goodwin at the Brookings Institution in 1972 specifically addressed the topic of the attitude of the poor, particularly the black poor, toward work. The question under study was: "Do the poor really want to work, or do they reject this form of activity, preferring welfare or other ways of getting money?" Social scientists have given little attention to this topic.[16] The principal conclusion of this study, which follows strict scientific methodology, was this:

> Evidence from this study unambiguously supports the following conclusion: poor people—males and females, blacks and whites, youths and adults—identify their self-esteem with work as strongly as do the nonpoor. They express as much willingness to take job training if unable to earn a living and to work even if they were to have an adequate income. They have, moreover, as high life aspirations as do the nonpoor and want the same things, among them a good education and a nice place to live. *This study reveals no differences between poor and nonpoor when it comes to life goals and wanting to work.*[17]

One of the complications in the motivations of black poor is their loss of confidence in themselves owing to the frustrations of their life. Goodwin's study has clear evidence that poor blacks are "very uncertain about their ability."[18] The study shows that both poor and nonpoor black fathers show great lack of confidence in their ability to succeed, whereas poor as well as more affluent white fathers are reasonably confident. Acceptability of welfare, on the other hand, follows economic rather than racial lines.[19]

An atmosphere of poverty without hope of success obviously inhibits expectations and self-estimate of worth. Another study shows that it is only after the third grade that black children begin to fall behind and that this seems to relate to their discovery of their low status in the society.[20] The message from the dominant and enormously impressive white society is a message of black inferiority. Around third grade, black children begin to hear this message and believe it. The American dream is not black. Black children do not emerge into a world of high expectations. They inherit a world of insult. And insult, again, is the root of all rebellion. As Aristotle said: "Men who are themselves dishonoured and who see others obtaining honours rise in rebellion."[21] To represent the black attitudes toward work, crime, and welfare as traceable to their finding crime and welfare "attractive" is both libelous and arrogant in the face of the facts. It is also uninformed.

Another study, in California, showed that the preference for work among black welfare recipients was almost the same as that of better-off black and white men.[22] Similar results were obtained in a New Orleans study which also showed that poor blacks displayed as much willingness to make special efforts, such as moving outside the city to get better jobs, as did nonpoor whites and blacks.[23] A nationwide study and a study in New York of AFDC (Aid to Families with Dependent Children) asked women whether they would prefer to work for pay or to stay at home.[24] Eighty per cent preferred work in the nationwide study, and 70 per cent in the New York study. A survey of both poor and affluent youth in New York asked: "Supposing that somebody just gave you the money you needed every week; would you like this better than working?" More than 72 per cent of *all* groups said they would rather be working.[25]

Robert B. Hill, using data collected by the Census Bureau, makes this observation about black poor: ". . . most of the black poor are poor despite the fact that they work. Sixty-two percent of poor black families have wage or salary earnings, compared to 53 percent of poor white families. The economic situation is so acute for these families that some of them also have to rely on public assistance to supplement their earnings. But despite the fact that 53 percent of the poor black families receive public assistance, only 36 percent of their total income comes from that source."[26] The jobs available to blacks are often inadequate to support them. As much as any group, they take the work that is available to them. As a black friend once said to me: "Show me the white man who wants to work so much that he will shine your shoes and hand you towels in a public toilet!"

I am not suggesting that there is no kind of attractiveness in crime or welfare for *any* black poor. Obviously, the rebellious spirit spawned of insult could at times find a certain "attractiveness" in hostile acts of self-enrichment, as well as in free gifts from the coffers of the dominant white man.[27] But, again, that has to be set against the profound alienation and hopelessness that blacks experience in our society. The most recent study by Louis Harris on *Attitudes Toward Racial and Religious Minorities and Toward Women,* gives chilling evidence of that alienation, reporting that 44 per cent of blacks say their young people feel "pretty hopeless about their chances to make it." Also, 40 per cent feel that their young "feel justified in ripping off whatever they can get." As the study puts it: "[Blacks] have virtually no faith that the white community can be expected to do much for their people who are seeking work."[28] Given those attitudes so broadly found among blacks, it is not surprising that a certain "attractiveness" might be found in attempting to take, one way or the other, from the oppressive and dominant white society. To speak of that "attractiveness," however, without noting the context of despair and disempowerment which is the animating mold of that "attractiveness," imputes a peculiar moral baseness to blacks. In point of fact, blacks actually respond well to genuine opportunity. A report of the Carnegie Council on Policy Studies in Higher Education relates that "evidence from several studies suggests that black students have higher degree aspirations than whites."[29] The new racism does not call blacks "shiftless" or explicitly call them a subspecies of the genus *human* as the more candid racism of the past did. What it does is ignore the devastation that lowest caste stigma inflicts upon blacks from early childhood. Much of what is seen as disruptive behavior and poor study habits springs from a realistic assessment of just what "nigger" status means. No matter what blacks do, a "job ceiling" hovers over their efforts limiting their possibilities of success. How do you motivate a child who discovers early on that a lid has been clamped down upon his possibilities by the overwhelming white society? The new racism takes such a child, who has been raped at the very center of his self-confidence, and then diagnoses his problem as a native penchant for illicit activities and welfare.

Some further examples will show the new face of racism. Harvard urbanologist Edward C. Banfield takes great pains to argue that all kinds of things such as class and recent immigrant status are more important than the race factor in explaining the deprivation blacks endure. Cultural differences, "and conceivably even biological ones as well," enter in. "If there is something about Jewish culture that makes the Jew tend to be upwardly mobile, there may be something about Negro culture that makes the Negro tend not to be."[30] Josef Diamond, the attorney for Marco De Funis, put it equally clearly: "The predominance of whites in the University law school may well be explained by a lack of inclination or aptitude on the part of blacks for such studies. . . . By the same logic that impels the preference of less qualified minorities to achieve racial balance in law, it might be argued that special treatment should be given to whites to achieve racial balance in athletics."[31] Banfield and Diamond here are both Jensenian in spirit and full of consolation for the "benign neglect" school of social justice. If biological and cultural factors are the causes of black lowest-caste status, those of us whose cultural and biological endowment has lofted us to the top can only sigh for those less nobly inclined. Surely we cannot remake them in our own virtuous image. Diamond is willing to say that the paucity of blacks in law school might indicate that blacks lack the aptitude for law studies. Given the number of lawyers and other professionals with less than outstanding intelligence, that is no slight damnation. The reference to athletic ability strengthens the genetic inferiority thesis that peeks through Diamond's remarks. He might as well have added a reference to black predominance in soft shoe dancing and shoe shining and asked for special treatment there for whites!

The same message of inferiority emerges in yet another form in the social science literature. A study by Robert Hall and Richard Kasten has this apparently good news: "The sixties saw the nearly complete elimination of racial bias in the way that the labor market assigned individuals to occupations. . . ."[32] Richard Freeman also reports "a virtual collapse in traditional discriminatory patterns in the labor market."[33] Now if this gospel of cheer is even partly true, how are we to interpret the latest statistics on unemployment, which still show black unemployment at twice that of whites and, among teen-agers, almost three times as high? The new racism absolves the discriminatory structures and indicts the victims.[34] The position here is that of Bull Connor. He just lacked the education to say it so well. His was the old racism.

Derrick A. Bell, himself a black and a professor of law at Harvard, goes to the heart of the matter: "The burden of racism has scarred us all, and there are few whites who at some level of their being do not believe that whites are superior, and even fewer blacks who do not recognize that feeling and resent it."[35] The allegation of inferiority is an attack on the dignity and meaning of one's personhood. This kind of prejudice strikes at the center of power in any individual—his or her own self-esteem. If this center is damaged, if the confidence needed to succeed is broken, the person is radically disempowered. "The American Triumph," James Baldwin asserts, "was to make black people despise themselves."[36] Knowing is a social phenomenon. We do not gaze at reality with limpid, direct, and unmediated knowledge. Rather, the symbols, myths, and images of that society give us our knowing matrix. If you are born black in a culture whose myths, symbols, and images consider black as degraded, it would take a colossal power and strong countercultural support to establish a high concept of one's self. As Joel Kovel, author of *White Racism: A Psychohistory,* puts it: "The accumulation of negative images forced upon blacks in America amounted to presenting them with one massive and destructive choice: either to hate one's self, as culture so systematically demanded, or to have no self at all, to be nothing. With the passage of time and abstraction, these alternatives amounted to the same thing. . . ."[37] Again, the conclusion of the *Report to the National Commission on the Causes and Prevention of Violence* says that slavery and the caste system produced in the "black pariah . . . a psychically crippling Negro dependency and even self-hatred which is largely immune to mere economic advance."[38]

The strange story of IQ has also been used—particularly by Jensen —in the assault on black persons. When Alfred Binet developed the first IQ testing method in 1905, he warned that they should not be used to prove genetic inferiority. He warned against the brutal pessimism of those who thought intelligence was a kind of fixed endowment. Writing for the Carnegie Council on Children, Richard de Lone blasts "Jensen's extremist assertion" that black and white IQ scores show genetic differences. As de Lone points out, the basic misperception regarding IQ tests is that there is some measurable talent called intelligence. Actually, the IQ test does not tell what a person can do nor even how much a person knows. It is fairly good in predicting how a student will perform in certain kinds of tests and thus, de Lone suggests, could be better called "school performance quotients." In the hands of the biased, however, the IQ test can prove anything. At the turn of the century it proved that Jews are innately feebleminded. Now it proves that blacks are. In fact, when environmental circumstances are similar, blacks do as well on IQ tests as whites. Also, it has been shown that black children whose IQ test scores seem to indicate that they lack certain cognitive abilities actually show those same abilities when tested in natural settings.[39]

Richard de Lone begins his excellent study, *Small Futures: Children, Inequality, and the Limits of Liberal Reform,* by discussing the situation of two second-graders who have identical IQ scores, but are of different socio-economic classes. The upper class child is four times more likely to enter college and twelve times more likely to complete it. He will probably have four more years of schooling than his lower class counterpart and he is twenty-seven times as likely to make it into the top ten per cent of all incomes. The lower class student has only one chance in eight of earning a median income.[40] The problems of the lower class student will be even worse if he is black as well as poor. Yet, both students have the same IQ. In this context, the IQ test is a diversionary tactic to distract from the real issue of social injustice and the redistributional changes needed to achieve a just society.

In view of all of this, the miracle is that blacks have been so little "attracted" to crime and so tenacious in their desire to improve themselves. The white scholars who report so disdainfully on the tardy work habits and motivational deficiencies of blacks in education are superficial and uncritical in the extreme when they do not set the situation of blacks in its devastating historical context. This is all the more anomalous in view of the narcissistic penchant of American scholars to pore over our past—compulsively dissecting it and rehashing it. Yet we consistently slight the significance of black history for an understanding of contemporary black problems. When we look at black American history the proper conclusion is that black achievement in this country in these circumstances is an epic in the history of the resilient human spirit.

Thus far, then, I have spoken of how the blacks fulfill the first two conditions for preferential aid. They have no alternatives open to them, since voluntary programs have been hopelessly ineffective and often a sham. Even governmental prescriptions have been doggedly resisted. Secondly, the bias against blacks is unparalleled in our experience and ultimately amounts to a denial of the worth of black persons. This disesteem, blacks testify, has even reached into the innermost core of black self-consciousness.

The third condition refers to the translation of this bias into the systems and conduits of power in the polity. If the bias were able to be contained in the heart of whites, that would in itself be a weakness in the society. It has not been and could not be so contained. We are social beings and our deepest feelings and valuations find social and systemic expression. The poison has come out and infected the controlling forces and structures of our social existence. The results have not just been unfortunate: they have been lethal. Depersonalizing, insystemed prejudice kills its victims. The maternal mortality rate for blacks is three times higher than that for whites. Infant mortality is twice as high. Blacks have a life expectancy of almost seven years less than whites.[41] Poorer, ghettoized blacks have an even lower life expectancy. Dr. James R. Dumpson notes that "One of the reasons that only 10.1 percent of all Social Security retirement beneficiaries are black is that twice that percentage receive their retirement benefits through the Social Security Disability benefits program."[42]

This testifies, as Dr. Dumpson points out, both to the poorer health of the black population and to the hazardous nature of their occupations. In the past twenty-five years the cancer death rate for blacks increased by 26 per cent while the rate for whites increased only by 5 per cent, a trend which seems to be accelerating. Among the causes of this, experts suggest conditions in the polluted ghettos, limited access to health programs, failure to be included in cancer screening programs, and poor nutrition.[43] White bias against blacks is killing blacks. It can do this because it has been built into the system and into the distributional processes of the society. It is systemic murder. And when this diseased social power does not kill blacks, it maims and limits their lives in the three most influential and interrelated areas of employment, housing, and education. In each of these areas racist influences affect opportunities and patterns of distribution.

SYSTEMIC UNEMPLOYMENT

Chief Justice Burger, in *Griggs v. Duke Power Co.,* acknowledged "built-in head winds" and "artificial, arbitrary, and unnecessary barriers to employment," barriers which "operate invidiously to discriminate on the basis of racial or other impermissible classification." Burger also acknowledged the existence of "barriers that have operated in the past to favor an identifiable group of white employees over other employees."[44] What this says is that fairness has not operated in the market place of jobs. Instead barriers and head winds have obstructed in multiple ways the efforts of blacks to find work and have favored whites as an identifiable group. These head winds and barriers—note well—are not individual torts or projects. They are built into the system. There is nothing amorphous or ineffective about them; they have very concrete results. Whites get hired and blacks don't.

Black unemployment is related to both housing and educational problems. The teeming masses of the ghettos constitute an excess of unskilled workers in one area. On top of that, firms have been leaving the center cities for the suburbs. In the period of slow economic growth in the late fifties, firms tended to close down their least productive plants, which were in the inner cities, and locate their new plants in the suburbs, in areas which would be more congenial to managerial employees.[45] In the period from 1960 to 1970 civilian employment in the central cities of the fifteen largest metropolitan areas declined by 836,000.[46] Many things contributed to this. The national expressway system was intended to bring the flow of life from the suburbs into the cities. In actual fact, however, these highways have facilitated and in effect subsidized the flight from the city by white residents and by industry and commerce. The result is reduced numbers of jobs and deepening segregation of the central cities. The loss is not offset by the number of blacks who can afford to commute to the suburbs for work.[47] Automation has struck largely at the unskilled—and therefore at large numbers of blacks. The U. S. Civil Rights Commission notes the adverse effect on blacks from word-of-mouth recruiting for new employees. In most cases these informal networks do not reach into the ghetto. Nepotism also operates, as some unions and employers favor relatives of current employees, thus again perpetuating white hiring patterns. The use by employers of arrest records is also cited. Many blacks have been subject to arrest on suspicion or on charges which in the suburbs would be handled by a call to the parents. Many blacks who would be honest and reliable are thereby excluded.[48] Even when there is governmental pressure to advertise more broadly for workers, the "old buddy system" can prevail, since it is simple enough to advertise and then hire whomsoever you wish. This is common practice in businesses and in universities.

Blacks did not share in the recovery from the 1975 recession. Labor Department statistics in the autumn of 1977 showed black unemployment double that of whites and higher than at any time since World War II. Black teen-age unemployment rose to an astonishing 40.4 per cent, or three times that of white teen-agers. In Milwaukee, a city where black problems rarely make national headlines, a poll in August 1978 produced some numbing statistics. Among all inner city blacks eighteen and older, only 42 per cent have jobs. The comparable figure for Milwaukee metropolitan area whites is around 75 per cent. In the crucial eighteen to twenty-four age bracket where life goals and attitudes are likely to take shape, only 29 per cent of the blacks are employed. (The poll also revealed that, contrary to the popular myth, most of the unemployed are receiving no income from welfare or unemployment compensation.)[49]

Again, the barriers against black success in seeking employment are multiple and often come from apparently benign sources. Increases in the minimum wage, for example, would seem calculated to bring special relief to blacks. However, one study by the Bureau of Labor Statistics showed that, in response to an increase in the minimum wage, companies did some of the following things: they changed equipment, plant layout, and work procedures and even went so far as to change product lines. This made it possible to discharge some low-paid employees, especially those least desirable to employers—black teen-agers.[50] Another example is found in Boston in 1965 when 125 jobs as coin collectors for Boston's metropolitan transit system were open. Because the wages were set high some three thousand persons took the examination (!) and, as a result, low-skilled persons who could have handled the job with ease had to compete to their own undoing with more highly qualified candidates.[51] Obviously, testing in such a case was unnecessary and prejudicial, since special skills were not necessary. But the point here is that improvements in the job market, even from benign sources, can—given the overall situation of blacks—add to the barriers to work. The intricacy of the black plight is thus further illuminated and we can better appreciate the inanity of appeals for mere non-discrimination and ad hoc litigation as a realistic way of dismantling the huge interlocking barriers that stand between blacks and equity in employment.

The power of the unions has not been directed sufficiently to black employment problems. Seniority systems, nepotism, and the old white buddy spirit have oppressed blacks. In some instances, segregated black unions have been merged into larger white locals with the apparent goal of integration in mind, but with the negative effect of subsuming black leadership and financial resources under white control.[52]

THE SCHOOL BLIGHT

Much of black joblessness also relates to the poor quality of education in ghetto schools. Such schools often are, in the phrasing of

Kenneth Clark, "custodial programs for the deprived."[53] These schools tend to be overcrowded, using old and run-down buildings, with programs and equipment and extracurricular activities far below the level of middle-class and suburban schools. Truancy is high. Retention and graduation rates are low. Students are often channeled into technical and vocational tracks that leave them ineligible for college. In 1957 in eight high schools in depressed areas, 25 per cent of the graduates received college preparatory diplomas. In 1967 that figure had fallen to 13 per cent.[54] Even in integrated school systems, culturally biased testing and tracking schemes can achieve an internal resegregation system in a way that is blatantly insulting to black students and deepens their sense of despair.[55] Theories about the genetic inferiority of the black are perfect rationalizations for the sad results of this system.

Another way of achieving the systematic degradation of blacks is by labeling students retarded on the basis of one IQ test or on grounds of disruptive behavior. A citizen task force in Boston discovered that this tactic was used to get troublesome students out of the classroom. The U. S. Civil Rights Commission reached the same conclusion about Chicago. In fact, in a remarkable statistic, the President's Committee on Mental Retardation reported in 1976 that about 90 per cent of all children diagnosed as retarded have no known organic problems at all but are victims of what is cynically called socioeconomic retardation.[56]

The results of efforts to educate blacks in sensitive ways that are suited to their needs do meet with extraordinary success. In the period of 1955–59 at the Northside Center for Child Development in New York, there was a crash program of remedial reading for one month in the summer. In that month of intelligent and serious teaching, the average child gained on the average of one school year in reading ability. Some of the better students gained more than two years in reading achievement. Because something meaningful was going on, the 104 children came eagerly and regularly. Attendance was never less than 85 per cent.[57]

A new and positive "pilot" approach to education was attempted in a junior high school on the periphery of Harlem. Using positive techniques, all inspired by the belief that the children could learn in spite of previous experience at this school, dramatic results were achieved. The drop-out rate fell by one-half; the number of students going to college rose from 4 per cent to 25 per cent—a sixfold increase. Eighty-one per cent were judged to have greater intellectual capacity than earlier IQ tests had shown. In somewhat more than two years, gains in reading scores advanced by 4.3 years compared to 1.7 years during a similar earlier period. And all of this was done without any revolutionary teaching methods but simply by the enthusiastic insistence on normal teaching methods.[58] The conclusion from this type of experience is that blacks are regularly maleducated and undereducated. The needs of black students are not met. And the failure is systemic, not ad hoc or individualized.

The concept of "institutional racism" is scorned by some white writers. But how else describe the broad social neglect of black educational needs? How else explain the fact that, of blacks who do make it to college, 71 per cent are in "low-level" colleges as opposed to 49 per cent of whites?[59] How else explain the fact that 75 per cent of all black Ph.D.s, 85 per cent of black physicians, 75 per cent of black officers in the armed forces, and 80 per cent of all black judges received their degrees from black colleges or graduate schools?[60] Would anyone represent this as the product of freedom of choice on the part of individual blacks? If blacks are congregated in the poorest city schools, in the low-level colleges, in all-black colleges, in segregated tracks of "integrated" schools, is there any realism in arguing that white society may be exonerated of all guilt for this persistent social fact? Is the racism operating here private and individualized or is this not a fair example of that dreaded term "institutional racism"?

HOUSING

In the field of housing, it is again apparent that institutional and social forces are at work. Again, the National Advisory Commission on Civil Disorders put it quite properly in institutional terms: "White society is deeply implicated in the ghetto. White institutions created it, white institutions maintain it, and white society condones it."[61] The commission called for new initiatives and experiments that

would change "the *system* of failure and frustration that now domi-
nates the ghetto and weakens our society."[62] Clearly the ghetto is not
what blacks want. By what the 1979 Harris poll properly characterizes as "a sizable majority"—68–17 per cent—blacks prefer to live
in integrated neighborhoods, not in all-black neighborhoods. Outside
the South, that majority is even larger: 74–12 per cent.[63] (These
figures would reflect favorable attitudes toward some good all-black
neighborhoods in the South with sensitively run schools, such as, for
example, in Atlanta.) It is a very safe assumption that no one would
prefer to live in a rat-infested ghetto. No one prefers to live in a situation in which fear is a constant fact of life. Fear for your children,
for yourself, and for your property suffuses the ghetto.

Some white social scientists compare black ghettos to other "concentrations" such as the "Little Italy" where many Italo-Americans
choose to dwell. The comparison is cruelly deceptive. Black ghetto
dwellers do not *choose* to dwell there as common sense and the
statistics given above suggest. Italo-Americans move in and out of
Little Italy. They also marry in and out of that community and
they intermarry with other ethnic groups. Their neighborhood is
sufficiently stable to support restaurants that attract the general population. "Redlining" does not threaten their neighborhood. Ethnic
pride and self-confidence are visible aspects of their life. The comparison of a Little Italy to a black ghetto is basically sick and misleading.

Ghetto living involves poor medical aid, poor legal aid, higher
amounts of mental stress and mental illness, poverty, and an overall
feeling of hopelessness. In some cases the actual concentration of so
many persons is overwhelming. It has been estimated, for example,
that if the population density of some of Harlem's worst blocks were
extended to all of New York City the entire population of the United
States could fit into just three of New York's boroughs![64] Add to all
of this that, while the actual conditions of ghetto life are successfully
ignored by whites, the actual conditions of white life are intensely
known by blacks. From this comes the ghetto's enervating sting of insult, stigma, and frustration.[65]

GAINS AND SLIPPAGE

The black situation has improved in some respects. There are a few more black elected officials now—although they are often elected in deteriorating cities and their numbers are not at all proportionate to the number of black citizens. There have been some gains in education. Affirmative action programs have helped many blacks. *At least in interviews with pollsters,* white attitudes seem to have ameliorated somewhat. These gains are exacting a terrible price, however, from blacks. The slightest indications of improvement fuel the great American myth of inevitable progress. This carries great gains for whites since, if things are improving, then we can let well enough alone. More of what we have been doing will do nicely. Meanwhile the caste system remains, and blacks are filled with a sense of *déjà vu.*

During the three hundred and sixty years the blacks have been in this country, they can point to only two periods of significant relief— from 1865 to 1877 and from 1961 to 1968.[66] Even these major efforts in their behalf were not marked by anything like a total effort. Blacks at the bottom of the economic scale were scarcely touched by these two reforming periods. And after each period there has been retrenchment. In the view of blacks, "the failure to mount and sustain an all-encompassing societal effort is intolerable."[67] What Gunnar Myrdal wrote in 1944 is abidingly true. An educational offensive against racial intolerance, going beyond the reiteration of the "glittering generalities" in the nation's political creed, has never been seriously attempted in America. It was Myrdal's hypothesis that the real battle for black rights must be waged in the white mind. Until that battle is won, significant judicial and legislative victories, such as *Brown* in 1954 and the civil rights legislation of 1964 and 1965, are largely hollow and will be deviously frustrated.

What blacks see is that the decade from 1969 to 1978 could tragically be called the "Decade of Lost Opportunities." From the black viewpoint, "the momentum to improve the quality of life in the ghettos of America, that grew out of the Civil Rights Movement of the 60's, the urban riots that followed, and the *Report of the Na-*

tional Advisory Commission on Civil Disorders, was allowed to falter and eventually disappear."[68] On many fronts, prospects look bleak. There is mounting interest in a balanced budget. The mood is one of general fiscal conservativeness. The economy is tightening. This traditionally has always hit blacks more than others. They are the last hired and the first fired. Financial aid for graduate studies is diminishing. Calls for the needed massive overhaul of black schools will generate little enthusiasm. To meet economic woes, even Democratic presidents will need to form strategic coalitions with those who are unenthusiastic about black rights. If the price for needed economic compromises is the neglect of black needs, that price is likely to be paid. It is the strong feeling of blacks that in the 1970s all three branches of the federal government showed diminishing forcefulness in responding to the black situation.[69] Many people (erstwhile liberals among them) warm themselves with the ideals of the civil rights movements but contend that the more you work at some problems the worse they get, and the victim is more to be blamed than we realized in the sixties, and maybe Jesse Jackson will save us all by getting the blacks to shape up with his push for excellence. Most of all there is that detached viewing of the black plight, an attitude that Gunnar Myrdal said "is philosophically made possible by the inherited Anglo-Saxon naïveté and lack of clarity regarding the value problem."[70] There is no passion for black causes. Persons who would die for the Panama Canal will not stir for civil rights. That is the enduring American problem.

Whites are overwhelmingly negative about giving any preferential relief to blacks. When it was proposed in the 1978 Harris poll that "minorities and women have to learn that they are entitled to no special consideration and must make it strictly on merit," whites agreed with gusto by a resounding 76–18 per cent. Whites react more benignly to remedial affirmative action. However, remedial affirmative action will not change the system and we are talking about in-systemed discrimination. We are talking about a shift in power. Merely remedial affirmative action is micropolitical; the problem, however, is macropolitical and so too must be the solution. As mentioned above, blacks are cut out of the crucial *loci* of power in the society. Even where the power looks as though it is opening to blacks, as when a greater number of them get elected at the local level, the power remains white. One scholar looked at the situation around Chicago, where many blacks are elected and appointed to municipal and state offices. His conclusion: "Negroes really hold less than 1 percent of the effective power . . . the power structure of Chicago is hardly less white than that of Mississippi."[71] Yale professor of law Owen M. Fiss makes the same point. Noting that there may be more black-dominated political agencies now—a black city council or a black mayor—he insists that these facts be put in context. "One facet of their context is the white domination of those extra-political agencies such as the banks, factories, and police, that severely circumscribe the power of the formal political agencies."[72]

The momentum of power in the society is tilted toward maintaining the caste system with its implied doctrine of white supremacy. Because of the economic crunch in which we now find ourselves, that momentum for preservation of the status quo is growing even stronger. In these circumstances, white calls for micropolitical and microeconomic remedial programs are sops thrown to the disempowered black caste. This is equivalent to colonial paternalism. There is nothing new in this, of course. It is but the latest example of our traditional affection for piddling approaches to the colossal systemic problems that beset black Americans. The need is for redistribution of the sort that will correct the dominant patterns of maldistribution. Preferential affirmative action does precisely that. It proceeds out of a recognition that the problem is systemic, not privatized and patient of ad hoc solutions. The blacks clearly meet the third criterion for preferential affirmative action—systemic disempowerment.

The fourth and final criterion for preferential relief is the visibility of the victim. Blacks obviously qualify. In slaving times it was said that the advantage of black slaves was that nature had branded them from head to toe. Thus one would think that this criterion need not be argued in any way. However, the more one studies the black problem the more one realizes that nothing can be taken for granted . . . not even their claim to visibility! Eliot Marshall, a senior editor of the *New Republic,* contributed to a fusillade of horror stories in that journal on the evils that would come with preferential affirmative action by projecting the need for unwieldy ancestor checks to de-

termine ethnic and racial status. Marshall worried that the Supreme
Court in the future could be consumed with questions like "Can a
person qualify as black if his only black relative was a grandmother
listed in the official records as 'mulatto'?"[73] (It should relieve Marshall's anxieties to reflect on the number of blacks who have been
identified as such without help from the Supreme Court.) Louisiana
law goes to the contorted extreme of stipulating that anyone who has
one thirty-second "Negro blood" is black.[74] In 1972 a Florida school
superintendent appealed from a district court school desegregation
order because it contained no definition of what a Negro is. The
court, with some consternation, labeled this maneuver "a last gasp in
the struggle against desegregation" and it alluded to the sensible criterion of the Department of Health, Education and Welfare, which
said that Negroes are those persons "considered by themselves, by
the school or by the community to be of African or Negro origin."
The court added with strained patience: "The record indicates that
in the past the School District has apparently had no difficulty identifying Negroes for the purposes of segregating them. For desegregation they can be identified with similar ease."[75] If someone is not
identifiably black, he would not qualify under the criteria I am setting up, by reason of this fourth criterion of visibility. Persons who
are not visibly black do not qualify for preferential relief, since one
of the purposes of black preference is to provide black role models.
Those who seem simply white do not fulfill this social need. The creation of role models is part of the redistribution process. When
members of a disempowered group do not see members of their
group in certain positions or professions, the message of exclusion is
emphatic. The appearance of significant numbers of group members
in these previously guarded preserves engenders hope and raises
aspirations. This contributes to the empowering process. Thus the
importance of visibility among the criteria.

My conclusion then is that blacks meet the tests for preferment, as
no other group in this nation does. There are three other disempowered groups in American society that can secondarily but ade-
quately meet the criteria: women, American Indians, and Mexican
and Puerto Rican Hispanics. Beyond these, there are other disadvantaged groups in the nation, all meriting special attention in a just

society. However, it is only the four groups that I have mentioned here who can, in my judgment, meet the necessary tests for enforced preferential affirmative action. Only these four are so systemically disempowered as to require the special redistributional relief of enforced preference.

WOMEN
AS A DISEMPOWERED GROUP

When I state that the need of blacks for preferential affirmative action is primary and paradigmatic, I do not anticipate inevitable applause from those men and women who are feminists or from other disempowered groups. In claiming a priority for blacks, am I not setting the dispossessed against one another? What gain could there be in comparing woes and deciding some beleaguered groups are worse than others?

The answer briefly is that, if there are differences, we have to make distinctions. And there are differences. The blacks have watched group after group join them in destitution and despair and then leave them there as that group left to join the main stream of affluence. Edward C. Banfield, who pleasures white folks with the thesis that blacks are just the latest wave of temporarily suffering migrants, notes the disdain of an 1832 visitor to Boston who deplored the indigence and idleness and filth of districts occupied by the Irish or Negroes.[76] In the period from 1885 to 1890, persons born in Ireland made up 12.6 per cent of the population but represented 10.4 per cent of the almshouse, 36.7 per cent of the workhouse, and 15.5 per cent of the prison populations.[77] Like the blacks, the Irish were allegedly notorious for sexual promiscuity and for their fatherless families.

The Irish, however, have escaped the slums and have been granted passports into many of the power structures.[78] The blacks remain in permanent economic depression in ghettos that grow larger and more dehumanizing. The blacks are painfully aware of the American penchant for preferring all causes to the black cause. Women, some Hispanics, and Indians do meet the criteria for preferential aid at this time. This, however, should not blur the fact that the black cause requires a special commitment, since it has a history of well-demonstrated and very special intractability. The passion to blur all good causes and not to distinguish distinct claims and needs has no merit. The error here is not academic or donnish. It has this practical import. It will mean that the blacks, once again, will watch the progress of others from the ghetto.

There is a further reason why we have to distinguish the claims of different groups. Preferential affirmative action is by its nature temporary. When the disempowered are empowered, when monopoly has lost its grip, preferential policies of this sort should cease and the normal dynamics of the market place, with enforced non-discrimination, should suffice. This will not happen at the same time for all the disempowered groups. Some will find relief more quickly and will lose their need for and thus their right to such relief. No two of the disempowered groups have the same problem or need. In each case, the etiology and the tenacity of the problem will vary, as will its susceptibility to relief. "We are all in this together" has a ring of egalitarian attractiveness to it, but it is a soft base for realistic policy.

Yet, of all groups, women would seem to have the best claim to having the deepest problem. After all, it has been argued that the history of subjugation of blacks began in the sixteenth century. The subjugation of women stretches back all the way to the dim dawn of prehistoric culture. Furthermore, it is argued that the liberation of women is a far more radical movement than the liberation of blacks or any other group. The subjugation of women is arguably the prototype of subjugation and oppression, which like an original sin has set the primordial pattern for oppression of other groups as well as for the destruction of our very ecological setting.[79] What indeed could compete with the elementary dislocation of sexism, which strikes devastatingly at the very meaning of the human male-female dyad, thus poisoning all subsequent human relationships! In what sense could the cause of women be secondary to the cause of blacks or of anyone else?

I do indeed grant that nothing matches the depth and potential revolutionary might of the attack on sexism. By distorting *female,* we have necessarily distorted *male* and thus *humanness* since male and female are the essential correlatives of humankind. You cannot distort one half of a correlative without distorting the other. The most imaginative thinker among us cannot conjure or picture the effects of so radical a split at the core of human meaning. We can only vaguely guess the impact this perversion has had on the development of civilization and its possibilities for perdurance. We have no clear idea of what our lives might be had this fatal distortion not undermined our history. The exploration of this distortion is beyond doubt the most profound movement in human self-understanding today. As Rosemary Reuther writes: "The women's movement is engaged in an effort to reach behind the history of civilization to a lost alternative."[80] The movement to go to the roots of sexism—which by its nature cannot be merely a "women's movement"—is a radical probe of the foundations of all human institutions which have been affected by this primeval blight. Its ultimate success is as distant as its prehistoric origins.

To all of which any black has the right to cry: "Don't tell me now that we are going to be asked to wait for all of that to happen before we get our rights!" The answer must be no. Granting, as I am disposed to do, the primatial significance of sexism, the special and immediate needs of blacks still stake out their unique and compelling claim. Even if one concedes some cause-effect relationship between sexist domination and racist domination, it would be a strange genetic fallacy to say that the current crisis of blacks must be downplayed until we attend to the skewed foundations of human civilization. That would be like refusing food to a starving man by alleging your preference for seeking out the root causes of poverty. Even though a case can be made that sexism has affected all of our social problems, we can still argue that the lethal prejudice against blacks be relieved as a first order of business. The black child who is malnourished and condemned to poor schools cannot be told to wait until the human race has worked out its sexual self-understanding. *Immediate essential needs have a non-negotiable priority*. Hence, a feminist—and I aspire to that title—can consistently press the cause against sexism and still grant the priority of black Americans at this time. There is no nobility in fixating upon the ultimate causes of evil if the immediate and most pressing effects go unattended. The immediate claims of blacks have never won our persistent attention. That they now should have it is my thesis.

Blacks have repeatedly been the victims of utilitarian thinking in this nation. In various ways, specific manifestations of the greatest good of the greatest number have always been put before black needs. And since the blacks are not the greatest number, the utilitarian mind set is their natural enemy—noble as it may appear in its patriotic dress and bedecked as it may be in the proclaimed prerogatives of the common good.

With all of this said in favor of black claims, the point at hand is that three other groups do meet the criteria for preferential treatment. Women fulfill the first criterion of depersonalizing prejudice with unfortunate ease. The prejudice against women, so ancient as to seem indigenous to the species, cuts to the quick of personal dignity. Woman has been impaled upon two myths, one which defines her essence and personhood in terms of her domesticity and sexual functioning, and the other which identifies her with the principle of evil.

In discussing these myths, I shall be arguing that women meet the first two criteria for preferment: the absence of alternatives and victimization through depersonalizing prejudice. The very depth and intransigence of the depersonalization suggest the impossibility of change without enforced preference.

Because the male does not get pregnant and cannot nurse a child, he was historically the one assigned the role of leaving the cave to meet the challenges of the hunt or of self-defense. From this there developed the myth that woman is a creature of *"die Kuche und die Kinder."* Tending kitchen and children is her quintessential role and fulfillment. In these contexts her true being is essentially revealed. Outside of domesticity, she lacks meaning. "She will be saved through motherhood," says the Christian Epistle to Timothy.[81] Without it she is anomalous, a thing apart and incomplete. This negativity perdured into the belatedly obsolescent word "spinster."

Sexual ethics is where myths show through. The functional domesticity that defined and demeaned woman appears, for example, in ancient Israel. Sexual infidelity was punishable by death for a woman. A man had greater freedom, as long as he did not offend the rights of another male. As biblical scholar Kenneth Grayston writes: "Since everything centered on the man, polygamy was the natural type of marriage for Israelites, for several wives do more than one to satisfy the demand for children. If a wife gave her husband insufficient children he might take secondary wives and concubines and be encouraged by his wife to do so."[82] Augustine expressed this depersonalization in its purity when he wrote: "I do not see what other help woman would be to man if the purpose of generating was eliminated."[83] No one would be so crude in modern times, but the myth of woman as sexual domestic functionary abides. The definition of a person in terms of one aspect of her personhood is straightforward depersonalization. Undisguised in this, of course, is a doctrine of male supremacy. Males are not limited in their self-definition by the sexual function. All of the challenges of reality are a legitimate sphere for their superior capacities.

The depersonalization of woman did not stop at this diminishment. Her inferiority attained sordid and hateful depths. Woman became the root of all evil. Simone de Beauvoir cites some examples of it. "Eve, given to Adam to be his companion, worked the ruin of mankind; when they wish to wreak vengeance upon man, the pagan gods invent woman; and it is the first-born of these female creatures, Pandora, who lets loose all the ills of suffering humanity. . . . Woman is thus dedicated to Evil. 'There is a good principle, which has created order, light, and man; and a bad principle, which has created chaos, darkness, and woman,' so says Pythagoras."[84] The myth, of course, is not as consistent as it is vicious. Arnold Toynbee points out the irony that, while women are defined as passive and diminished creatures, they are still credited with causing our major catastrophes.[85] The hatred of woman did not remain merely "academic." Anthropologists note the use of female infanticide as a means of population control even though it inconveniently led to a marked surplus of adult males over females.[86] Also, in the Middle Ages, the venom flowed over into the paranoid witch hunts of the sixteenth and seventeenth centuries. It is estimated that more than a million woman died in the witch hunts of this period.[87]

The modern debasement of woman is more contorted because it wears a mask of benignity and feigned admiration. Thus the Supreme Court in 1872, while sustaining the exclusion of women from the

practice of law, was ablush with admiration for the timidity and deli-
cacy of the female sex. (But, then, who would hand over the affairs
of state and law to the timid and the delicate?) The Catholic bishops
of Massachusetts in 1920, while opposing women's suffrage, magnan-
imously feared the loss of that "respect and dignity" that the unen-
franchised woman enjoyed in her home.[88] The denigration of women
is profoundly expressed and reinforced in the organized religions that
exclude women from the ministry and priesthood. This hatred
reaches profound levels in the Roman Catholic Church, where not
only is a woman excluded from the priesthood, but even a man who
is contaminated by marriage to a woman is forbidden to function as
a priest. In the political order, the long denial of the vote and the
horror that greets the Equal Rights Amendment show the same exclusion, fear, and ultimately hatred that enter into the long-tenured,
culturally ensconced depersonalization of women.

A copious literature documenting this depersonalization of women
has appeared in recent years. These few data are offered as illus-
trative of the fact that women easily fulfill the first two criteria for
preferment. The illness here is the kind against which weak medi-
cines will avail nothing. There are no realistic alternatives to enforced preference. The weakness of social voluntarism discussed
above apply here also. Secondly and clearly, the radical prejudice
against women is depersonalizing.

The third condition for meriting preference is that the prejudice
become systemic and institutional, in such wise as to create the "built-
in head winds" that frustrate the best efforts of the group members.
Again, documentation has poured out on this score. I shall offer only
some examples of the problems that women face. In a most visible
way, women have been successfully excluded from the centers of
power in government, finance, the professions, journalism, organized
religions, et cetera. Women's salaries have been traditionally lower
than men's and even now many low-paying jobs are reserved for
women. Most jobs do not provide day care for children but rather
presume that there is a wife at home to handle domestic needs and the
children. Almost 4.5 million women with children under six are now
employed but only 6 per cent of these children are in day-care centers, because space is either not available or not affordable. These

women have to struggle to get relatives, neighbors, or others to care for their children, creating multiple problems and stress for the mothers and the children.[89] Employers at every level are, in effect, still prejudiced against pregnancy. Men are perceived as more reliable since this can't happen to them. Myths about mental instability during menstruation are still widely held—even by executives who are rather unstable themselves on a regular basis after "three-martini lunches." The tendency to see women as sexual targets limits their employability. Often, the discrimination is not due to particular reference to any of these factors but to an ingrained conviction of women's basic inferiority. An article in *Science* in 1973 reported that academic department chairmen evaluated equivalent credentials less favorably if they were told they belonged to a woman rather than a man.[90] Ultimately, we are not that far removed from the view that was defended into this century that education would so tax the limited mental resources of women that it could cause sterility![91]

Again, my listing here is suggestive, not exhaustive. The case is overwhelming that women do indeed also meet the criterion of built-in, systemic resistance. The powers and structures of the society constitute a white male monopoly. Though the approaches and tactics are often different from those used against blacks, women are effectively victimized and deprived.

The fourth criterion of visibility is, as with the blacks, obvious. Women cannot pass over into the dominant white male aristocracy.

Beyond all reasonable doubt, then, women do qualify for preferential affirmative action. Indeed, they seem to qualify so well that the question arises again of why I would see their case as less urgent than that of blacks. Even these brief data seem to argue that women, rather than blacks, are the paradigmatic victims of the white male ascendancy. In fact, however, white women are better off than blacks for these reasons:

First, white women are in a more socially advantageous position than blacks. As a group they are not nutritionally deprived, nor does the quiet immobilizing despair of the ghetto engulf them. As a group, women have not been deprived of solid basic education at the elementary and intermediate levels. They have not been confined to the worst schools in the system. Women are found in every social class and are not as a group immersed in poverty.[92] Women are present in the white male world. They are not, like blacks, "invisible" persons. Men marry them and sons are born of them. Foremen, deans, and influential employers have wives and mothers but are not likely to have even one close black friend. In a word, white women are, by nature, infiltrated into the white male world in ways that give them significant leverage. A white woman hungry for liberation has more going for her than do blacks who are even geographically removed from white male power. Not to sense the strategic advantages that women enjoy in fighting for their rights would be insensitive and would be another example of the perennial belittling of the black caste problems in this nation. If there are those who would argue this point I would invite them to look back at the partial listing I gave of black disadvantagement in our system and ask whether women match that. (See pp. 130–53.)

Secondly, the advantages of women are showing up in recent statistics. A report of the Carnegie Council on Policy Studies in Higher Education shows the significant gains women have made in entering the "gateways of power" represented by higher education. In the past decade the number of women admitted to institutions of higher education has increased from 10 to 25 per cent.[93]

In 1964 women earned 1,535 doctorates while men earned 12,955. By 1974 a quarter of the doctorates were earned by women and it is projected that by 1985 women will receive a third of all doctoral degrees.[94] Enrollment of women in ABA-approved law schools increased from 4.3 per cent in 1966 to 25.5 per cent in 1976.[95] Enrollment of women in medical schools increased from 9 per cent in 1968 to 25 per cent in 1976 while underrepresented minorities in that same period increased only from 3 to 9 per cent.[96] In schools that offer graduate management degrees, the representation of women increased from 8 to 22 per cent between 1971 and 1975.[97] Blacks increased in that period from 2.2 per cent in 1971 to 3.7 per cent in 1975.[98] Clearly the educational and other advantages that women have in their fight for equity is paying off. As recently as 1974, some have argued that women have so many advantages that preferential affirmative action is already unnecessary to meet their needs.[99] The fact that their needs were not met until such preference was accorded disproves this contention. Also, the depth and long tenure of the sexist problem attest to the naïveté of suggesting that male power will voluntarily divest itself of its privileges. Still, the conclusion stands. Women can do better than blacks and are doing so.

AMERICAN INDIANS
AS A DISEMPOWERED GROUP

Depersonalizing prejudice is always genocidal in intent. That intent is often impeded but in the case of the American Indian it was vigorously acted out. White settlers, from the time of their arrival on this continent, began encroaching on Indian rights. As the nation grew and became expansive in spirit and in policy, the Indians were brutally removed from their historic territories. With all the rhetoric about the Indians being a nation within a nation, they were never treated that way. Justice Marshall was closer to honesty when he wrote in 1831: "[The Indians] are in a state of pupilage. Their relation to the United States resembles that of a ward to his guardian."[100] The "guardian," of course, was anything but benign.

With the dawning of the nineteenth century the image of the Indian became more and more that of the savage. They were seen in the popular mythology as cruel practitioners of "pre-Christian" or bloody rites and in general an obstacle to white America's "manifest destiny" to evangelize the continent and eventually the world with its brand of civilization. Inasmuch as the Indians were different and thus an obstacle to that destiny, the official policy became "removal." That policy was carried out. The Indian Removal Act of 1830 authorized the President to negotiate "treaties" with the Indians to the end of getting them all west of the Mississippi. Good faith on the part of the whites was in small supply in these dealings. There was no respect for the "savages" such as would undergird a genuine treaty. And when the Indians refused to negotiate about their removal, as did the Cherokees and the Seminoles, the army "effected their removal."

Manifest destiny, of course, could not be stopped by a river, and so even the lands to which the Indians were consigned in the West were engulfed. By 1887 the entire Indian land base west of the Mississippi had shrunk to under 140 million acres. By 1934 they were down to 48 million acres—almost half of that barren and unusable. By as early as the middle of the nineteenth century the Indian population had been reduced to one third of its size in colonial times. Even peaceful tribes which had gone so far as to adopt Christianity and the economic folkways of the white Americans were slaughtered or sent on the "trail of tears" to the West.

The treatment of the Indian as subpersonal and thus negligible continues. As an Indian woman in Mankato, Minnesota, said in a recent interview, the white men "may have wanted to save us, but they have destroyed us . . . there have been three suicides on our reservation during the last two weeks. We have been beaten down too many times. Many of us have no self-esteem."[101] The suicide rate of Indians is double that of the general population. Unemployment runs at 45 per cent as opposed to 6 per cent for the white population. Four times as many Indians as whites live in overcrowded housing by the standards of the general population. Two thirds of rural Indian homes do not have water. Only 18 per cent entered college, as against 50 per cent for white Americans. Median family income for 1971 was $4,000.[102]

Even this short account of the Indian plight shows that they fulfill the first two criteria for preferential affirmative action. The prejudice against them is radical, depersonalizing, in-cultured, in-systemed, and lethal. Voluntary alternatives offer no hope in a nation that perpetrated genocide. As to visibility, Indians have been considered Caucasian and thus can assimilate if they so choose in a way that has not been open to blacks. However, they do meet the criterion of visibility since they may be distinctive by reason of their names and appearance, and are often rendered identifiable by the educational deprivations they have suffered as well as by the special difficulties they have in adapting to urban culture.

Since the Indian unemployment and educational problems are worse than those of blacks—not to mention the historic genocidal policies inflicted on them—why not list the Indians as the paradigmatic recipients of affirmative action? One should readily concede the tragic incomparability of many of the statistics of the Indian plight.

The Indian problem, however, is unique and not paradigmatic because of the strong Indian desire for separation from the main national society. Also, Indians who did wish to integrate into the white society would meet less resistance than blacks. Symbolic of this is the fact that intermarriage with whites is more possible for Indians than it has been for blacks. Assimilation, if desired, is more feasible for Indians. Again, the Indian problem is different from that of any other group because of the strong Indian desire to separate from white society, to hold onto their land bases, and to maintain tribal self-rule. In the past two decades Congress and the courts have been tilting to the position that the American Constitution does not apply to Indian reservations. In general, reservation Indians seem to have approved such decisions.[103]

Therefore, though blacks may be seen as the prime claimants among those groups seeking integration in the society, the special tragedy of the Indian should not be missed. The total Indian population in the 1970 census was only 792,730. It is an enduring scandal that the needs of this diminished group could still meet with cold neglect. In fact, worse than neglect, there are bills afloat in Congress to further strip the Indians. These bills would reduce Indian control over their reservations, restrict tribal rights to waters flowing through their reservations, and take away fishing rights granted by nineteenth-century treaties. Such bills are given little chance of passage, but their appearance, plus the continuing pattern of neglect, testify that the savage in this tragic story is still the white man.

DISEMPOWERED HISPANICS

The complexion of America is changing and so too is its accent. If it is projected that by 1994 non-whites will make up 20 per cent of our eighteen-year-old population, it is estimated that, as of now, Hispanics number 19 million and that number is increasing rapidly. The movement of Mexicans into this country represents a modern exodus with estimates of up to one million persons per year crossing the border. There is, of course, no such thing as painless exodus. Such a transmigration inevitably presents massive problems for social and distributive justice. To "promote the general welfare" amid the misery caused by such dislocations is a supreme challenge.

The term "Hispanic" covers a varied multitude, including Mexican Americans (Chicanos), Puerto Ricans, Cubans, and persons from Central or South America. Not all of these groups are suffering or disempowered. The Cuban migration to this country was not an exodus of the lowest economic class seeking an alternative to destitution. Upper- and middle-class Cubans were fleeing Castro's Communism and they arrived with skills and money and with the psychological security born of success in their homeland. Thus nearly two thirds of the Hispanics in the Miami area own their own homes. Cuban Americans are found in large numbers in comfortable suburban settings such as Coral Cables, Kendall, and Westchester. As Cuban writer José Sanchez-Boudy boasts: "We have been the most successful immigrants this country has received since it was founded."[104] Aside from the successful Cubans, there are other aristocratic Hispanics who settled in the Southwest before the *Mayflower* reached Plymouth Harbor. In no way could "Hispanics" be listed without qualification as a "disempowered group." The criterion of "Spanish surname" is worth little in determining the drastic need that merits preferential affirmative action. Indeed, to discredit preferential affirmative action programs, critics happily point to those well-heeled Hispanics who do not need and do not deserve preferential care. It is well to admit that this is a special problem. Finding those Hispanics who need special help is not as simple as finding blacks and finding women. Hispanics too, it can be argued, do not have the same need of successful role models. Hispanics have "made it" in this country, suggesting that other Hispanics can too. Hispanics are generally classified as Caucasian. Hispanic blood does not stigmatize. Intermarriage is not abhorrent. Culturally, the Hispanics have preserved and been fortified by their traditions. They were not stripped of their cultural assets and uprooted as the blacks were. Neither were they mythologized into inferior status from prehistoric times as women have been. The temptation, then, is to say that Hispanics do not qualify for preferential affirmative action, since the problems they face are less intractable and since it is administratively impossible to sort out the needy from the self-sufficient among them. Such a conclusion, however, is shortsighted. It would only illustrate how easily we cry "unnecessary" and "infeasible" when aid to the gored oxen of others is at issue. There is discoverable and drastic need among Hispanics. In many significant ways we as a nation rely on the plight of these people and profit from it. It is thus unbelievable to say that we cannot find the problem and treat it.

The two groups of Hispanics who most obviously qualify for special aid are the Chicanos and the Puerto Ricans. It is these groups who contribute to the gloomy data underlying the following general statistics on "Hispanics." Nearly 27 per cent of all Hispanic families in the United States earn under $7,000 a year. Only 40 per cent have completed high school, versus 47 per cent for blacks and 67 per cent for whites. In urban ghetto situations the Hispanic school dropout rate is almost 85 per cent.[105]

The Chicanos are the largest deprived group of Hispanics. Their deprivation is an old story. Immigrants from Mexico had begun establishing settlements in what is now our Southwest as early as 1550. Until the 1820s these areas were isolated and scarcely penetrated by explorers or traders. After the Mexican-American War in 1848 they became part of the United States. About 75,000 Mexicans accepted American citizenship along with promises of protection but they quickly began to experience the sufferings of a conquered people. All the bitterness of the war fell upon their heads, as non-Hispanic whites (Anglos) began their rapacious discovery of the new lands. There was no interest in or respect for the culture and history of the Mexican Americans. The grab for land was on and the Spanish-speaking inhabitants were little more than a source of cheap labor. Upper-class Hispanics collaborated with Anglos in the oppression of the Chicanos. Resistance to this oppression was minimal and unsuccessful. The economy of the Southwest was greatly changed in the first part of this century with federally financed irrigation and the increased demand for mass-produced fruits and vegetables. It is estimated that Mexican Americans provided about 75 per cent of the labor that grew these crops. In addition, most of the cotton field workers, 60 per cent of the mine workers, and 80 per cent of the railroad workers in the Western states between 1910 and 1930 were Mexican American. With the depression, the usefulness of these people ceased, and half a million Mexican Americans—possibly half of them American citizens—were dumped back into Mexico, many of them dying in the parched deserts of northern Mexico. Cattle cars full of human cargo, such as one associates with the Nazi movement of Jews, rolled through the Midwest and the Southwest to dispose of what had become surplus labor.

Ghettoization is still a fact of Chicano life, a fact that is complicated and solidified by the linguistic isolation of Hispanic ghettos. The impact of this communication problem on employment is enormous. In the Southwest the unemployment rate of Chicanos is twice that of Anglos and this statistic does not even reflect the chronic underemployment that is the lot of farm workers. In 1960 almost 80 per cent of all Chicano workers held unskilled or semiskilled jobs.[106] Also, even though there are some campuses in the Southwest which have substantial numbers of Spanish-speaking students, there is no system of Chicano or Puerto Rican colleges comparable to the black colleges in Southern and border states. There is also no comparable support system like the United Negro College Fund.[107]

The situation for Puerto Ricans is even worse. Puerto Ricans are the least-educated, least-employed, and the least-paid minority in this country. Of Puerto Ricans in the mainland United States, 72.1 per cent speak Spanish as their first language. More than a million of them reside in New York. Like the Chicanos, they are treated as non-white partly because of their ghettoized existence and partly because the gene pool from which Chicanos, Puerto Ricans, and other Latinos come includes Indians and blacks as well as Caucasians. Thus the Latinos feel the heat of the black analogue of persecution that is indigenous to the American soul. At times the Latinos even become the blacks' "niggers" as persecution also comes from that quarter. Discrimination in housing, employment, voting, and education are part of both the Chicano and Puerto Rican story as our judicial history shows.[108] In the crucial area of education, University of Wisconsin president Robert M. O'Neil judges that the "conditions in the elementary and secondary schools in the barrios (both rural and urban) seem to be worse than those in the black ghettoes."[109]

It does not seem an excessive conclusion that Chicanos and Puerto Ricans, strapped as they are in this economic setting by linguistic and educational problems and the effects of ghetto existence, are in no position to break free from the grip of poverty. The prejudice against them is depersonalizing and systemic. They face head winds and barriers over which they have no control. They are rendered visible by their language, their names, their residence, and their educational history. They are identifiable. Chicanos and Puerto Ricans meet the four criteria for preferential affirmative action.

I insist, then, that it is senseless to establish "Hispanic surnamed" as a category for preference. This simply confuses dissimilar groups. The Nicaraguans in San Francisco, for example, probably have had the same problems that any immigrant group with a foreign language has had. This does mean that they should receive appropriate assistance in a just society. This assistance, however, does not include preferential affirmative action since they do not meet the criteria for this special aid. Some may wish to argue that incoming Colombians represent a crisis comparable in all details to that of the Chicanos and Puerto Ricans. If they do meet the criteria, they too could qualify for preferential affirmative action. The burden of proof should be borne by those who would defend the thesis that any group qualifies, but the criteria I have suggested are not easily met.

Chinese and Japanese Americans have indeed suffered in their history. They are, however, well established and have achieved education and occupational and economic status. I do not see how they could meet the criteria for preferential affirmative action.[110] Their inclusion among the lists of minorities simply works against those who truly need this assistance.

The uncritical proliferation of minority claimants for preferential affirmative action undercuts the whole program and plays into the hands of the critics of this work of social and distributive justice. There are many forms of discrimination that operate in this country and the government should be concerned to forestall that discrimination when possible. Thus the "Guidelines on Discrimination because of Religion or National Origin" are on target when they state: "Members of various religious and ethnic groups, primarily but not exclusively of Eastern, Middle, and Southern European ancestry, such as Jews, Catholics, Italians, Greeks, and Slavic groups, continue to be excluded from executive, middle-management and other job levels because of discrimination based upon their religion and/or national origin."[111] The WASP ascendancy in this nation is still intact. This could be due to the fact that WASPs are brighter, more talented, and more industrious. However, with a bias signaled by my surname, I do not believe this to be the case. But, beyond my bias, there are, blessedly, other more objective criteria which suggest that there is no such natural aristocracy in this land or elsewhere. Exclusionary clubs of various sorts operate effectively in every society. This is a problem in social and distributive justice. However, it would be nonsense to imply that Jews, Catholics, and middle Europeans all deserve to be listed for preference and that companies should be sent out to locate x number of Catholic welders and Eskimo shop stewards to meet the needs of a just society.

Let me conclude this chapter with a necessary reference to that last refuge of scoundrels. As I spell out my criteria for preference, thus attempting to meet a glaring need in this area, I can hear the scoffers decrying the absolute infeasibility of sorting out the deserving from the non-deserving in our society. It would all be unbearably complicated. Unmanageable. An administrative nightmare. Summarily, my reply is that we were able to sort out groups to disempower and exploit them; we can sort them out to correct matters. Complexity is there and I do not deny it. But we deal with complexity valiantly in the world of taxation, corporate mergers, and other business and political dealings that do not threaten our class status. The complexity of the remedy is no excuse for continued injustice.

CHAPTER EIGHT

Answering the Objections

In Chapter Three I gave a summation of the principal arguments against preferential affirmative action. Throughout the book I have actually spoken to all of them in a specific or in a generic way. Here I shall give a focused response to each, noting that the weight of my replies depends upon the substance of the theory of justice I have offered. First to the philosophical objections:

THE PHILOSOPHICAL OBJECTIONS

1) *Preferential affirmative action is "reverse discrimination."* (See p. 32.)

Preferential affirmative action is not "reverse discrimination" since it does not involve arbitrary or invidious discrimination. It is rather an effort to reverse the arbitrary and invidious discrimination that has produced a white male quota system and kept it in existence for two centuries. To end a discriminatory monopoly is not discriminatory. It is rather a termination of discrimination. The journalistic use of the expression "reverse discrimination" even in quotes is doing a disservice to truth by publishing and implanting a false and distorting symbol in the popular imagination.

"Reverse discrimination" implies that preferential affirmative action is now doing to us white males what we did to the blacks *et al*. This would be true only if preferential affirmative action required the "niggerization" of white males—to use with apologies that cruel term that connotes the spirit and effects of the caste system. But in what sense are we planning to systematically insult white males and put them in the lowest caste in society? In what sense does preferential affirmative action plan to decrease the life span of white males and their wives and children? Is this policy geared to making white males hate themselves and be ashamed of their physical appearance? Will it make white male unemployment double that of blacks and will it reduce white male salary to 60 per cent of that of blacks? Will it confine white males to ghettos where there are more rats than people and no hope? Et cetera, et cetera, et cetera. To truly *reverse* the discriminatory process would require all of that. Obviously, none of that is contemplated or possible. The term "reverse discrimination" houses a big lie.

It also betrays an ignorance of social and distributive justice. It is innocent of the sociology of power and is at root a crude and unnuanced form of individualistic philosophy. Significantly, it blesses the status quo since it would not permit the just work of dismantling a monopoly. It ignores the reality of group identity and power in society and shows no conception of our natural sociality. My whole discussion of justice was speaking to the inadequacy of such a lightsome philosophy.

2)   *Groups have no rights; only individuals have rights.* (See p. 32.)

Again this is individualism, pure and all too simple. It ignores the fact that a group is more than the sum of its individual parts. There is nothing morally or politically irrelevant about what a group can do to individuals or to other groups. And what remarkable aplomb it takes for persons basking in the perquisites of group membership (white male) to deny steadfastly the relevance of group membership when deprived groups come seeking a piece of the action. At its core this objection is undiluted racism and sexism. If white males are up, and blacks and women are down, and if this has nothing to do with group membership, then one must concede the aristocratic superiority of white males. Of course, in the real world, group membership is overwhelmingly important and every legal system, including our own, recognizes it.

The most obvious example of the social, moral, and political significance and power of human grouping is found in what the Anglo-Saxon group has managed to do in this country. As the conclusion of the study *Violence in America* puts it, "The original dominant immigrant group, the so-called Anglo-Saxons, effectively preempted the crucial levers of economic and political power in government, commerce and the professions."[1]

This elite group—as a group—also managed to act against other groups—as groups. They restricted the immigration of certain groups, confined the Indians to barren reservations, and reduced blacks, as a group, to degraded caste status.

One is tempted to give this objection the back of the hand and dismiss it as patently absurd, but this would be an ill-advised retreat. Supposedly serious folks are out there arguing that group identity is meaningless and that our courts may traffic only in the individual deeds of individual doers. It is obvious what they are up to since such stark individualism would foreclose on any effort to deal directly with a disempowered group. A quick look at the record should show that a group is a recognized entity in social, legal, judicial, and political life.

The equal protection clause of our Constitution had as its primary intent the needs of a distinct group, the newly freed blacks.[2] Blacks, of course, point out that they were not chosen as individuals on a meritocratic test of their farming abilities but were chosen for enslavement as a group. Veterans are treated as a group and given benefits as a group even though some risked life and limb and others had a relatively easy tour of duty. In other words, individual merit is not the issue in veterans' benefits. Group identity is. Professor of law Alfred Blumrosen noted that the Supreme Court in the *Griggs* decision viewed "discrimination not only as an isolated act by an aberrant individual wrongdoer that affects only an individual complainant, but also as the operation of industrial-relations systems that adversely affect minority group members."[3] Laws against child labor view children as a needful group requiring protection as a group. The Supreme Court also upheld group treatment in *Morton v. Mancari* in 1974 when it unanimously supported a federal statute giving Indians a preference for employment in the Bureau of Indian Affairs.[4] The

Brown decision, in 1954, certainly treated a problem that blacks as a group had.

And finally, in international affairs, group identity is basic. The establishment of Israel is a prime example of group identity and group need. The declaration and prosecution of modern war is an action by one group on another. Group identity affects our status and one's status affects what opportunities one has or lacks. When subjected status has been imposed on a distinguishable group, it is a work of social and distributive justice to remove the stigma and relieve the strangle hold of inferior status. In rights language, one could say that such a group has a right to that relief. The "never as groups, only as individuals" objection is nonsense, but for those who are oppressed as a group it is objectionable and even deadly nonsense.

3) *By merit alone.* (See p. 32.)

Our newly blooming love affair with a meritocracy is not edifying. The sudden stress on merit criteria as dispossessed groups appear at the gates is immediately suspicious. The implication is that the white male establishment, which is not being threatened by these new demands, always worked, in the past, on a strict merit system. By some kind of litmus test, we always knew who was the best applicant to be bus driver, mailman, corporate executive, college student, professor, et cetera. Of course there never was a litmus test. The old adage, "It's not what you know but who you know . . ." was none too cynical. An enormous amount of subjectivity enters into all hiring and admissions. The meritocratic rhetoric further implies that, since males dominate all the major centers of power, they deserve to. The appeal to merit is a symptom of consummate gall!

In fact the old buddy system always prevailed. Most workers in a plant got their jobs when they heard from a buddy that "They need a man in the shop," et cetera. This word did not get to the ghetto, whose residents are cut off from this all-important network of the employment system unless they too are hired there in sufficient numbers. Relatives of reliable employees always had an advantage. Many jobs do not require merit but simply trainability. And when better qualifications are the issue, as with admission to professional schools, these "merits" often derive not from Horatio Alger pluck but from being born into upper-class privileges. Thus the "merit" of the better qualified is often not merited but simply bequeathed and inherited like royal blood.

More basically—and this is generally ignored in the discussion—"merit" is a loaded word containing a social philosophy. It can house either egoistic individualism or social conscience. It can mean that the individual, asocially considered, deserves something or that society and the common good deserve something. From the second perspective, being black or a woman could be counted as merit, given the racist and sexist monopolies that strap society, depriving it of the contributions of blacks and women. From the social perspective, being black and qualified might make you more qualified since the society needs to spring blacks out of isolation and into the productive main stream of national life. A black professor who can alleviate the racism of his white students and inspire learning and hope in his black students is a better teacher for that.

Since blacks, women, certain Hispanics, and Indians are more qualified than others to meet the society's need for ending monopoly and caste, being a member of those groups is a qualification. The meritocratic principle, fleshed out with a philosophy not only of individual justice but also of social and distributive justice, actually supports preferential affirmative action. Among a candidate's qualifications are his or her qualifications to meet society's needs. Meritocracy is not the tidy little weapon that opponents of preferential affirmative action think it is. One thinks of the sly old man who was asked how he was. He queried in reply, "Compared to what?" Merit judgment is a comparative judgment, and one that has to factor in both the individual and the social reality of persons.

There are, of course, situations in which the talents and skills of the candidate are definitive. There can be no quotas or numerical goals for graduation. Graduation says that a person has fulfilled certain requirements and acquired certain skills. If this is not true, the graduation is a farce and a subversion of justice. Remedial help and special programs may be necessary along the way, but he or she who cannot cut the mustard should not pass a course or receive a degree. Also, when skills become more and more the issue, as with brain surgeons and airplane pilots, race, sex, or ethnic origin is not the issue; skill is. Here is where social and individual good blend since it is for the good of all that the most talented fill the roles requiring high and rare skills.

4)   *Equality.* (See p. 32.)

I have attacked above (pp. 99–103, 127) the confusion of justice and equality. Equality, of course, will not leave our political lexicon because I have attacked it. If we must stay with the term, let us concede that equal rights mean that no one is denied his or her minimal due as persons. However, reaching such an ideal requires corrective preferential inequalities. Certain inequalities are required to get equal rights. This means that I would accept the idea of "minimal due egalitarianism" without buying into the absurdity of across-the-board egalitarianism. But because of the confusion that equality talk engenders, my urging is that we move to clear-minded discussion of what justice entails and leave equality aside as much as possible.

THE PRAGMATIC OBJECTIONS

1)   *Preferential redistribution leads to backlash.* (See pp. 32–33.)

One may note here that backlash reveals bias. There was no backlash against veterans, with all the preferential treatment they have long enjoyed. Also, backlash is often misdirected. As McGeorge Bundy notes, "Most of the competition the white males face comes from other white males."[5]

Also, given the statistics mentioned above about the extraordinary success of women in the years of affirmative action, it is clear that women have more to do with the rejection of white males than blacks or other minorities do. Yet there are strong intimations abroad that blacks lurk behind every rejected white male. Again, as McGeorge Bundy notes, in 1975–76 there were about 35,000 white applicants for medical school and 22,000 of them were not accepted. In the same year the total number of minority students accepted was 1,400. Ninety-three per cent of the whites would still not have been accepted if no minorities had entered![6] The backlashers should be more discriminating in their aim—unless, of course, it is the desire to maintain the caste system that really motivates them. If this be the case, then the backlash argument is another form of anti-black threat.

However, it should be added that the reasons why I suggest strict criteria for preference is to minimize backlash whether nobly or igno-bly motivated. Enlightened government seeks to anticipate and fore-stall tension and my arguments have that in mind. Also, as far as possible, efforts should be made to aid those who are disadvantaged by a policy of preferential affirmative action.

2) *Wrong victims, wrong beneficiaries.* (See p. 33.)

Equality and individualized accounting are not intrinsic to social and distributive justice. Only someone caught at individualistic levels of awareness could expect it to be otherwise. Group problems cannot be addressed by an analysis of all the problems of all the individuals in the group. This is absolutely infeasible. Also, attending to group problems does not allow for the individual indictment of all the malefactors who contributed to the problem. The Brown decision ending segregated schools inconvenienced a number of people whose racist sins might have been minor whereas wealthy racists may not have been inconvenienced at all. Such is the way with massive group policies. Those who already have served their country heroically may still be pressed into jury duty or be forced to give up their homes through eminent domain. Also, as mentioned above, preferential aid to well-off blacks provides role models and thus indirectly aids poorer blacks. Finally, it should be noted here that affirmative action requirements provide an easy alibi for admissions and hiring officers. Many alleged "victims" are not victims at all. "We'd love to have you, but these federal requirements . . ." The fact is they may not love to have you and would not have you even in the absence of affirmative action regulations.

3) *More government intrusion into business and academe.* (See p. 32.)

First, regarding academe, preferential affirmative action is not a threat to academic freedom or integrity. There should be no challenge to the right of the university to decide who is qualified to teach and who is not. There should be no compulsion to take in unqualified or unqualifiable students to meet government rules. When this happens it is a serious abuse. Indeed, it would be racism or sexism to let in people who are unqualified and unqualifiable just because they are black and/or female. It would imply a judgment that if we must have blacks, et cetera, we must have unqualified people. If blacks cannot qualify even with remedial help, they should not be admitted.

Also, in business, there is no need to hire the incompetent. It is a caricature of affirmative action to say otherwise. I have quoted above the experience of businessmen who found that affirmative action regulations forced them to become more sophisticated in management. American business has a long history of worrying about its managerial chastity in the face of government interests. (It is often pointed out that this same fear does not manifest itself when government is looked to for bail-out or depletion allowance.)

Basically, the point at issue here is that neither business nor academic institutions exist in a moral vacuum. They are, in fact, agents of social and distributive justice. They are not private in the sense of being withdrawn from the public domain. Their policies have impact on the common good and so that impact must meet the requirements of moral reason. Their decisions affect the flow of power and privilege in society. Also, businesses and academic institutions must recognize that their good is not divorced from the common good even though short-term thinking might make it seem so. Ultimately, all flourishing is threatened if the health of the society is impaired. For this reason the natural relationship of business and academe to government is not adversarial but collaborative. Recognition of this fact of life changes the whole discussion of "government intrusion." The dismantling of a caste system and the enfranchisement of feminine genius is good both for General Motors and for the country. Governmental insistence here is supplemental, not intrusive.

Since in the present state of civilization private goals and the dynamics of profit often overshadow the common good, and since ad hoc virtuous responses would disadvantage the virtuous, governmental pressure is needed. In the case of preferential affirmative action, this could take more effective forms than are now employed. A. T. & T., which has complied admirably under appropriate pressure, is in many ways an example to other industries. However, the court proceedings leading to this happy eventuality consumed much time and commitment of personnel on the part of the Equal Employment Opportunity Commission. It would not be possible, with their limited staff, to pursue all of the top five hundred corporations—much less the smaller businesses. Similarly, it is not possible to monitor the compliance of the three thousand colleges and universities in the nation. There is an alternative method that should be considered. Professor Christopher Stone, author of *Where the Law Ends: The Social Control of Corporate Behavior,* suggests that in the area of ecological compliance the court could appoint a temporary vice-president for environmental affairs. Something similar could be done to oversee affirmative action affairs. This vice-president for affirmative action would be appointed when there was substantial evidence of noncompliance and would be paid by the business or university but be answerable to the court regarding his specific mandate. He or she should be an acknowledged expert in the field. Having an internal position in the corporation, such an officer could redirect policy and be commissioned to return periodically to check and report to the court. Such an officer might discover that the prima facie evidence against the corporation was misleading and that the company was not guilty of simulated compliance. At any rate, his or her mere presence would be an enormous inducement toward genuine compliance. The current system of slapping at individual corporations in the hope that others will get the idea and follow suit has obvious limitations. It is a scatter-shot approach to enforcement. As it is, corporations like A. T. & T. are complying in ways that most other corporations are not. This is unfair.

This state of affairs also encourages paper compliance. A corporation (including a university) will have an affirmative action officer, cover its documents and brochures with protestations of affirmative action compliance, advertise for hiring in ways that will reach all sectors of the population, insist on the signing of affirmative action forms for every hiring—and still leave the old buddy system in the saddle. It is easy to go through the motions and hire whomever you want and a number of businesses and universities do precisely that. The posturing of compliance may even be enough to get them through the unlikely event of investigation. Feigned compliance would be much more difficult to sustain under the investigative eye of a court-appointed internal officer who could discover how business is really done—over and under the table.

There is another way in which academic institutions and government could collaborate—and in which the institutions would do well in doing good. We are in the anomalous situation of having a glut of teachers in a student-starved market, while the educational needs of minorities are abounding and unmet. The number of eighteen-year-olds was expected to peak at 4.2 million in 1977 and is expected to decline to 3.5 million by the mid-1980s. The projected decline would level off only after 1994.[7] Almost 20 per cent of the eighteen-year-olds will be non-white by 1994 and the number of Hispanics by that time is likely to make them the largest minority in the country. Both groups have extensive educational needs. Given the special vernacular that many blacks inherit in their segregated existence and the lack of facility in English that afflicts many Hispanics, and given the dropout rate and the inferior school situation, we have a huge need and market for education. Government and educators would be natural allies in developing a system of vouchers and continuing education for adults. Many people, after their "school years" are over, are more educable and this is especially true for deprived groups. Minority students will respond in a better school situation. Most of their schools are holding operations. As one despairing teacher put it: "We don't teach; we ride herd."

Our halfhearted approach to minority education is a drain on our national resources. People are not pouring into our usual educational openings, so we study the situation and lament and leave the nation's glaring educational needs and opportunities unattended. This is neither bright, nor just, nor constitutional since it represents a refusal to "promote the general welfare."

4) *Race certification: who's black and who's white?* (See p. 33.)

This objection I have spoken to above (pp. 151–52). I also was discussing it in arguing the visibility of each of the four groups who qualify for preference.

5) *How to set the quota or target number?* (See pp. 33–34.)

Let us admit that inflexible quotas can be irrational. No one can be required to hire unavailable people. If there are no Puerto Ricans in Montana, you can't be required to import them to meet an abstract quota. Another absurdity was exemplified at the University of California (Berkeley) Law School in 1972. Black students wanted their "share" of admitted blacks to be based on the national demography. Chicanos wanted figures based on California statistics. Asian students, who do not even meet the criteria of need that I offer, wanted proportions based on the immediate San Francisco Asian population. Had all demands been met, half the entering class would have been from minorities and if the quotas were inflexible there would have been no quality control.[8] Obviously, more reasonable approaches were worked out at the law school. Inflexible quotas do not match the flexibility of reality. They are not defensible. The guiding principle for flexible quotas or goals is the breakup of monopolies by bringing in ascertainable numbers of available persons from the previously excluded four groups. Surely that does not present insurmountable challenges to the human mind. The goal for a suburban plant should be based on the metropolitan population. (The suburb where it is located might be lily-white and that might be why it is located there.) State universities can set reasonable targets, with an eye to both the nearby and state-wide population. Professional schools should view the underrepresentation of various groups in the particular profession. A particular school, like Dartmouth, might specialize in Indian education. A Southwestern school might seek to attract Chicanos. Such regional specialization makes sense and should not be prevented by nationwide rigidities. The protracted and often pedantic debate on the distinction between quotas and goals is misplaced and unnecessary. It also, at times, seems a smoke screen for underlying resistance to the whole idea of redistribution.

As to the suggestion that, once begun, there will be no end to numerical goals, this too is wrong. The preference should continue until the monopoly-breaking goal is achieved and until it is clear that the same inequities will not obtain if the program ends. I cited Professor Blumrosen's concrete suggestion regarding blacks. He says that when their unemployment rate is no longer double that of the white race but is running at one and one half to one and when the median income levels of minorities is 80 to 85 per cent rather than 60 per cent, preference could be ended.[9] Given the momentum of past practices, the system of numerical goals should be called off cautiously. The old forces that established the monopoly situation may be waiting in the wings and may quickly reassert themselves. Ideally, once appropriate proportionality has been achieved, the normal dynamics of the market place will allow continued balance and equity. The newly employed minorities and women can act as conduits for employment opportunity news. Prejudice will hopefully subside with the experience of an integrated work force. By its nature, a policy of preference is temporary.

6) *Some monopolies are benign; so too are some housing concentrations.* (See p. 34.)

I have spoken of this above (p. 148). If you don't know the difference between a Little Italy and a black or Hispanic ghetto, visit a ghetto. Regarding ethnic-occupational links, it is true that some groups incline to certain kinds of work because of their background. It is also true that this is less the case today, and it is further true that benign tendencies like this can be discerned by persons of good will. The very examples offered indicate how flimsy a problem this is. Nathan Glazer speaks of Irish policemen and Italian fruit dealers and Sidney Hook wants to protect the benign preferences of Swedes for tugboat work in New York.[10] One senses that these examples are a little dated and might not represent the main concern of these gentlemen. A more serious example comes in references to basketball. The National Basketball Association is becoming predominantly black. Must we in all justice insist on a proportional representation of white males, thus banishing blacks from one of their successes? Again, this is sophistry, but the objection is raised and must be spoken to.

Two points can be made here. First of all, professional sports involve highly refined and unusual skills and physical abilities. Where rare skills are involved, only a merit system makes sense. We shouldn't think of numerical proportions when picking a national chess team or selecting athletes for the Olympics. Here, as in brain surgery, the ideal is to get the best to the top. Even this ideal, of course, will be stricken by racism and sexism and other prejudice. We have no idea of how much talent lies buried in our disempowered groups who do not have the circumstances in which excellence may flower. Thus even in this supposedly purified merit calculation, class privilege tells. Also, it has been pointed out that in spite of their growing numbers in professional sports blacks still face discrimination. Second-string or substitute players are usually white. The black has to excel to make it. In competition between black and white "journeymen," the nod tends to go to the white. It is noteworthy that the batting averages of black players in the major leagues between 1953 and 1970 averaged twenty points higher than the averages for white players.[11] In other words, even where fierce competitive passions are involved and where profit depends on victory, racist infection operates.

7) *Class, not race, is the issue.* (See p. 34.)

It should be conceded that class, with the false consciousness it engenders, is a vital consideration in social analysis. However, racism and sexism are not confined within the category of class. Women, first of all, are found in all classes; sexism crosses class lines. Also, blacks are the perpetual underclass. Something more than class is involved. Middle classification is easier for some groups than for others and it has proved uniquely difficult for blacks. All of the factors of the black plight that I have listed above militate against the idea that class is the key to black liberation. In fact an approach based on class will ensure the continued degradation of blacks. Many persons are disadvantaged but not radically disempowered by class factors. White disadvantaged people have more going for them and they are quick to distinguish themselves from blacks in recognition of this. To broaden preferential affirmative action to include all those disadvantaged by low-class status blurs the unique problems of the disempowered groups who exist amid the disadvantaged.

8) *Black doctors and lawyers will not go back to serve their own people.* (See p. 34.)

In reply it can be said that, even if black professionals followed the lead of whites and chose to feast upon the already overserved "fat cats," a social goal would be achieved by their very existence in those professions. The professions would be enriched by the presence of black culture and perspectives. Medical research would be likely to pay more attention to specifically black medical problems if blacks were more present in medicine. And role models are provided, affecting black career hopes and educational motivation.

Statistics on how many black professionals go back to serve blacks are hard to come by. The California court in the Bakke case did recognize that minority doctors were more likely to practice in minority areas than a white doctor.[12] Supportive of this was a survey conducted between 1965 and 1970 of health centers operated by the Office of Economic Opportunity. It showed that, whereas only 2 per cent of practicing doctors were black during that period, 17 per cent of the OEO doctors were blacks.[13]

A wry thought suggests itself here. Those who raise this objection as an argument against preference for blacks could indeed be the very ones who would never consider going to a black physician or lawyer —thus making it necessary for those professionals to find clients among their own people where they would be more welcome. Since many whites would not choose a black doctor, where else will that doctor go to practice but back to his own people? Owing to preferential affirmative action, more blacks are getting into the professions. There is a reasonable likelihood that future studies will show that these people will return to help other blacks.

9) *Affirmative action horrors stories.* (See 34–35.)

A number of horror stories which are welcomed and published by opponents of preferential affirmative action make the rounds. These involve maladministration, unrealistic and even silly demands on the part of affirmative action agencies, et cetera. We can fairly assume that not all of these allegations are apocryphal and many are true. Does it follow then that the entire project should be scrapped? An ancient axiom puts it this way: *Abusus non tollit usum* (Because something is abused does not mean that it cannot be intelligently used).

This is another of those arguments that would seem to conceal the real project of the arguers. The sign of this is that similar arguments would not be used to attack abuse-ridden programs that are found congenial. One could accumulate a massive dossier of abuses in the Department of Defense or in the Social Security system. Here, however, the general assumption is that abuses call for correction, not for the dismantling of the entire project. The same holds for the affirmative action program.

THE LEGAL OBJECTIONS

1) *The equal protection clause of the Fourteenth Amendment excludes the very notion of preference.* (See p. 35.)

It is true that "equality" achieved constitutional status in the Fourteenth Amendment. However, no one could defend the thesis that the amendment imposed radical and complete egalitarianism on this nation. As Professor Owen M. Fiss of Yale University says, "When asked what the Equal Protection Clause means, an informed lawyer . . . is likely to respond that the Clause prohibits discrimination."[14] Discrimination, etymologically, merely means making a distinction where there is a difference. So constitutional literature goes further and qualifies the kind of discrimination that is offensive. The equal protection clause is seen to prohibit "arbitrary" or "invidious" discrimination.[15] The jurists thereby are advising us that equal protection does not mean that everyone is to be treated the same but that we are to be treated "equally" only in the sense that everyone should be protected against *arbitrary* and *invidious* discrimination.

Conceptually, therefore, the equal protection clause of the Fourteenth Amendment does not forbid preferential restitutional treatment of an offended group if that serves to end the hostile pattern of discrimination. It only forbids arbitrary and invidious preference. It would conceptually support preferential treatment of a disempowered group if this would help to empower that group so that its members could escape the invidious discrimination which they are suffering as a group.

Remember too that the original purpose of the Fourteenth Amendment was to help blacks. It is therefore no gentle irony that pedantic quibbles over the wording of this amendment are now used to block the "equality" for blacks that was the prime purpose of the amendment. And it is indeed quibbling to resist curative preference for blacks out of a strained, abstract, and historical fixation on the word "equal." The key word in the phrase "equal protection" is not *equal* but *protection*. J. tenBroek, author of *Equal Under Law,* says that it was because protection of the laws was denied to some people that the term "equal" arose. In his view, the term "full" could have served the same purpose.[16] Given the lubricity of the term "equal," it is a tragedy that "full" was not used. At any rate the key to understanding the relevance of the Fourteenth Amendment to preferential affirmative action is to realize that blacks and other disempowered groups are invidiously unprotected and discriminated against. Ending such a state of affairs is the quintessential purpose of the Fourteenth Amendment. The Fourteenth Amendment, therefore, is not an argument against but an argument for preferential relief. Preference used against an invidious monopoly is not invidious. To say that it is is to logically deny the very notion of redistribution, and thus the possibility of justice for victims of social monopolies.

This speaks to the other arguments given above (p. 35). These arguments are based upon the Civil Rights Acts of 1964 and 1968 and the Equal Employment Opportunity Act of 1972. What these provisions did was to forbid invidious discrimination against anyone on the basis of color, race, sex, or national origin. Paragraph 703(j) of Title VII even criticizes "preferential treatment." This has been seized upon as legal grounds for denying preferential affirmative action as though the statutes required us to be color-blind, sex-blind, and religion-blind in the administration of justice. Obviously this would totally undercut preferential affirmative action.

This is not what these statutes mean and this is not the way they have been used by the courts. Rather these paragraphs have been seen as "mini-equal-protection clauses."[17] They reassert our constitutional opposition to invidious discrimination against anyone, white, black, or other. They do not require us to be blind to a person's race, sex, or religion whenever there has been discrimination on any of those grounds. In fact, as Professor Blumrosen writes, "The actions of Congress in 1972, in rejecting proposed amendments to Title VII which would have prohibited 'discrimination in reverse' . . . confirm the view that Congress intended to permit effective affirmative action remedies where discrimination was found, including the use of numerical standards. . . ."[18] What these clauses prohibited was a mechanical allocation of quotas based on demographics without reference to discrimination. The courts have so understood these statutes and been quite conscious of race, sex, and religion when discrimination was found.[19] The Weber decision confirms this.

The whole debate on these statutory clauses is tedious and punctilious in the extreme. Common sense plays little part in the efforts to wrench a prohibition of preferential affirmative action from these texts. In the background of this effort, among other things, is a dogmatic Lockean individualism that would paralyze government in the face of the evil that groups can inflict on groups. This leaves the caste-making and caste-sustaining power of the white American male home free. That bottom-line conclusion should be borne in mind as one reads through the learned agonizings over a paragraph 601 or a 703(j).

THE OBJECTIONS OF STRATEGIC NAÏVETÉ

1) *Progress was being made, so let's have more of the same.* (See pp. 35–36.)

This objection means that affirmative action is unnecessary. It says that the progress of recent years probably would have come about anyhow even without preferential affirmative action. The weakness of this position should be apparent but it might help to give a few examples. In 1967–68, the last year before special admissions to medical schools came into significance, the percentage of blacks in white medical schools was 0.6 per cent. By 1977, after preferential affirmative action, the number had risen to 5 per cent of the total.[20] Evidence submitted in the Bakke case reports that at Davis Medical School, in the two years prior to special admissions, only two blacks and one Mexican American were admitted. Between 1970 and 1974, with special admissions in effect, thirty-three Chicano students, twenty-six blacks, and one American Indian were admitted.[21] There is no reason to believe that this influx of qualified minorities would have happened without preferential considerations. And these minorities are qualified. Their attrition rates are higher than those of whites but are comparable to the attrition rates of whites some thirty or forty years ago when, it may be assumed, medical learning was less complex. McGeorge Bundy is on target in urging middle-aged critics of affirmative action in the medical profession to ask if those with records as good as their own should be considered under-qualified.[22]

The dramatic increase of women in various schools is witness to the effectiveness of preferential admissions and it is implausible to suggest that this change would have come about on a "business as usual" basis. Indeed, the formidable resistance to affirmative action shows that, without this pressure, little would have changed.

2)   *Preference makes blacks* et al. *look bad.* (See p. 36.)

Given the way white males have held their chins up high while awash with preferential treatment all these years, one somehow has to hope that minorities and women will have similar grit and will bear their preferment with equal aplomb.

3)   *Blacks as latest immigrants.* (See p. 36.)

No immigrants experienced slavery or an enduring caste system. And the blacks arrived in 1619. Latest immigrants?

4)   *Find alternatives to preference.* (See p. 36.)

Fine. But meantime, in the absence of effective alternatives, let us stick with this modest means that does work.

5)   *Blacks are culturally unattuned to the demands of the work place.* (See p. 36.)

I have cited studies showing that blacks want to work as much as others (pp. 136–39). And anyone who would criticize black work habits on the job must be prepared to assess the responsibilities of the white society which has systematically assaulted black self-confidence. (See pp. 140–45.)

6)   *"Societal discrimination"* and *"institutional racism"* are non-viable concepts. (See p. 37.)

If this is true, then all persons who are not part of the white male aristocracy are inferior.

REDUCTIO AD ABSURDUM OBJECTIONS:

1)   *The unending line of groups begging preference.* (See p. 37.)

The criteria I have suggested seem to be met only by blacks, women, Chicanos, Puerto Ricans, and Indians. The objection implies that we cannot make distinctions where there are differences.

2)   *Preference means graduating and hiring incompetents.* (See p. 37.)

There can be no preference for graduation or for positions requiring high and rare skills. Preference enables the societally disenfranchised to be allowed to try to qualify.

3)   *Preferential affirmative action reinstitutes the hereditary birthright of feudalism.* (See p. 37.)

If one must resort to the past for analogues, affirmative action is not comparable to the creation of a noble class but to the freeing of slaves. It addresses the needs of those whose birth left them deprived of rights, not endowed with privileges.

4) *Affirmative action success statistics are like the fake body counts of Vietnam.* (See p. 38.)

Now really! I would, however, concede that lying and juggling of figures is done by employers to give the impression of compliance. This indicts not the program but only the liars. To Miro Todorovich's suggestion that this program shows the same interventionism that our foreign policy did in Vietnam, I can only hope he'll come to see the differences.

5) *We cannot make reparations for all past wrongs.* (See p. 38.)

True enough. But *present* disempowerment is the issue in preferential affirmative action. The past has only evidentiary importance to show the depths and intractability of the present problem. Preferential policy does not offer reparations of money; it modifies the unfair distributional patterns in the direction of justice. There is no need to add the Etruscans to the list of offended minorities.

6) *Too complicated to administer.* (See p. 38.)

If we cannot handle complication, then we must flee modernity. The criteria I offered bring what simplification is necessary and possible. The appointment by a court of a temporary vice-president for affirmative action in the presence of substantial evidence of non-compliance would also cut through much obfuscatory red tape.

IN FINE

Thomas Jefferson spoke good sense to early America when he urged that "the object is to bring into action that mass of talents which lies buried in poverty in every country."[23] Affirmative action is a belated attempt to liberate those groups whose talents have been buried in literal poverty and in the more subtle poverty of sexism. The white male aristocracy has long reigned on the assumption that white male talent was our only reliable national resource. The end of this self-defeating hubris is past due. However, the long-learned habits of dominance and exclusion are not easily changed. Effective affirmative action is broadly resisted. The situation is not unlike that of one hundred years ago when efforts to enfranchise the freed slaves in American life were quickly blunted. In the spirit that characterizes contemporary resistance to affirmative action, the Supreme Court then declared: "When man has emerged from slavery, and by the aid of beneficent legislation has shaken off the inseparable concomitants of that state, there must be some state in the progress of his elevation when he takes the rank of a mere citizen and ceases to be the special favorite of the laws."[24] Those pompous words ushered in the subsequent century of American apartheid. What the Court was saying in 1883 was that we had done enough for the disempowered blacks. There is a strong disposition today to say again "Fare thee well" to groups who have been effectively disempowered. The times, however, are different. We are at great remove from 1883. The spirit and the temper of the dispossessed are more urgent. If even the modest redistributional efforts of affirmative action are successfully resisted, the price of injustice will finally have to be paid. Doing justice exacts its own price, but we have reached a point where continued injustice will be even more costly.

NOTES

CHAPTER TWO

1. Frederick J. Turner, *The Significance of the Frontier in American History*, p. 200, in A Readex Microprint of pp. 197–227 of the *Annual Report of the American Historical Association* for the Year 1893. © Readex Microprint Corporation (1966).

2. Nathan Glazer, *Affirmative Discrimination: Ethnic Inequality and Public Policy* (New York: Basic Books, 1975), p. 15.

3. Ibid., p. 7.

4. Ibid., p. 22.

5. Quoted in Yehoshua Arieli, *Individualism and Nationalism in American Ideology* (Cambridge, Mass.: Harvard University Press, 1964), p. 67.

6. Quoted, ibid., p. 46.

7. Stanley M. Elkins, *Slavery* (New York: Grosset & Dunlap, 1963), p. 61.

8. Ibid., p. 61. See also p. 63.

9. John Codman Hurd, *The Law of Freedom and Bondage in the United States* (Boston: Little, Brown, 1858), Vol. 1, p. 303.

10. Sylvester Judd, *A Moral Review of the Revolutionary War* (Hallowell, Me.: Glazier, Masters & Smith, Printers, 1842), p. 38.

11. Ibid., p. 40.

12. See Hugh Davis Graham and Ted Robert Gurr, *Violence in America: Historical and Comparative Perspectives* (New York: Bantam Books, 1969), p. 66.

13. Richard Maxwell Brown, "Historical Patterns of Violence in America," ibid., p. 67.

14. Frederick J. Turner, op. cit., p. 204.

15. Charles A. Beard, *The Idea of National Interest* (New York: The Macmillan Company, 1934), p. 52.

16. See ibid., p. 70.

17. Carl Schurz, quoted in ibid., p. 395.

18. Quoted without reference in Hans J. Morgenthau, *Politics Among Nations* (3rd Ed.; New York: Alfred A. Knopf, 1962), pp. 36–37.

19. Quoted in Arieli, op. cit., p. 335.

20. Quoted, ibid., p. 334.

21. Quoted, ibid., p. 336.

22. Richard Hofstadter, *The American Political Tradition* (New York: Vintage Books, 1954), p. vii.

23. Robert Nozick, *Anarchy, State, and Utopia* (New York: Basic Books, 1974), p. ix.

24. Ibid., p. 33.

25. Ibid., p. ix.

26. Ibid., p. 169.

27. Richard Hofstadter, pp. 329–30.

28. Quoted, ibid., p. 331. Even outside of hard times, American individualism was not untouched by the concept of "the common good." Enlightened self-interest leads to common good considerations. This, however, is a distant relative of genuine social justice.

29. Carnegie Samuel Calian, *The Gospel According to the Wall Street Journal* (Atlanta: John Knox Press, 1975).

30. William Roscoe Thayer, *Life and Letters of John Hay* (Boston: Houghton Mifflin), Vol. I, pp. 6–7. Quoted by Reinhold Niebuhr, *Moral Man and Immoral Society* (New York: Scribner's, 1932, 1960), p. 125.

31. Quoted in Hans Kohn, *American Nationalism: An Interpretive Essay* (New York: Collier Books, 1961), p. 143.

32. Reinhold Niebuhr wrote about the attitudes of privileged classes and concluded: "The moral attitudes of dominant and privileged groups are characterized by universal self deception and hypocrisy." Niebuhr, op. cit., p. 117. This hypocrisy reveals itself in language which regularly commingles and confuses terms of affluence and of virtue. Thus words like "gentle" and "noble" with all of their positive moral content were co-opted to refer to the aristocratic "gentlemen and noblemen." Contrariwise, words like "villain" or "churl" were used to show a lack of moral worth in the poor. Niebuhr, op. cit., pp. 125–27.

CHAPTER THREE

1. To Rev. James Madison, October 28, 1785, quoted in Yehoshua Arieli, *Individualism and Nationalism in American Ideology* (Cambridge, Mass.: Harvard University Press, 1964), p. 159.

2. See ibid.

3. Elaine A. Alexander and Lawrence A. Alexander, "The New Racism: An Analysis of the Use of Racial and Ethnic Criteria in Decision-Making," *San Diego Law Review* 9:190 (1972), p. 198.

4. The United States Commission on Civil Rights, *Statement on Affirmative Action,* Clearinghouse Publication 54 (October 1977), p. 2.

5. *Griggs v. Duke Power Co.* (1971) 401 U.S. 432.

6. *International Brotherhood of Teamsters v. United States* (1977), 97 Sup. Ct. 1843, 1856–57 n. 20.

7. Actually, even remedial affirmative action involves some element of preference since it requires money that must be drawn from general resources. Such money meets the needs of some at the expense of others. That is preferential.

8. This expression is that of Lee Nisbet, who argues that the affirmative action programs are not liberal or progressive. "The essence of liberalism has always been concerned with the welfare, rights and responsibilities of *individuals qua individuals,* not the masses or classes or other such linguistic abstractions." Lee Nisbet, "Affirmative Action—A Liberal Program?" in *Reverse Discrimination,* ed. by Barry R. Gross (Buffalo, N.Y.: Prometheus Books, 1977), p. 52.

9. Alan H. Goldman, "Affirmative Action," in *Equality and Preferential Treatment,* ed. by Marshall Cohen, Thomas Nagel, and Thomas Scanlon (Princeton, N.J.: Princeton University Press, 1977), p. 205. Originally published in *Philosophy and Public Affairs,* 5 (Winter, 1976). Emphasis added.

10. Aristotle, *Politics,* 1282b. Quotations from Aristotle are from Richard McKeon, ed., *The Basic Works of Aristotle* (New York: Random House, 1941).

11. John Kaplan, "Equal Justice in an Unequal World: Equality for the Negro—The Problem of Special Treatment," *Northwestern University Law Review,* 61 (1966), p. 379.

12. *Legislative History of the Equal Employment Opportunity Act of 1972 . . . ,* Subcommittee on Labor of the Committee on Labor and Public Welfare, U. S. Senate, 92nd Congress, 2nd session, November 1972, pp. 209–11.

13. For an extensive discussion of the legal arguments, see the *Brief for the United States as Amicus Curiae* in *The Regents of the University of California, Petitioner v. Allan Bakke.*

14. Eliot Marshall, "The Logical Next Step: Race Certification," *New Republic,* 177 (October 15, 1977), p. 20.

15. Edward C. Banfield, *The Unheavenly City: The Nature and Future of Our Urban Crisis* (Boston: Little, Brown, 1968, 1970), p. 105.

16. 98 S. Ct. 2733, 2757 (1978).

17. Nathan Glazer, *Affirmative Discrimination: Ethnic Inequality and Public Policy* (New York: Basic Books, 1975), p. 15.

18. Virginia Black, "The Erosion of Legal Principles in the Creation of Legal Policies," in Barry R. Gross, op. cit., p. 181. Reprinted from *Ethics,* 84 (January 1974), pp. 93–115.

19. Paul Seabury, "HEW and the Universities," in Gross, op. cit., p. 112.

20. Miro M. Todorovich, "Discrimination in Higher Education: A Debate on Faculty Employment," ibid., p. 37.

21. 98 S. Ct. 2733, 2757 (1978).

22. Winton H. Manning, Warren W. Willingham, and Hunter M. Breland and Associates, *Selective Admissions in Higher Education: Public Policy and Academic Policy* (San Francisco: Jossey-Bass Publishers, 1977), p. 24.

23. 98 S. Ct. 2733, 2763 (1978).

24. Ibid., 2757.

25. Ibid., 2763.

26. Ibid.

27. Ibid., 2764.

28. Ibid.

29. Ibid., 2762.

30. "Hence, the purpose of helping certain groups whom the faculty of the Davis Medical School perceived as victims of 'societal discrimination' does not justify a classification that imposes disadvantages upon persons like respondent, who bear no responsibility for whatever harm the beneficiaries of special admissions are thought to have suffered." Ibid., 2759.

31. Ibid., 2757.

32. Ibid., 2755.

33. Ibid., 2762, 2765.

34. Ibid., 2762.

35. Ibid., 2763, 2765.

36. Ibid., 2763.

37. Ibid., 2765.

38. Ibid., 2766.

39. Ibid., 2763.

40. Ibid., 2762.

41. Alan Dershowitz, "Powell's Beau Ideal," *New Republic,* 179 (July 22, 1978), p. 15.

42. Thomas Nagel, "Introduction," *Equality and Preferential Treatment,* p. viii.

43. 98 S. Ct. 2733, 2766 (1978).

44. Alfred W. Blumrosen, "Quotas, Common Sense, and Law in Labor Relations: Three Dimensions of Equal Opportunity," *Rutgers Law Review,* 27 (1974), p. 692.

CHAPTER FOUR

1. Aristotle, *Nichomachean Ethics,* 1155a. For a fuller discussion of the foundational moral experience which finds its first articulation in justice, see Daniel C. Maguire, *The Moral Choice* (Garden City: Doubleday, 1978; Minneapolis: Winston Press, 1979), Chapter 3. Though *suum cuique,* to each his/her own, is the quintessential statement of what justice imports, the ancient literature offers broader and richer appreciations of the notion. Cicero, who reflects a whole tradition in this matter, says that "justice is a predilection for giving to each his/her own and for protecting generously and equitably the common good of persons." This is my translation of his words: "Quae animi affectio suum cuique tribuens atque hanc, quam dico, societatem coniunctionis humanae munifice et aeque tuens justitia dicitur." *De Officiis,* L. i, Cap. 5, #15. Ambrose extends this tradition. "Justice, which renders to each his/her own, does not lay claim to the goods of another and even neglects its own interests in the interests of an equitable common life." "Justitia, quae suum cuique tribuit, alienum non vindicat, utilitatem propriam negligit, ut communem aequitatem custodiat." *De Officiis Ministrorum,* L. i, Cap. 24, #115. And Ulpian described justice as "a constant and perpetual willingness to give to each his/her own." *Dig.* i, I, 10, pr. Each of these definitions imports the value of every person, the presence of affectivity in the notion of justice, and a concern for the common good. I submit that the theory of justice that I offer in this book and in *The Moral Choice* is an adaptive extension of that tradition. Readers of *The Moral Choice* will notice that I do not follow in a mechanical way the model of method that is the structure of that book. They will also notice, I trust, that no aspect or element of that model of method is unrepresented in this book.

2. See Daniel C. Maguire, *Death By Choice* (Garden City: Double-

day, 1974; New York: Schocken Books, 1975), pp. 203–9 for further arguments against the morality of capital punishment.

3. See Giorgio Del Vecchio, *Justice: An Historical and Philosophical Essay* (Edinburgh: University Press, 1952), pp. 53, 68–69, n. 15. See William T. Blackstone, "Reverse Discrimination and Compensatory Justice," *Social Theory and Practice*, 3 (1975), pp. 253–88. Blackstone works off the assumption that there are but two main categories of justice in Aristotle and then exemplifies the weakness of this truncation.

4. An excellent treatment of the tripartite nature of justice is found in Josef Pieper, *Justice* (New York: Pantheon Books, 1955). This has been republished in Josef Pieper, *The Four Cardinal Virtues* (New York: Harcourt, Brace & World, 1965).

5. The confusion on the forms of justice and the befuddling multiplication of these forms resulted from efforts to give justice a new definition in every situation to which it applied—and it applies to the whole of life. To mint a new title for justice in every distinct situation of rendering to each his own allows for infinite and unhelpful proliferation. To give a sampling of this melee: I will list some of the kinds of justice mentioned in the literature: vindictive, judicial, familial, antipeponthotic, synallagmatic, commutative, legal, social, distributive, retributive, attributive, recognitive, providential, syndical, corporative, reparatory, penal, and cosmopolitical. The multiplicity bears witness to the breadth of application that justice has as well as to the felt need for meaningful definitions of the term. Justice talk has further been confused by a long tradition of treating justice as universal virtue, the sum of all goodness. Plato was a mighty force in this direction. See *The Republic,* I. 6, 331 E; I. 7, 332 D; IV. 10, 433 A. This remained as a tension in Aristotle and also in Thomas Aquinas. Finally, justice was taken as just one virtue among the many, missing the fact that it is the primary and foundational category of communal existence.

6. Thomas Aquinas, *Summa Theologica,* II II q. 51, a.1, ad 3.

7. To Rev. James Madison, October 28, 1785, quoted in Yehoshua Arieli, *Individualism and Nationalism in American Ideology* (Cambridge, Mass.: Harvard University Press, 1964), p. 159.

8. Pieper reports this as the opinion of philosophy professor Chungsho Lo, a onetime member of the Unesco Commission. See Josef Pieper, *Justice,* p. 116, n. 15.

9. Ronald Dworkin, *Taking Rights Seriously* (Cambridge, Mass.: Harvard University Press, 1977), p. xi. Dworkin goes on to say that this characterization of rights does not have any "special metaphysical char-

acter." Actually, it certainly does have a metaphysical character, showing again how metaphysics is a term on the loose in much philosophical discourse.

10. For this reason, this form of justice has been called "commutative," from the Latin *commutatio,* meaning exchange. This kind of justice regulates the competing claims that occur in exchanges between individuals.

11. Martin Buber, *I and Thou* (2nd ed.; New York: Scribner's, 1958), p. 8.

12. Quoted by Arieli, op. cit., p. 41.

13. Robert Nozick, *Anarchy, State, and Utopia* (New York: Basic Books, 1974), p. 169.

14. Aristotle, *Politics,* I. 2. 1253.

15. Jethro K. Lieberman, "The Relativity of Injury," *Philosophy and Public Affairs* (Fall, 1977), p. 73.

16. Richard H. de Lone, *Small Futures: Children, Inequality, and the Limits of Liberal Reform* (New York: Harcourt Brace Jovanovich, 1979), p. 179.

17. Koji Taira, "Japan—the New Corporate State?" *The Wilson Quarterly,* 3 (Spring, 1979), p. 53.

18. A. D. Lindsay, *The Essentials of Democracy* (2nd ed.; Oxford: Clarendon Press, 1935), p. 71.

19. Quoted in Eric Voegelin, *The New Science of Politics* (Chicago: University of Chicago Press, 1952), pp. 56–58.

20. Ibid., p. 59.

21. I am taking liberties with the term "nation" here, having in mind a distinguishable societal grouping. The grouping may include a number of national entities which are culturally conjoined. There are various configurations, even hemispheric in breadth, which we might employ as vehicles of interpretation. Certain interpretations of reality are found in nations of the Far East that would not be found in the West. But at any rate we do obey the philosophical injunction "Know thyself!" *through political media* as well as through private and interpersonal forms of sociality. Knowledge is, among other things, political in nature. Since the goal here is an understanding of our ultimate reality and is thus transcendent in its significance, the high stakes are reflected in the language of sacredness. "Everything is full of gods!" as Thales said, and this is certainly so in national self-consciousness. Sacred truths for which men die are at issue. The seriousness is dreadful.

22. Thomas Aquinas, *Commentary on the Nichomachean Ethics of*

Aristotle, 8, 9; #1658. *Justitia consistit in communicatione.* I translate *communicatione* with some freedom, but without distortion. The cognate "communication" would be misleading. "Living with one another" is another possible rendering, but "sharing" seems best.

CHAPTER FIVE

1. Josef Pieper, *Justice,* op. cit., p. 85.

2. Plutarch, *Banquet of the Seven Wise Men,* Chapter 11.

3. Admittedly, even individualized crime will have associated sociological dimensions which add to its complexity. Still, the difference I am citing does obtain.

4. Hugh Davis Graham and Ted Robert Gurr, *The History of Violence in America* (New York: Bantam Books, 1969), p. 794.

5. 98 S. Ct. 2733, 2758 (1978).

6. *Report of the National Advisory Commission on Civil Disorders (Special Introduction by Tom Wicker)* (New York: Bantam Books, 1968), p. 2. It is worth noting that the eleven-member commission that produced this report were persons known for their moderation. Radicals and militants of any race were purposely excluded. As a result, the membership was almost all white male, moderate, cautious, and middle class. For comments on this commission, see Faustine Childress Jones, *The Changing Mood in America: Eroding Commitment?* (Washington, D.C.: Howard University Press, 1977), pp. 29–30.

7. Ibid. The Supreme Court cannot say that it is not its job to "change the system," that such an enterprise is for the legislature. The Brown decision in 1954 is just one obvious example of the Supreme Court changing the system and attacking an in-systemed pattern of discrimination.

8. *Toward a Long Range Plan for Federal Financial Support for Higher Education,* by Alice Rivilin, U. S. Department of Health, Education and Welfare (Washington, D.C.: Government Printing Office, 1969), pp. 18–19.

9. I again insist that government is not the only subject of distributive justice. It is, however, the most powerful and the principal agency of distributive justice.

10. I have written further of this neglected paradox at the center of human life in my book *The Moral Choice* (Garden City: Doubleday, 1978). See pp. 74–80 *et passim.*

CHAPTER SIX

1. Significantly, when the notion of giving to each according to his needs was first used in 1850, it too was presented as a dictate of equality. See Gregory Vlastos, "Justice and Equality," in Richard B. Brandt, ed., *Social Justice* (Englewood Cliffs, N.J.: Prentice-Hall, 1962), p. 42, n. 31.

2. Aristotle, *Politics,* III. 11. 1282b. As with everyone who would have equality carry a lot of the weight of justice, Aristotle had to start making distinctions. His use of geometric and arithmetic proportion as a way of saving his usage of equality shows the problems. See, for example, Book 5 of his *Nichomachean Ethics.*

3. Alfred W. Blumrosen, "Quotas, Common Sense, and Law in Labor Relations: Three Dimensions of Equal Opportunity," *Rutgers Law Review,* 27 (1974), p. 682.

4. See Monroe H. Freedman, "Equality in the Administration of Criminal Justice," in J. Roland Pennock and John W. Chapman, eds., *Equality* (New York: Atherton Press, 1967), p. 251.

5. George F. Kennan, *American Diplomacy: 1900–1950* (New York: A Mentor Book, 1951), p. 59.

6. See Plutarch, *Banquet of the Seven Wise Men,* Chapter 11.

7. See *A Study of Attitudes Toward Racial and Religious Minorities and Toward Women,* prepared for The National Conference of Christians and Jews by Louis Harris and Associates, Inc. (November 1978).

8. One might allege that the abolition of slavery was a white initiative, thus providing a glorious exception to the dire rule. However, the abolition of slavery issued into a second enslavement in the form of caste. The glories of the white man in all of this are dim indeed.

9. See Ralph Linton, "The Problem of Universal Values," in Robert F. Spencer, ed., *Method and Perspective in Anthropology: Papers in Honor of Wilson D. Wallis* (Minneapolis: University of Minnesota Press, 1954), p. 157.

10. See Irenaus Eibl-Eibesfeldt, *Love and Hate: The Natural History of Behavior Patterns* (New York: Holt, Rinehart and Winston, 1971), p. 226.

11. Ibid., p. 244.

12. Blumrosen, op. cit., p. 679.

13. Ibid., p. 680.

14. Ibid., pp. 680–81. See also Alfred W. Blumrosen, "Strangers in Paradise: *Griggs v. Duke Power Co.* and the Concept of Employment Discrimination," *Michigan Law Review,* 71-59 (November 1972), pp. 59–107.

15. Faustine Childress Jones, *The Changing Mood in America: Eroding Commitment?* (Washington, D.C.: Howard University Press, 1977), p. 228.

16. A. T. & T., acting on the terms of the consent decree which was called by Judge Higginbotham "the largest and most impressive civil rights settlement in the history of this nation," produced extraordinary results. (See *EEOC v. American T. & T. Co.,* 365 F. Supp. at 1108, 5 FEP Cases at 644 [3rd Cir. 1973].) In the period of 1972–75, A. T. & T. increased the number of women at the second level of management and above by 60 per cent and 120 per cent on craft jobs. The company paid over $50 million for back pay and other charges in the first year alone to comply with equal pay for equal work. See Theodore V. Purcell, "Management and Affirmative Action in the Late Seventies," *Equal Rights and Industrial Relations,* 1977 Industrial Relations Research Association Series, pp. 81–84. It is very difficult to imagine any of this happening out of a sudden birth of moral passion in the upper management of A. T. & T. A similar message is found in the medical school situation. In the school year 1967–68, only 0.6 per cent of the students in the white medical schools (i.e., excluding Howard and Meharry) were black. After the ten-year effort under the pressure of affirmative action programs blacks are 5 per cent of the total. It is, as McGeorge Bundy writes, "an extraordinary transformation." See McGeorge Bundy, "The Issue Before the Court: Who Gets Ahead in America?" *Atlantic* 240 (November 1977), p. 44.

17. Thomas Jefferson, letter to M. Correa, November 25, 1817.

18. Herbert Marcuse, *Aggression und Anpassung in der Industriegesellschaft* (Frankfurt), p. 11. Quoted in Eibl-Eibesfeldt, op. cit., p. 244.

19. Robert L. Carter, Dorothy Kenyon, Peter Marcuse, Loren Miller, *Equality* (New York: Pantheon Books, 1965), p. 35.

20. Blacks will be 15.4 per cent and other non-whites will be 3.9 per cent of the eighteen-year-old population by 1994. See Winton H. Manning, Warren W. Willingham, and Hunter M. Breland and Associates, *Selective Admissions in Higher Education: Public Policy and Academic Policy* (San Francisco: Jossey-Bass Publishers, 1977), pp. 78, 154.

21. Quoted in Ruth G. Shaeffer, *Discrimination in Employment, 1973–1975* (New York: Conference Board, 1975), pp. 30–31.

22. Kenneth B. Clark, "The Wonder Is There Have Been So Few Riots," *New York Times Magazine* (September 5, 1965), p. 10.

23. Thomas Paine, *Works,* ed. by J. P. Mendum (Boston: 1878), pp. 454–55. Quoted in Pennock and Chapman, op. cit., p. 248.

24. See Faustine Childress Jones, op. cit.

25. Ibid., Chapter III.

26. Howard Schuman and Shirley Hatchett, *Black Racial Attitudes: Trends and Complexities* (Ann Arbor: University of Michigan Survey Research Center, 1974), p. 15.

27. Ibid., pp. 74–75.

28. Quoted in Reinhold Niebuhr, *Moral Man and Immoral Society* (New York: Scribner's, 1932, 1960), p. 163.

29. See Mary Harrington Hall, "Conversation with the President of the American Psychological Association, The Psychology of Universality: Abraham H. Maslow," *Psychology Today* (July 1968), p. 35.

30. J. Glenn Gray, *The Warriors: Reflections on Men in Battle* (New York, Evanston, and London: Harper & Row, Harper Torchbook, 1959), p. 212.

31. Emil Brunner, *Justice and the Social Order* (London: Lutterworth Press, 1945), p. 7.

32. One happy exception to Catholic and broader Christian and Jewish indifference is Project Equality. Project Equality is a national program of the interfaith community to utilize their purchasing and hiring power to achieve effective affirmative action. For information about this program, write Project Equality, 1442 North Farwell Ave., Suite 210, Milwaukee, Wisconsin 53202. Also the Catholic Archdiocese has adopted a policy of formal support for Project Equality, harnessing archdiocesan purchasing power in the cause of affirmative action and nondiscrimination.

33. The debate on affirmative action has been unhappily impaled on the differences between quotas and goals or targets. Obviously, *Bakke* was saying that flexible quotas are part of the approved Harvard Plan. *Weber* also approved flexible quotas. We could all agree that irrationally inflexible quotas are unacceptable, stop the semantic quibble, and get down to the substance. Verbal squabbles, of course, can be an avoidance tactic.

34. See Charles Abrams, "Foreword," in Robert L. Carter, Dorothy Kenyon, Peter Marcuse, Loren Miller, *Equality* (New York: Pantheon Books, 1965), p. ix.

35. See Faustine Childress Jones, op. cit., p. 44.

36. Ibid., p. 238. One could approve of the principle of preference employed in the creation of Israel without approving of the specifics of the case.

37. See Aristotle, *Nichomachean Ethics,* Book V, Chapter 10.

38. It was, I believe, the philosopher Arthur Schopenhauer who first referred to philosophers as civil servants.

39. Aristotle, *Nichomachean Ethics,* 1132a. W. D. Ross translates it as "animate justice." See McKeon, op. cit., p. 1009. The Greek is δικαιον εμψυχον.

40. The term "living intellect" is that of John Henry Newman, *A Grammar of Assent* (Garden City: Doubleday Image Books, 1955), p. 277.

41. These are the words of Giorgio Del Vecchio in his *Justice: An Historical and Philosophical Essay* (Edinburgh: University Press, 1952), p. 73. Del Vecchio adds: "It is in this philosophical orientation that the superiority of Roman Jurisprudence lies as compared with the modern positivist schools." In a similar spirit would be Mr. Justice Cardozo when he wrote: "What we are seeking is not merely the justice that one receives when his rights and duties are determined by the law as it is; what we are seeking is the justice to which law in its making should conform." Benjamin Cardozo, *The Growth of the Law* (New Haven: Yale University Press, 1927), p. 87.

42. Aristotle, *Nichomachean Ethics,* 1132a.

43. In speaking of this base of willingness, I am not succumbing to the simplicities of contractarian thinking. The basis of the state is still our natural sociality which leads us to consent. The consent follows from our sociality; it is derivative and expressive of it. The consent is still the cart in its proper secondary place. It is our sociality that legitimates and requires consent.

44. *The Merchant of Venice,* Act IV, Scene 1.

45. Thomas Aquinas, *Commentary on the Gospel of Matthew,* 5, 2.

46. Deuteronomy 15:4. On the Jubilee Year, see Leviticus 25:8–55. Certainly the Jubilee legislation was resisted in practice. Such is the way the best efforts of law are met. The conception, however, and the attempt were heroic and monumental.

47. Proverbs 10:15.

48. Dr. Trude Weiss-Rosmarin, "The Editor's Quarter," *Jewish Spectator,* 43 (Spring, 1978), p. 3.

49. As Stephen Charles Mott writes: "The provisions of the Year of Jubilees are exemplary of what Biblical justice is." "Egalitarian Aspects

of the Biblical Theory of Justice," *Selected Papers* from the Nineteenth Annual Meeting of the American Society of Christian Ethics, p. 18.

CHAPTER SEVEN

1. Aristotle, *Nichomachean Ethics,* 1132b.

2. Loren Miller, "Equality," in Robert L. Carter, Dorothy Kenyon, Peter Marcuse, Loren Miller, *Equality* (New York: Pantheon Books, 1965), p. 29.

3. Owen M. Fiss, "Groups and the Equal Protection Clause," in *Equality and Preferential Treatment,* ed. by Marshall Cohen, Thomas Nagel, and Thomas Scanlon (Princeton, N.J.: Princeton University Press, 1977), p. 139. Fiss is giving arguments here that *may* be mounted as arguments for black preference.

4. Robert M. O'Neil, *Discriminating Against Discrimination: Preferential Admissions and the De Funis Case* (Bloomington: Indiana University Press, 1975), p. 113. O'Neil is speaking here about admissions to professional schools.

5. See Leon Poliakov, *The Aryan Myth: A History of Racist and Nationalist Ideas in Europe* (New York: A Meridian Book, 1971, 1974), pp. 7–8, 142–43, *et passim.*

6. Ibid., pp. 136, 143.

7. See *Oeuvres complètes de Voltaire,* ed. Moland, Vol. XII, pp. 192, 210. Quoted in Poliakov, op. cit., pp. 175–76.

8. Edward Long, *History of Jamaica,* excerpted in Winthrop D. Jordan, ed., *The Negro Versus Equality, 1762–1826* (Chicago: Rand McNally, 1969), p. 29. On the authority of *History of Jamaica,* see Poliakov, op. cit., p. 178.

9. *Dred Scott v. Sandford* (1857) 60 U.S. (19 How.) 393.

10. Opinion of Judge Crenshaw in *Brandon et al. v. Planters' and Merchants' Bank of Huntsville* (January 1838) Stewart's Ala. Report, 320, quoted in Stanley M. Elkins, *Slavery* (New York: Grosset & Dunlap, 1963), p. 59.

11. *Plessy v. Ferguson* (1896) 163 U.S. 537, at 563.

12. Lerone Bennett, Jr., *Before the Mayflower* (New York: Penguin Books, 1966), p. 236.

13. Derrick A. Bell, Jr., "The Real Cost of Racial Equality," *Civil Liberties Review Surve*y (Summer, 1974), p. 94.

14. Dorothy Burnham, "Jensenism: The New Pseudoscience of Racism," *Freedomways*, 10 (Second Quarter, 1971), p. 156.

15. Nathan Glazer, *Affirmative Discrimination* (New York: Basic Books, 1975), pp. 71–72.

16. See Leonard Goodwin, *Do the Poor Want to Work?: A Social-Psychological Study of Work Orientations* (Washington, D.C.: The Brookings Institution, 1972), p. ix.

17. Ibid., p. 112. Emphasis added.

18. Ibid., p. 117.

19. Ibid., p. 81.

20. *Youth in the Ghetto, A Study of the Consequences of Powerlessness and a Blueprint for Change,* pp. 239–40. Quoted in John Kaplan, "Equal Justice in an Unequal World: Equality for the Negro—The Problem of Special Treatment," *Northwestern University Law Review*, 61 (July–August 1966), p. 402.

21. Aristotle, *Politics*, 1302b.

22. Irelan, Moles, and O'Shea, "Ethnicity, Poverty, and Selected Attitudes." Quoted in Goodwin, op. cit., p. 5.

23. Leonard Reissman, "Readiness to Succeed: Mobility Aspirations and Modernism Among the Poor," *Urban Affairs Quarterly*, 4 (March 1969), pp. 379–95.

24. Perry Levinson, "How Employable Are AFDC Women?," *Welfare in Review*, 8 (July–August 1970), p. 16.

25. Cited by Goodwin from a New York University Graduate School of Social Work study, pp. 5–6. Several other studies arriving at similar conclusions are reported on in *The State of Black America*, 1978, a publication of the National Urban League, Inc. (January 17, 1978), pp. 202–3.

26. Robert B. Hill, *The Strengths of Black Families* (New York: Emerson Hall, 1972), p. 6.

27. Leonard Goodwin admits that the attractiveness of income from illegal activities and welfare payments has not been thoroughly explored. Yet the hypothesis he offers from the divergent findings is that poor people lose interest in work when they discover that success evades their efforts to find work. See Goodwin, op. cit., pp. 7–8.

28. *A Study of Attitudes Toward Racial and Religious Minorities and Toward Women,* prepared for The National Conference of Christians and Jews by Louis Harris and Associates, Inc. (November 1978), p. 32.

29. Winton H. Manning, Warren W. Willingham, and Hunter M.

Breland and Associates, *Selective Admissions in Higher Education* (San Francisco: Jossey-Bass Publishers, 1977), p. 28.

30. Edward C. Banfield, *The Unheavenly City: The Nature and Future of Our Urban Crisis* (Boston: Little, Brown, 1968, 1970), p. 73.

31. Quoted in Robert M. O'Neil, op. cit., p. 38.

32. Robert E. Hall and Richard A. Kasten, "The Relative Occupational Success of Blacks and Whites," *Brookings Papers on Economic Activity* (Washington, D.C.: The Brookings Institute, 1973), 3, pp. 785, 791–92.

33. Richard B. Freeman, "Changes in the Labor Market for Black Americans, 1948–1972," ibid., 1, p. 118.

34. Edward C. Banfield, op. cit., p. 105. Banfield is here citing and approving a study by Michael J. Piore, an M.I.T. economist, on the undisciplined nature of blacks.

35. Derrick A. Bell, Jr., op. cit., 97.

36. James Baldwin, "An Open Letter to My Sister, Angela Y. Davis," in Angela Davis, ed., *If They Come in the Morning,* quoted in Derrick A. Bell, Jr., "Racism in American Courts: Cause for Black Disruption or Despair?," *California Law Review* 61 (January, 1973), p. 203.

37. Quoted in Derrick A. Bell, Jr., "Racism in American Courts," p. 202.

38. Hugh Davis Graham and Ted Robert Gurr, *Violence in America: Historical and Comparative Perspectives* (New York: Bantam Books, 1969), p. 794. See also John U. Ogbu, *Minority Education and Caste: The American System in Cross-Cultural Perspective* (New York: Academic Press, 1978). Ogbu argues that the poor performance of black children in most school settings can be best understood as proceeding from perfectly accurate assessments of the limited opportunities available to the subordinate caste. He relates similar responses found in cross-cultural studies of caste societies around the world. Richard de Lone, in his *Small Futures: Children, Inequality, and the Limits of Liberal Reform* (New York: Harcourt Brace Jovanovich, 1979), p. 156, speaks of "a developmental master setting, differentiating the situation of subordinate caste members from that of dominant caste members." He notes that black parents inevitably tend to transmit in various ways in their child-rearing, the social, emotional, and cognitive qualities required by their social status. In effect what is communicated here is a sense of hopelessness. Again, to take the victims of this tragedy of dehumanization and point to them as inferior beings who are drawn by the "attractions" of dole and

crime (as Glazer, Banfield, *et al.* have done), touches the nadir of cynicism.

39. See Richard H. de Lone, *Small Futures: Children, Inequality, and the Limits of Liberal Reform* (New York: Harcourt Brace Jovanovich, 1979), pp. 120–26, p. 146.

40. Ibid., pp. 3–4.

41. Cited in Thomas Rainbow Morse and Anthony Joseph Rusciano, "Case Comments: *Bakke* v. *The Regents of the University of California,*" *New England Law Review,* 12 (1977), p. 751, n. 155.

42. James R. Dumpson, "Social Welfare," in *The State of Black America,* 1978, a publication of the National Urban League, Inc. (January 17, 1978), p. 130.

43. "Cancer Rate Rises for Blacks, Declines for Whites," *Milwaukee Journal,* February 18, 1979.

44. *Griggs v. Duke Power Co.* (1971) 401 U.S. 429–33.

45. See Nathan Glazer, op. cit., p. 150.

46. Ibid.

47. See Edward C. Banfield, op. cit., pp. 14–15.

48. See The United States Commission on Civil Rights *Statement on Affirmative Action,* Clearinghouse Publication 54 (October 1977), pp. 2–3.

49. The poll was conducted by the Milwaukee *Journal,* where the results were published on August 20, 1978.

50. See Norman J. Samuels, "Plant Adjustments to the $1 Minimum Wage," *Monthly Labor Review,* 81 (October 1958), p. 1137.

51. See Edward C. Banfield, op. cit., p. 99.

52. See Derrick A. Bell, Jr., "The Real Cost of Racial Equality," p. 95.

53. See Kenneth B. Clark, *Dark Ghetto: Dilemmas of Social Power* (New York: Harper & Row, 1965), p. 141.

54. See Robert M. O'Neil, op. cit., p. 104.

55. See Derrick A. Bell, Jr., "The Real Cost of Racial Equality," p. 84.

56. See the report of the President's Committee on Mental Retardation, *Mental Retardation: Century of Decision* (Washington, D.C., March, 1976).

57. Kenneth B. Clark, op. cit., p. 140.

58. Ibid., pp. 141–43.

59. See *Selective Admissions in Higher Education,* pp. 78–79.

60. See Robert M. O'Neil, op. cit., pp. 120–21.

61. *Report of the National Advisory Commission on Civil Disorders* (New York: Bantam Books, 1968), p. 2.

62. Ibid. Emphasis added.

63. *A Study of Attitudes Toward Racial and Religious Minorities and Toward Women,* p. 33.

64. See John Kaplan, op. cit., p. 390. Kaplan cites in this regard the *Report of the U. S. Commission on Civil Rights,* 267 (1959).

65. The very existence of the ghetto is a mark of rejection. Ghettos were preceded by white flight. Eighty per cent of the increase in black population in the period from 1950 to 1969 occurred within the twelve central cities while 90 per cent of the white population increase occurred outside the central cities. In the twenty-four urban areas with populations of more than one million people, 100 per cent of the white population increase occurred in the suburbs. See Derrick A. Bell, Jr., *Race, Racism, and American Law* (Boston, Toronto: Little, Brown, 1973), pp. 720–21. A *Newsweek* survey pointed out that between 1967 and 1969 the white "escape rate" from the central cities tripled to an annual average of nearly half a million. See "Report from Black America," *Newsweek,* June 30, 1969, p. 32. This massive transmigration sends an unmistakable message of insult to black Americans.

66. See Faustine Childress Jones, p. 37.

67. Ibid.

68. *The State of Black America,* 1978, p. 173.

69. See Faustine Childress Jones, *The Changing Mood in America* (Washington, D.C.: Howard University Press, 1977), pp. 184–229.

70. Gunnar Myrdal, "Foreword," in Kenneth B. Clark, op. cit., p. x.

71. R. M. Baron, "Black Powerlessness in Chicago," *Trans-Action,* 6 (November 1968), p. 33.

72. Owen M. Fiss, "Groups and the Equal Protection Clause," op. cit., pp. 129–30.

73. Eliot Marshall, "The Logical Next Step: Race Certification," *New Republic,* 177 (October 15, 1977), p. 20.

74. See Robert M. O'Neil, op. cit., p. 135. O'Neil reports that this law was recently sustained by the Louisiana Supreme Court against the claim that its existence discriminated against blacks.

75. *United States v. Flagler County School District* (5th Cir. 1972), 457 F. 2nd, 1402.

76. Edward C. Banfield, op. cit., p. 56.

77. Ibid., p. 59.

78. There is still warm and effective prejudice against Irish and Catho-

lics, but it does not leave its victims ghettoized and desperate—just keenly aware of the enduring WASP hegemony.

79. For a strong argument in this wise, see Rosemary Radford Reuther, *New Woman, New Earth: Sexist Ideologies and Human Liberation* (New York: Seabury Press, 1975).

80. Ibid., p. 25.

81. 1 Timothy 2:15.

82. Kenneth Grayston, "Marriage," in Alan Richardson, ed., *A Theological Word Book of the Bible* (New York: Macmillan, 1962), p. 139. Grayston refers to Genesis 16:1ff.; 30:1ff.

83. Augustine, *On Genesis According to the Letter* 9–7 (Vienna: *Corpus Scriptorum Ecclesiasticorum,* 1866), 28:275.

84. Simone de Beauvoir, *The Second Sex* (New York: Bantam Books, 1961), p. 74.

85. See Arnold Toynbee, *A Study of History,* abridgments of Vols. VII–X by D. C. Somervell (New York and London: Oxford University Press, 1957), p. 142.

86. See Ralph Linton, "The Natural History of the Family," in Ruth Nanda Anshen, ed., *The Family: Its Function and Destiny* (New York: Harper, 1959), p. 40.

87. See Rosemary Radford Reuther, op. cit., pp. 18–19, and Part II.

88. Cited by Rosemary Radford Reuther, ibid., p. 22.

89. See "What's 'Best' for the Child," *Wilson Quarterly,* 3 (Spring, 1979), pp. 34–35.

90. See A. Y. Lewin and L. Duchan, "Women in Academia," *Science,* 176 (1972), pp. 457–59.

91. See Rosemary Radford Reuther, op. cit., p. 22.

92. I would insist, however, that women are not in the upper classes in the same way that men are. They do not have all the privileges and opportunities that men enjoy at the affluent levels of life.

93. Winton H. Manning, Warren W. Willingham, and Hunter Breland and Associates, op. cit., p. 67.

94. Ibid., pp. 91, 162. In 1975 the figures for doctoral degrees were 7,600 for women and 28,500 for men; in 1985, the projected figure is 28,900 for men and 14,000 for women.

95. Ibid., p. 98.

96. Ibid., p. 115.

97. Ibid., p. 118.

98. Ibid., p. 119.

99. See Alfred W. Blumrosen, "Quotas, Common Sense, and Law in

Labor Relations: Three Dimensions of Equal Opportunity," *Rutgers Law Review,* 27 (1974), p. 676, n. 4.

100. 30 U.S. (5 Pet.), I, 1831, at 17.

101. See "The Fate of the Indian," *National Catholic Reporter* (July 15, 1977).

102. See Robert A. Hecht, "The Right to Remain Indian," *Commonweal,* 106 (March 30, 1979), pp. 176–79. See also Derrick A. Bell, Jr., *Race, Racism, and American Law,* pp. 59–69; Gary B. Nash and Richard Weiss, *The Great Fear: Race in the Mind of America* (New York: Holt, Rinehart and Winston, 1970).

103. Robert A. Hecht, op. cit., pp. 176–79. It is, of course, true that only 28 per cent of the Indians live on reservations, with 50 per cent living in urban areas. These figures, however, are hard to interpret. Life on the reservations is so often trying and employment so difficult to find, that Indians would be forced to the cities even if they preferred a good tribal existence. At any rate, those Indians who do move to the cities suffer a kind of culture shock. They have been ill prepared for such a transition. Social and distributive justice requires that the nation react sensitively and generously to their needs and to the rights that flow from those needs.

104. "It's Your Turn in the Sun," *Newsweek* (October 16, 1978), p. 51.

105. Ibid., p. 50.

106. See Derrick A. Bell, Jr., *Race, Racism, and American Law,* pp. 76–81; *De Funis versus Odegaard and the University of Washington,* ed. by Ann Fagan Giner (Dobbs Ferry, N.Y.: Oceana Publications, 1974), pp. 926–43.

107. See Robert M. O'Neil, op. cit., pp. 55–62.

108. See *Hernandez v. Texas* (1954), 347 U.S. 475. On school segregation, see *Keyes v. School Dist. No. 1* (1973), Denver, 93 Sup. Ct. 2686, 2691–92; *Cisneros v. Corpus Christi I.S.D.* (5th Cir. 1972) 459 F. 2nd, 13. On the denial of political rights, see *Graves v. Barnes* (W.D. Texas 1972) 343 F. Supp. 704, aff'd sub nom., *White v. Regester* (1973) 93 Sup. Ct. 2332, 2340–41.

109. Robert M. O'Neil, op. cit., p. 60.

110. Regarding the situation of Oriental-Americans in graduate and professional schools, see Winton H. Manning, Warren W. Willingham, and Hunter Breland and Associates, op. cit., pp. 212–21. See Talcott Parsons, "Some Theoretical Considerations on the Nature and Trends of Change of Ethnicity," in *Ethnicity,* ed. Nathan Glazer and Daniel Moyni-

han (Cambridge: Harvard, 1975), pp. 73–74. It was after completing the manuscript of this book that I encountered Richard H. de Lone's book *Small Futures: Children, Inequality, and the Limits of Liberal Reform.* I found support there for my contention that only certain groups have a distinctively disempowered status. In his discussion of caste as a master setting, he points out four groups as occupying a lower caste setting: blacks, Mexican Americans, Puerto Rican Americans, and Native Americans, p. 153. He speaks of the uniquely depressed socioeconomic status of these groups as opposed to conditions due to "mere prejudice." He does not, however, in his fine study sufficiently distinguish the special status and problems of blacks.

111. *Federal Register,* "Guidelines on Discrimination because of Religion or National Origin," January 19, 1973, Part (b) of 60–50.1.

CHAPTER EIGHT

1. Hugh Davis Graham and Ted Robert Gurr, *Violence in America* (New York: Bantam Books, 1969), p. 794.

2. See Owen M. Fiss, "Groups and the Equal Protection Clause," in *Equality and Preferential Treatment,* ed. by Marshall Cohen, Thomas Nagel, and Thomas Scanlon (Princeton, N.J.: Princeton University Press, 1977), p. 124 *et passim.*

3. Alfred W. Blumrosen, "Strangers in Paradise: *Griggs v. Duke Power Co.* and the Concept of Employment Discrimination," *Michigan Law Review,* 71:59 (November 1972), p. 62. Owen M. Fiss also says that Justice Powell uses the social group category in *San Antonio Ind. School District v. Rodriguez.* See Owen M. Fiss, op. cit., p. 133, n. 72.

4. *Morton v. Mancari* (1974), 94 Sup. Ct. 2474.

5. McGeorge Bundy, "The Issue Before the Court: Who Gets Ahead in America?" *Atlantic* 240 (November 1977), p. 49.

6. Ibid.

7. See Winton H. Manning, Warren W. Willingham, and Hunter Breland and Associates, *Selective Admissions in Higher Education* (San Francisco: Jossey-Bass Publishers, 1977), pp. 77–80.

8. See Robert M. O'Neil, *Discriminating Against Discrimination* (Bloomington: Indiana University Press, 1975), p. 132.

9. Alfred W. Blumrosen, "Quotas, Common Sense, and Law in Labor Relations: Three Dimensions of Equal Opportunity," *Rutgers Law Re-*

view, 27 (1974), p. 695. See also Robert M. O'Neil, op. cit., pp. 157–58.

10. Nathan Glazer, *Affirmative Discrimination* (New York: Basic Books, 1975), p. 203. Sidney Hook, "Discrimination, Color Blindness and the Quota System," in *Reverse Discrimination,* ed. by Barry R. Gross (Buffalo, N.Y.: Prometheus Books, 1977), p. 85.

11. See Derrick A. Bell, Jr., *Race, Racism, and American Law* (Boston, Toronto: Little, Brown, 1973), pp. 372–73.

12. *Bakke,* 132 Cal. Rptr. at 695.

13. See Thomas Rainbow Morse and Anthony Joseph Rusciano, "Case Comments: *Bakke* v. *The Regents of the University of California,*" *New England Law Review,* 12 (1977), p. 752, n. 158.

14. Owen M. Fiss, "Groups and the Equal Protection Clause," op. cit., p. 85. After I had completed this manuscript, Ronald Dworkin published a penetrating commentary on the legislative theories operative in *Weber.* Dworkin points out the simplism in the approach of Burger and Rehnquist in interpreting paragraph 703(a) of Title VII of the Civil Rights Act, almost as though one could interpret the act by staring at the words Congress used and backing this up by the discovery of the precise "legislative intent" behind the act. On the contrary, Dworkin offers a different theory of legislation which he calls a "coherence theory." "This supposes that a statute should be interpreted to advance the policies or principles that furnish the best political justification for the statute." "How to Read the Civil Rights Act," *New York Review of Books,* 26 (December 20, 1979), p. 41. According to this theory, says Dworkin, an interpretation is better than another "if it provides a more accurate or more sensitive or sounder analysis of the underlying moral principles." (Ibid.) Dworkin supports the Weber decision and sees it as a step that "will seem more important than the Court's hesitant shuffle in *Bakke,*" p. 43.

15. See ibid., p. 86.

16. Ibid., p. 96, n. 16.

17. The language is that of Owen M. Fiss, ibid., p. 100, n. 23.

18. Alfred W. Blumrosen, "Quotas, Common Sense, and Law in Labor Relations," op. cit., p. 692.

19. As Blumrosen says (ibid.), the political realities surrounding 703(j) involved a concern with statutory overkill. There was a desire to avoid the logical extreme of dividing the nation's employment everywhere along racial and sex lines (p. 690). The *amicus curiae* brief of the United States in *Bakke* notes that the judicial treatment of 703(j) is in-

structive. "The courts have recognized in it an attempt by Congress to differentiate between using race to rectify previous discrimination and using race to attain racial balance for its own sake" (p. 53, n. 67). Owen M. Fiss notes this same understanding and the fact that religion, sex, and color have been permissible criteria and that we are not committed by law to blindness in these areas. See Fiss, op. cit., p. 99.

20. See McGeorge Bundy, op. cit., p. 44.
21. See T. R. Morse and A. J. Rusciano, op. cit., p. 746, n. 133.
22. McGeorge Bundy, op. cit., p. 47.
23. Thomas Jefferson, *Letter to M. Correa,* November 25, 1817.
24. *Civil Rights Cases* (1883) 109 U.S. 3, 25.